THE•PILLAR•OF CELESTIAL•FIRE

AND THE

LOST SCIENCE OF THE ANCIENT SEERS

BY

ROBERT COX

Sunstar

PUBLISHING LTD.

THE PILLAR OF CELESTIAL FIRE
AND THE LOST SCIENCE OF THE ANCIENT SEERS
by Robert Cox

© United States Copyright, 1997
Sunstar Publishing, Ltd.
116 North Court Street
Fairfield, Iowa 52556

Cover Design: Therese Cross

LCCN: 97-066694
ISBN: 1-887472-30-4

Printed in the U.S.A.

Readers interested in obtaining further information on the subject
matter of this book are invited to correspond with
The Secretary, Sunstar Publishing, Ltd.
116 North Court Street, Fairfield, Iowa 52556
For more Sunstar Books: http://www.newagepage.com

To the Enlightened Seers
both modern and ancient
who have devoted their lives
to the betterment of humanity

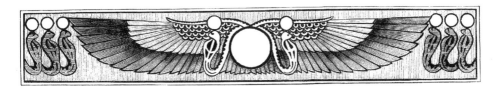

CONTENTS

ACKNOWLEDGMENTS ix

PREFACE x

1. INTRODUCTION 1
   • Collective Consciousness and the Cosmic Life Force • The Pillar
   of Celestial Fire • The Sacred Science and the Philosopher's Stone
   • Siddhis, or Perfections of Life • The Three Means of Spiritual
   Evolution • The Ravages and Promise of Time

2. THE COSMIC CLOCK—PRECESSION OF THE EQUINOXES . . .13
   • Major Epochal Transformations Every 13,000 Years

3. THE REVELATION OF JOHN 20
   • The Divine Messenger • The Wheel of Time • Emanations of
   Divine Power • The Seven Layers of Universal Life • The Four
   Living Creatures • The Sphinx

4. THE NATURE OF PURE KNOWLEDGE 29
   • Pure Consciousness • Nonlocal Intuition • The Unmanifest
   Blueprint of Creation • Expressions of Pure Knowledge

5. THE SACRED SCIENCE OF THE SEERS 36
   • Experience of Subtle Matter-Energy • Subtle Matter Technologies

6. THE HOLOGRAPHIC SPECTRUM OF CREATION 41
   • Frequency Bands of Consciousness • Holograms of Primordial
   Sound and Light • The Mechanics of Creation • The 108 Bands
   of the Spectrum

7. THE SEVEN-LAYERED STRUCTURE OF THE UNIVERSE 47
   • The Inner Celestial Regions • The Highest Heaven • The One
   Supreme Being and the Gods • The Universal Being • The Tree of Life

8. THE MILKY WAY GALAXY 59

  • Cosmic Life Spans • The Subtle Body of the Galactic Being •
  The Central Star of the Galactic Being • The Worlds of Light at the
  Galactic Center • Galactic Civilization

9. THE DIVINE KA 68

  • The Universal Song of Divine Love • The Crystalline Heart of the
  Sun • The Divine Ka in the Human Heart • The Vedic Tradition •
  The Egyptian Tradition

10. THE MORTAL SOUL 78

  • Subtle Matter Metabolism • Subtle Matter Generation • Polarized
  Subtle Matter • Condensed Subtle Matter • Streams of Subtle Matter

11. THE THEORY OF MORPHIC FIELDS 84

  • Morphic Resonance • Subtle Matter as Morphic Fields • Subtle
  Beings as Morphic Fields • Three Types of Subtle Beings •
  Mechanics of Morphic Resonance • Superluminal Transfers of
  Matter, Energy, and Information • Exotic Matter • Negative Matter-
  Energy • The Spiritual Name of the Soul • The Concept of
  Spiritual Purity

12. THE PRINCIPLE OF DIVINE CORRESPONDENCE 96

  • "As Above, So Below" • A Hypothetical Journey • The Seed and
  the Tree

13. THE IMMORTAL SOUL 102

  • The Higher Self • The Sons and Daughters of Immortality • The
  Marriage of Heaven and Earth • Polarized and Unpolarized Subtle
  Matter—Chitta and Chitta-Vritti

14. THE COSMIC NETWORK OF CELESTIAL RAYS 113

  • The Science of Astrology • The Three Main Celestial Rays • The
  Two Paths of Enlightenment

15. ERIDANUS—THE RIVER OF CELESTIAL FIRE 123

16. COOKING WITH CELESTIAL FIRE 128

  • Subtle Fusion or Tapas • The Judgment Day

17. THE DIVINE MESSENGER .133

18. THE PLEIADIAN CONNECTION 146

• The Pleiades in the Greek Tradition • The Pleiades in the
Polynesian Tradition • The Pleiades in the Mesoamerican Tradition
• The Pleiades in the Vedic Tradition • The Pleiades in the
Mesopotamian Tradition

19. THE DIVINE COVENANT 154

• Subtle Matter Technologies

20. THE FOUR AGES OF HUMAN CIVILIZATION 158

• The Celestial Yugas or Ages • Krita or Sat Yuga: The Golden Age
• Treta Yuga: The Silver Age • Dwapara Yuga: The Bronze Age •
Kali Yuga: The Iron Age • The Present Time of Transition

21. THE SOLAR AND LUNAR RACES 169

• Integrating Earth's Planetary Awareness

22. THE SPIRITUAL FOUNDATIONS OF HUMAN CIVILIZATION .174

23. THE ANTEDILUVIAN WORLD 177

• The Nature Spirits and Terrestrial Gods • The Innocent
Reflection of the Age • The Antediluvian End Times

24. THE SHIFT OF THE GEOGRAPHIC POLES 186

• The Magnetic Interaction of the Stream of Celestial Fire • The
Gravitational Interaction of the Stream of Celestial Fire • Earth-
Crust Displacement • Evidence of Pole Shifts • Earth, Water and
Fire • The Survivors • A New Illumination

25. ANCIENT LEGENDS OF THE FLOOD 198

• The Legend of Utnapishtim • Mesoamerican Legends of the Flood
• Chinese and Vedic Legends of the Flood • The Legend of Atlantis

26. THE TRADITION OF ENLIGHTENED SEERS 204

27. THE ANCIENT VEDIC TRADITION 207

• The Vedic Rishis • The Sacred Mantras • The Universal
Language of Nature • The Secret of Divine Invocation • The
Tradition of Oral Recitation • The Status of the Vedic Literature

28. THE ANCIENT EGYPTIAN CIVILIZATION 219
  • Egyptian Prehistory • The Ancient Esoteric Tradition • A Secret
  Radiation Technology • The Breath of the Serpent • The Djed Pillar
  • The Mortuary Rites • The Process of Spiritual Ascension • The
  Myth of Osiris • The Golden Basis of Spiritual Resurrection • The
  Giver of Eternal Life • The Pillar of Light • The Chamber of Light •
  The Bread of Life • Levitation Technology? • The Builder Gods and
  the New World Order • The Hidden Legacy • The Lost Tradition

29. THE TRADITION OF ALCHEMY 255
  • Hermetic Alchemy • Vedic Alchemy • Chinese Alchemy •
  Hebrew Alchemy • The Aquarian Legacy

30. CHURNING THE OCEAN OF CONSCIOUSNESS 270
  • Yagya • Churning the Milky Ocean • The Alchemical
  Significance of the Churning Process

31. THE ALCHEMICAL STONE, SALT, OR ASH 278

32. THE RITES OF IMMORTALITY 284
  • Traditions of Immortality • The Mechanics of Ascension •
  Preparation of the Soma

33. THE SECRET PURPOSE OF THE PYRAMIDS 295
  • Gateways to the Cosmos • The Pyramids of Giza and the Orion
  Constellation • The Great Seal of the United States

34. THE ARK OF THE COVENANT 302

35. THE NEED OF THE TIME 308
  • The Light of the Dawn • A Vision of Possibilities • A Time for
  Spiritual Rejuvenation • Centers of Light

ABOUT THE AUTHOR 317

THE CELESTIAL SCIENCE FOUNDATION 318

NOTES 320

REFERENCES 335

INDEX 340

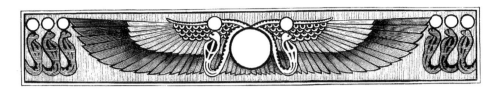

ACKNOWLEDGMENTS

There is no way to express the debt of gratitude that I owe to all of my teachers, both sacred and mundane, ancient and modern, who have laid the foundations of knowledge upon which this book stands. Without them this book could not have been conceived, much less written.

Most importantly, I would like to pay tribute to the great enlightened Seers who were the founders of the most ancient traditions of sacred knowledge around the world. These traditions may be compared to underground streams of life-giving water. These streams have been there all along; but up until recently only a few have known of their existence and enjoyed their life-giving essence. However, now that we are experiencing the birth of an information age, these long-hidden streams have begun to rise to the surface and flow together. They have begun to rise up and flow into a magical pool from which anyone may drink. Having slaked my own thirst from this rising pool of pure knowledge, I have filled a ladle with its crystal waters, and now offer a taste to all those who are ready and willing to receive it.

Although the waters contained in this sacred pool are universal, belonging to all traditions, I owe a special debt of gratitude to my teacher, His Holiness Maharishi Mahesh Yogi, who taught me how to drink from this pool. Without his profound teachings I suspect that I would still be wandering in a waterless desert with the life-giving essence out of reach. I thus wish to express my heartfelt gratitude to him and to the Holy Tradition of Vedic Seers to which he belongs.

I also would like to thank all those who have supported in various ways my research efforts over the years. In particular, I would like to thank Tom Stanley, Dick Mays, and Olivia Crawford for their continued support and encouragement. And on a very personal level, I would like to thank Diane Haffar for her sustaining love and patience, and my Mom, Melva Cox, for being there when it counted most.

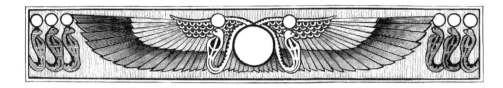

PREFACE

After reading the early versions of this book, several individuals posed the question: "Where did this knowledge come from?" Invariably my reply was that it came from many different sources. Originally it came from intuitive vision and spiritual cognition, but subsequently it was developed, enhanced, and refined through logical inference, the construction of analogies and models, and constant reference to the authoritative texts of both the ancient spiritual and modern scientific traditions.

Although some portions of this book are stated in a factual style, this entire book should be viewed as a statement of opinion. The opinions and conclusions presented here have been well thought out, and are based upon solid foundations, but I am not infallible, and no reasonable individual should accept my opinions as divine edicts or irrefutable statements of fact. Like everyone else, I am continuously engaged in a process of "seeing" and "understanding" the Universe more and more clearly.

Just as it is possible to carry an oak tree in the palm of one's hand by grasping an acorn, so also, it is possible to see and comprehend the essence of the Universe as a whole by operating on the level of pure consciousness. But the type of universal knowledge that first dawns on the level of pure consciousness is more or less general in its nature, and falls far short of complete knowledge. Complete knowledge implies the ability to know the abstract essence of everything along with its full detail. Such detailed knowledge of the Universe culminates in omniscience. Omniscience is a lofty goal even for the most enlightened Seers. Generally speaking, true omniscience is reserved for the celestial beings that dwell at the very center of the Universe.

I thus consider myself to be a perpetual student. I always am eager to learn more, even if it means that some closely held ideas and opinions must be rejected, modified, or replaced by new ones that are even closer to the

Truth. This is how our knowledge becomes more refined and complete. I have experienced this process of refinement throughout the entire course of my life, and I have no reason to suppose that it will cease. Nevertheless, at a certain point we must begin to act upon the knowledge that we have been given.

For years now, I have delayed writing this book to allow the knowledge to become more refined, that is, to become closer to the Truth. But at this point, I can delay no longer. The urgency of the time compels me to share a small portion of the knowledge that I have gained, so that others may traverse the same path of understanding much more quickly than myself.

Throughout this book, I have used the first person plural "we" rather than the first person singular "I" to refer to my opinions and conclusions. This was done for various reasons, the most important of which is purely intuitive. It just felt right to do so. This feeling is based upon an appreciation of the fact that we as human beings all are collective entities. We know from modern science that although each human being experiences itself as a single entity, it actually is a collective entity composed of billions of cells, each of which is a tiny organism or being. This alone would justify the use of the term "we." However, there is much more to it than that.

From the ancient Sacred Science, we learn that each human being may be compared to a cell in the collective awareness of a vast yet invisible cosmic being. This cosmic being, in turn, may be viewed as a cell in an even larger cosmic being, and that one as part of a higher being, and so on, until at the very end of the "way of ways" one comes to the Supreme Being, who is the highest Self, beyond whom there is no other. Although all of the cosmic beings leading up to the Supreme Being are collective entities, embracing vast numbers of souls within themselves, they experience themselves as individuals, just as we do.

There is thus a vast chain of beings in the miracle of God's creation, of which we are but a single link. Those selves in the chain that lie above our own position in the spiritual hierarchy may be understood as aspects of our "higher Self," while those that lie below us may be understood as aspects of our "lower self." As we proceed upwards on the chain we progress towards absolute Unity, and as we proceed downwards we progress towards infinite diversity. So our notion of an isolated self which is denoted by the word "I" is ultimately an illusion. In truth, we participate in the breath of the entire Universe with every thought, word, and deed.

This is especially true when it comes to receiving spiritual insight. Such insight comes to us through the grace of the Creator. Before we receive it, it must cascade through the awareness of at least seven different cosmic beings, all of whom are agencies of the Creator and aspects of our own higher Self. Although the details of these mechanics are too technical to be elaborated here, they illustrate the fact that cognition and exposition of knowledge is a collective endeavor that involves the assistance and guidance of many unseen benefactors.

I have chosen to use the pronoun "we" rather than "I" throughout this book to honor and recognize the contributions of these benefactors. However, the fact that such unseen benefactors are involved in the process of receiving and expressing knowledge does not ensure that the expression of knowledge is without error. It is our job to properly interpret, understand, and express the knowledge that we are given. No matter how pure is the water in the pool, if the cup is dirty, the water that it holds and carries also will be dirty.

Generally speaking, the knowledge presented here represents a blend of the inner spiritual and the outer scientific approaches to gaining knowledge. In this regard, I consider myself to be a true alchemist. For years I have been engaged in both deep spiritual practice as well as alchemical research in the laboratory to uncover deeper and deeper layers of knowledge concerning the ultimate relationship between consciousness and matter.

In my view, this combination of inner and outer approaches to gaining knowledge is essential. The results derived from these approaches must be complementary and mutually supportive if knowledge is to be both spiritually meaningful and practical in this world. And in this scientific age, we want knowledge that is practical. If it is not practical, that is, if the knowledge does not affect or influence the way that we actually experience and operate within this world, then of what use is it?

It is on the basis of this practical approach to knowledge that I have written this book. This book has not been written as a dry academic exercise. It has been written with passion and fervor by one who himself is on a journey of perpetual self-discovery. Furthermore, it is presented with a practical aim in mind. Its purpose is to uncover the spiritual, philosophical, historical, and scientific background of an extremely important body of knowledge. This knowledge pertains to a sacred alchemical science that once was shared by ancient Seers around our planet. I hold that the essence of this Sacred Science was lost several thousand years ago, and now is being rediscovered and reconstructed by researchers around the world.

There is no doubt that this Sacred Science is destined to play a critical role in the profound spiritual, scientific, and social transformation that is almost upon us. In my opinion, this transformation, which sometimes is referred to as the "Second Coming," the "Judgment Day," the "Descent of Heaven on Earth," the "Rapture," etc., is not due to anything that we as human beings have done in the past, or that we will do in the future. It is an inevitable consequence of certain celestial mechanics that are beyond the reach of human influence. I believe that these mechanics are about to deliver an immense flood of celestial fire or cosmic life force to our planet. When this wave of cosmic life force washes over our planet, everything will be transformed and changed in ways that are almost unimaginable. Although we cannot alter the inevitability of this transformation, we can change the way in which this transformation will influence us. To survive the wave of celestial fire and flourish in the new Golden Age that will dawn in its wake, we must begin to prepare ourselves to receive it.

To prepare ourselves, a new scientific understanding of the Universe, which is based upon both spiritual and physical principles, must dawn in human awareness. In addition, certain sacred technologies associated with this science must be made available to the world's population. This book was written to lay the foundation for the dissemination of this Sacred Science and its associated technologies. Several additional books are planned, which will delve more deeply into the various subjects touched upon here, and present new knowledge as it unfolds.

Fortunately, the knowledge presented here is now being received by various individuals all around our planet. In truth, I am just one of many voices crying out in the wilderness. It will take a chorus of many voices crying out together to awaken the sleeping giant of humanity. I have done nothing other than add one more small voice to the rising crescendo.

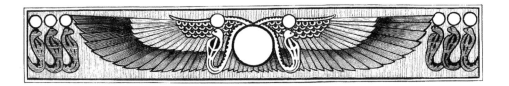

1. INTRODUCTION

There are times in the history of human civilization when changes from one epoch to another must occur, when everything that has been built up over thousands of years must come crashing down, and a new world must be constructed based upon new principles and new knowledge. It is at these times that a new perspective on the purpose of human civilization and life as a whole becomes established, a perspective that may endure for thousands of years, until hoary with age and stiff with meaningless tradition, the original inspiration becomes lost, and a new holistic perspective must arise once again.

Such cycles of transformation are not unique to human civilization. They have occurred on our planet since the first creatures spawned in the seas and crawled upon the Earth. Indeed, such cycles are endemic to all life. They are reflected in the birth, growth, decay, and death of all living things, which die only to be reborn, and begin the cycle anew on more evolved levels of development.

Although such changes are essential to all forms of life, our entire planet is now on the verge of an epochal transformation of a scope and power unprecedented in our recorded history. This type of earth-shaking transformation has not occurred for at least 13,000 years, since the end of the last Ice Age.

Some have called this impending transformation the "Judgment Day," and others have hailed it as the dawn of Heaven on Earth. Whatever it may be called, it most certainly will affect everything that we know and have known for thousands of years, in ways that are almost unimaginable.

Regardless of how one might feel about this event, there is absolutely nothing that can be done to avoid it—because it is not the result of human endeavor. It is part of a Divine Plan. Just as warm spring breezes follow the cold winds of winter, each Dark Age of humanity is followed by an Age of Light. This cycle has been built into the framework of the Universe since the beginning of time, and it is administered with clockwork precision by an all-knowing Cosmic Intelligence.

We are not the first civilization to face such a transformation. Vast and enduring civilizations have flowered on the Earth before, some far more advanced than our own. Yet the uncompromising wheel of time has ground them to dust and scattered them to the four corners of the Earth. Our present civilization is but a crude reflection of that ancient glory. And yet it too will follow in their path, and soon.

However, we should not despair. Our civilization will not be destroyed totally. It will be transformed, transfigured, and replaced by a new civilization, a civilization that will be filled with spiritual grandeur and scientific achievements incomparably superior to anything with which we are now familiar. In this book we will explore the mechanics of this transformation in light of the wisdom of the enlightened Seers of the most ancient traditions of knowledge on Earth.

Collective Consciousness and the Cosmic Life Force

The mechanics of the impending global transformation are both celestial and technological in nature. The celestial mechanics are governed by long cycles of time, extending over many thousands of years. The ancient Seers used these cycles to chart the rise and fall of collective consciousness on our planet.

The collective consciousness of our planet may be understood as the sum of all forms of individual consciousness on Earth. The collective consciousness includes not only the awareness of the entire human population, but also the elementary awarenesses of all the minerals, plants, and animals which make up the Earth. This vast collection of individual beings forms a single cosmic awareness. It constitutes a single Planetary Being that we call "Mother Earth."

The awareness of Mother Earth rises and falls in accordance with the cycles of time. These cycles determine the onset of the Ages of Light and the Ages of Darkness. During each Age of Light the collective consciousness of our planet is elevated to a high level of spiritual knowledge, and during each Age of Darkness it falls into the depths of spiritual ignorance.

The rise and fall of collective consciousness is a spiritually ordained phenomenon that is nonlocally administered by Cosmic Intelligence. However, it also can be viewed from a scientific perspective. The collective consciousness of the Earth is directly tied to the level of *cosmic life force* or *luminous subtle matter* present on the Earth at any given time.

Luminous subtle matter is that which provides the link or connection between pure consciousness and ordinary matter. It is the subtle luminous substance that enables consciousness to be reflected within the field of material Creation. The ancient Vedic tradition calls this subtle substance *chitta* (mind stuff); the Taoist tradition calls it *chi* (electromagnetic life force).

Whatever it is called, this luminous subtle matter is the key to the Sacred Science of the ancient Seers. It is the key to all methods of spiritual evolution, and to all the miracles performed by the ancient Seers. It also is the key to understanding the rise and fall of collective consciousness on Earth throughout the ages.

The rise and fall of collective consciousness is related to the varying level of luminous life force present on our planet over time. The higher the density of cosmic life force on Earth, the more profound is the connection between the body of the Earth and the field of universal pure consciousness. When this connection is fully awakened, the Earth and all of her inhabitants enjoy a Golden Age, and the collective consciousness of our planet is exalted to high levels of spiritual realization.

When the density of cosmic life force is reduced, the connection between the spiritual and material aspects of life becomes weak, and the Earth and all of her inhabitants experience an Age of Darkness. During such periods, the collective consciousness of our planet is overshadowed by the material side of life. All of the magic, mystery, and spiritual glory of life becomes increasingly hidden behind the mechanistic veil of material Nature, and life becomes miserable. Individual life becomes wracked with suffering and stunted by unfulfilled desires. A materialistic world view comes to dominate in collective awareness, and the spiritual side of life remains largely forgotten and ignored.

Although our world now has been immersed in spiritual darkness for thousands of years, this darkness cannot endure much longer. According to the cycles of time mapped out by the ancient Seers, the Earth and all of her inhabitants soon are destined to receive an enormous infusion of cosmic life force. At this moment in history, we stand in the gap between the end of one cycle and the beginning of another. The long Dark Age is ending and a new Golden Age is about to dawn.

The Pillar of Celestial Fire

In order to initiate the new Golden Age, the life force of the Creator must descend into our midst and be infused into the depths of our souls and the very fabric of the Earth. The "life force of the Creator" is not a euphemism. It describes an actual physical-spiritual force that periodically descends upon our planet in accordance with an ancient cosmic rhythm. It descends as a wave of luminous subtle matter or *celestial fire*.

The wave of celestial fire emanates from the heavenly regions at the center of the Universe. It is carried to the Earth from those regions by an invisible pillar of celestial fire that lies in the direction of the Pleiades constellation. We believe that the proper understanding of this phenomena is critical for the well-being of the human race. In fact, that understanding constitutes the essential message of this book.

The pillar of celestial fire may be understood as a vast stream of cosmic life force filled with the Divine Presence of God. It's unique function is to uphold the intimate relationship between Heaven and Earth. It connects our planet with the blazing glory of Heaven at the center of the Universe.

However, the pillar of celestial fire cannot be seen through a telescope. This is because it is not composed of ordinary matter. It is composed of luminous subtle matter. This type of matter is too subtle to be seen with our ordinary eyes. It can be seen only through the spiritual eye—the eye of pure consciousness. Nevertheless, it is very real, and has been described in various ways by Seers throughout the ages.

Metaphorically speaking, the pillar of celestial fire may be compared to a cosmic umbilical cord. Through this golden cord of subtle matter-energy the life-breath of the Creator flows to our embryonic world at the beginning of each new cycle of Ages, infusing Light and Life into every atom and cell on Earth.

The life-breath of the Creator flows along the cosmic umbilical cord as a wave of celestial fire. This wave already has been unleashed and now is on its way to our world. When the wave of celestial fire washes over our world, everything that we know will be changed irrevocably. The Earth will become infused with the Divine Presence. It will be set on fire with the ineffable glory of Heaven.

Although this transformation is inevitable, the character of the transformation—whether it is gradual and gentle, or sudden and violent—is within our own hands. The wave of celestial fire is coming. It is our job to prepare ourselves and the entire Earth to receive it.

To do this, over the next decade or so we must dramatically increase the density of the subtle life force within ourselves and within the Earth. We must acclimate ourselves to the increasing spiritual Light that will dawn at the time of Illumination. We must raise the spiritual vibration of our planet, so that we can resonate with the powerful wave of cosmic life force that is about to descend upon us.

The Sacred Science and the Philosopher's Stone
To assist in this preparation, many souls have been inspired with new knowledge, and some have been given pieces of a great and mysterious puzzle. This puzzle pertains to the Sacred Science and technology that was prevalent during the previous Golden Age, but

which has since been lost. In some of Earth's more ancient civilizations, this Sacred Science and technology was used to bestow spiritual enlightenment, perfect health, and physical immortality upon the people. Although entire cultures once cherished this knowledge as their most precious sacred wisdom, today only a vague memory of it remains.

The memory of this lost science holds a deep secret—the secret of how to infuse consciousness into ordinary matter. On a spiritual level, this knowledge was used in sacred rituals to infuse celestial fire into the Earth and invoke the blessings of Heaven for all humanity. On a material level, it provided methods to produce and utilize a sacred substance, which in different traditions variously was called the Philosopher's Stone, the alchemical Salt, or the holy Ash.

The ancient Seers used this substance in various ways. They consumed it to rejuvenate their minds and bodies; they used it in their rituals to generate an abundance of luminous subtle matter or celestial fire; and they used it in their sacred technologies to perform miraculous feats.

According to alchemical texts belonging to different ancient traditions, the sacred alchemical substance consisted of certain metals, such as silver, gold, and mercury, that had been alchemically prepared, or fully "spiritualized." When these metals were alchemically prepared, they no longer appeared or functioned as ordinary metals. They took on the appearance of a crushed white stone or powder that was filled with the Light of Life. This spiritualized metallic powder was the fabled Philosopher's Stone, Salt or Ash.

Although this material could be prepared alchemically from metallic ore, it also was available in trace amounts in many natural herbs. The ancients Seers thus used both crushed minerals and crushed herbs as sources of the sacred Stone.

The Stone was deemed to have miraculous powers. When a small quantity of the Stone was mixed with molten metal and heated in an alchemical furnace, it was capable of transmuting many times its original weight of base metal into pure gold. When it was consumed it was capable of healing and rejuvenating the body, and of filling the mind and soul with the Light of Life.

When the Stone was prepared in a solid dry form, it sometimes was fashioned into wafers and called *Manna* or the Bread of the Presence. When it was prepared in a liquid form it was called *Soma* or the Elixir of Immortality. Regardless of the name it was given, or the form in which it was prepared, the ancient Seers viewed it as the ambrosial "food of the gods," and believed it to be the key to perfect health, spiritual enlightenment, and physical immortality.

The ancient texts proclaim that upon consuming certain preparations of this sacred material those who were afflicted with the infirmities of old age were restored to the prime of their youth. They grew lustrous hair and youthful limbs. Their faces and forms became transformed into that of beautiful adolescents. They became eternally young and insusceptible to disease or injury.[1]

In addition, they became filled with the Light of Life and gained direct intuitive knowledge of God. Indeed, they were said to possess all the extraordinary powers and privileges of enlightened Seers.

Siddhis, or Perfections of Life

In the Vedic tradition, these powers were called *siddhis* (perfections). Eighteen principal siddhis are mentioned. Although these siddhis normally were considered attainable only through the practice of meditation and yoga, the Vedic alchemical texts claimed that all of the siddhis also were attainable by consuming, or merely being within the proximity of the alchemically prepared substances.[2]

The eighteen principal siddhis include the ability: (1) to make one's body huge; (2) to make one's body very small; (3) to make one's body very light or very heavy; (4) to experience the Universe through the senses of other beings; (5) to enjoy the pleasures belonging to other worlds; (6) to direct Nature according to one's will; (7) to have no attachment to worldly desires; (8) to continuously enjoy the highest spiritual bliss; (9) to be free from hunger, thirst, and old age; (10 and 11) to see and hear things from a great distance; (12) to move or travel at enormous speeds; (13) to take any form at will; (14) to temporarily leave one's own body and enter into any other body; (15) to permanently leave one's mortal frame at will; (16)

to participate in the cosmic activities of the celestial beings; (17) to obtain all desires by mere intention; and (18) to exercise unobstructed authority over all beings.[3]

Although eighteen principal siddhis generally are listed, there are many others that are mentioned, including the ability to live for hundreds or even thousands of years; to know past, present, and future; to speak and understand all languages; to have complete power over all animals; to remain unaffected by heat and cold, etc.

Such extraordinary powers were not unique to the Vedic tradition. Esoteric schools of the Kabbalah within the Hebrew tradition also relate the various extraordinary powers obtainable through the application of the Sacred Science. One sixteenth-century manuscript lists twenty-two such powers, including the ability: (1) to behold God face-to-face without dying, and to converse with the celestial beings that command the celestial hosts; (2) to rise above all griefs and fears; (3) to reign with all Heaven and to be served by all Hell; (4) to rule one's own health and life, and to be able to influence those of others; (5) to be neither surprised by misfortunes, overwhelmed by disasters, nor conquered by enemies; (6) to know the reason of the past, present, and future; (7) to possess the secret of the resurrection of the dead and the key to immortality; (8) to find the Philosophical Stone; (9) to possess the Universal Medicine; (10) to know the laws of perpetual motion and to prove the quadrature of the circle; (11) to change into gold not only all metals, but also the earth itself, and even the refuse of the earth; (12) to subdue the most ferocious animals and have power to pronounce those words which paralyze and charm serpents; (13) to have the cosmic intuition that gives rise to the Universal Science; (14) to speak learnedly on all subjects, without preparation and without study; (15) to know at a glance the deep things of the souls of men and the mysteries of the hearts of women; (16) to force Nature to release one (from mortal bondage) at will; (17) to foresee all future events which do not depend on a superior free will, or on an indiscernible cause; (18) to give at once and to all the most efficacious consolations and the most wholesome counsels; (19) to triumph over adversaries; (20) to conquer love and hate; (21) to have the secret of wealth, and to be always its master and never its slave, (22) to enjoy even poverty and never become abject or miserable.[4]

Although these remarkable powers are extraordinarily wide-ranging, we believe that they all derive from a single cause—the infusion of the Light of Life (or cosmic life force) into the body, mind, and soul of the individual. When one is filled with the Light of Life, one becomes intimately connected and correlated with the Universal Consciousness that rules all of Creation. As a result, one's individual life breathes the breath of universal life, and one shares in the powers and privileges of Divine Sovereignty. This exalted state has been the goal of seekers of wisdom throughout the ages in virtually every esoteric tradition around the planet.

The Three Means of Spiritual Evolution
Generally speaking, this exalted state of spiritual realization can be achieved in three ways: (i) through internal means, which involve meditation, prayer, chanting, and performing sacred rituals; (ii) through external means, which involve producing and utilizing the sacred Stone; and (iii) through Divine Grace, which involves the descent of cosmic life force through the emanations of the celestial beings. The first two means of attaining spiritual exaltation are effected by human beings, and in principle can be pursued at any time. The third means is not controlled by human intelligence, but is in the hands of God.

When a new Golden Age dawns, all three means of spiritual evolution become available. Thus, just prior to each new Golden Age, many teachers, some with prophetic messages for the human race, arise to propound the glories of meditation, and the efficacy of chanting sacred sounds and performing sacred rituals. These teachers attract many people into otherwise long-forgotten practices and traditions, thus revitalizing the internal path of spiritual evolution. Is it any surprise that for the last twenty-five years the number of such teachers on our planet has been steadily growing?

In addition, at the beginning of each new Golden Age the secrets of the Sacred Science begin to manifest once again in the collective awareness, enabling certain individuals to rediscover the methods to produce and utilize the sacred Stone. This opens the external, or alchemical path of spiritual evolution to those who are not able or prone to follow the internal path.

Based upon recent scientific discoveries and developments, we predict that the external path soon will be available to the entire planet. This will enable a large portion of the population to rapidly rejuvenate their minds and bodies in preparation for the coming Illumination.

Finally, at the beginning of each new Golden Age, the cosmic life force on Earth spontaneously begins to increase in its density and potency. This is caused by the flood of celestial fire descending along the cosmic umbilical cord that connects our planet to the center of the Universe.

As the tide of cosmic life force rises, it causes the spiritual awareness of the entire human population to become more elevated—without any doing whatsoever. It is not difficult to see that this tide has been rising steadily for some time now. By the year 2000, the rate of its increase should become noticeable to almost everyone.

As the old cycle finally comes to its end (sometime around 2010–2012 A.D.), this rapidly rising tide of spiritual Light will cause more and more people to "wake up" and make good use of the internal and external means of evolution. This will enable progressively larger portions of the population to prepare themselves for the ultimate day of Illumination. At that time, the rate of increase of cosmic life force will turn almost vertical, and the flood of celestial fire will completely envelop the Earth.

Although we have delineated three separate means of evolution, they are not completely independent, nor are they equally efficacious in their results. They are hierarchically related to one another.

Those who merely bathe in the rising tide of cosmic life force without doing anything to further their spiritual evolution will enjoy one result. Those who actively strive to enhance their evolution by utilizing the alchemical means of evolution will enjoy another higher, more beneficial result. Finally, those who employ both the internal (spiritual) and external (alchemical) means of evolution will enjoy the most powerful result, and will evolve rapidly towards the status of enlightened Seers.

We believe that all three means taken together will yield the most everlasting results. Taken together, these three means will enable the seeker to fulfill his or her highest aspirations in both material and spiritual realms, and to attain the state of complete spiritual enlightenment and physical immortality.

To our knowledge, the three means of spiritual evolution have not been available to the general population at large in any previous epoch of recorded history. Our generation thus faces a unique opportunity.

This is not to say that this opportunity has never occurred before. We believe that it did occur during the previous Golden Age. According to our interpretation of the cycles of time mapped out by the ancient Seers, that Age lasted for about 5,000 years, and occurred between 11,000 B.C. and 6000 B.C. It thus took place long before existing historical records began to be kept. Nevertheless, intimations of this past Golden Age exist in virtually all of the most ancient traditions of knowledge.

The Ravages and Promise of Time

The fundamental premise of this book is that during the previous Golden Age the people of Earth enjoyed a high level of spiritual awareness, and the Sacred Science was known to ancient Seers all around the world. These included the Vedic Seers of ancient India, the Taoist masters of ancient China, the high priests of Old Kingdom Egypt, and the original Biblical patriarchs.

Unfortunately, their knowledge of the Sacred Science has not survived the ravages of time. It has been lost for thousands of years. Many have tried to resurrect it over the millennia, but with little success. Its revival was destined to wait until the present time—a time that marks the onset of a new Golden Age.

Now that we stand at the threshold of a new cycle of Ages, this knowledge has begun to flood into our collective consciousness once again. Various souls have begun to receive different pieces of the puzzle of this mysterious Sacred Science, and are now beginning to put the pieces together. The lost science is being reconstructed, and the miraculous material—the sacred Stone, Salt, or Ash—may soon be available once again.[5]

The reconstruction of the ancient Sacred Science is of paramount impor-tance to the entire human race. Its importance cannot be conveyed in just a few words. It promises to deliver miraculous spiritual and healing methods that will far surpass anything glimpsed by modern science. In addition, it may open the door to unprecedented industrial and technological advances that will make our wildest science fantasies come true.

We have written this book in an attempt to place the knowledge of the Sacred Science in its proper perspective—to give some idea of the profound role that it has played in some of the most ancient spiritual, philosophical, and cultural traditions on Earth, and to point out the urgent need for its complete revival in light of the profound cosmic transformation that is almost upon us.

The history associated with this Sacred Science is very ancient. It reaches back into the predawn history of the human race. Yet we believe that it is immensely relevant to our modern world. In our view, the rediscovery of the Sacred Science and its most glorious product—the "food of the gods"—heralds the dawn of a new Golden Age, where the highest aspirations of mankind will be fulfilled, and life once again will be truly worth living.

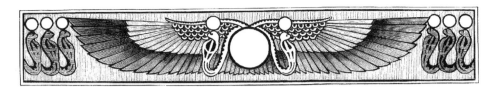

2. THE COSMIC CLOCK—
PRECESSION OF THE EQUINOXES

The dawn of a new Golden Age is not a chance phenomenon. It is part of a Divine Plan that is administered by Cosmic Intelligence. Many of the ancient civilizations that flourished thousands of years ago were aware of this Divine Plan, and used the movements of the stars in the celestial Heavens to map the cyclic unfoldment of this Plan over extremely long periods, spanning many thousands of years.

In accordance with the principle "as above, so below," the ancient Seers believed that the cycles of human evolution on Earth were deeply correlated with periodically recurring events in the Heavens. In particular, the transformation from one epoch of human civilization to another was marked with reference to the *precession of the equinoxes.*

The precession of equinoxes is an astronomical phenomenon caused by the very slow revolution of the Earth's axis against the background of the fixed stars. Technically speaking, it involves the slow pivoting of the Earth's axis with respect to the plane of the ecliptic. This motion resembles the slow wobbling of a spinning top as it is winding down. However, unlike a spinning top, it takes about 26,000 years for the slowly wobbling axis of the Earth to complete one revolution.

To the ancient Seers, the precession of the equinoxes was not just an obscure astronomical observation. It was an important and meaningful part of their lives, which was immortalized in their monuments and temples. Indeed, a number of the most mysterious of the ancient ruins, including Stonehenge, the Pyramids, and various Mayan temples, are aligned precisely with celestial events that are governed by the precession of the equinoxes.

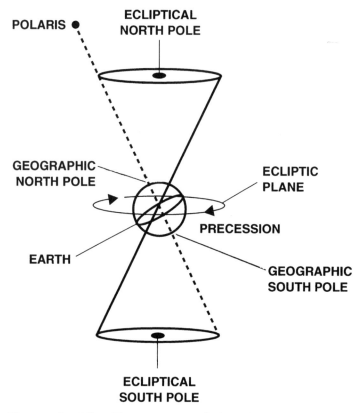

Figure 1—The Precession of the Equinoxes

The precession of the equinoxes involves a slow wobbling of the Earth's axis around the ecliptical North Pole. A full rotational cycle takes about 25,920 years (or according to modern observations, exactly 25,776 years).

Although many experts in the study of ancient civilizations may relegate these alignments to mere coincidence, the ancient Seers who designed these monuments were not prone to arbitrary whims of fancy. They were great and practical visionaries who saw the Universe as a seamless web composed of many invisible threads, each of which carries a unique set of divine correspondences.

In the eyes of the ancient Seers, the human physiology, the Earth, and the starry Heavens all were intrinsically and intimately interconnected in ways that are unimaginable to our modern rational intellects.[6] To the ancient

Seers, these correspondences obeyed the ancient and universal dictum "As above, so below." The Seers were able to see these correspondences because they viewed the Universe through the faculty of nonlocal intuition, rather than solely through the eyes of the rational intellect. In the light of pure consciousness, everything in the Universe appears infinitely correlated with every other thing.

By means of their intuitive vision, the ancient Seers cognized the deep connections between cyclic events in the starry Heavens unfolding over many thousands of years, and the rise and fall of human civilizations on Earth. The most important of these cyclic events corresponds to the precession of the equinoxes.

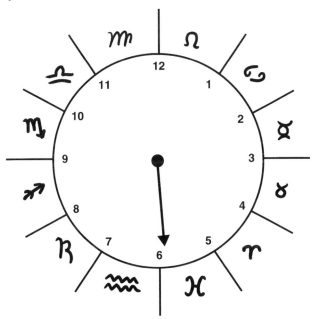

Figure 2—The Cosmic Clock

The movement of the twelve signs of the zodiac through the equinoctial point associated with the precessional cycle may be viewed as the movement of a cosmic hour hand around a Cosmic Clock. The hour hand of the Cosmic Clock sweeps through each of the zodiacal signs over a period of approximately 2,160 years. At the present time, the cosmic hour hand points to the end of the Age of Pisces and the beginning of the Age of Aquarius.

The precession of the equinoxes may be understood as the Earth's own *Cosmic Clock*. The twelve "hours" on this Clock are marked by the twelve signs of the zodiac, consisting of thirty degrees of arc each. The slow moving "hour hand" of the Clock corresponds to the steady precession of the spring equinox, which sweeps through all twelve signs of the zodiac over a period of approximately 25,920 years.

Each hour on the Cosmic Clock thus corresponds to a period of approximately 2,160 years. This is the time it takes for the hour hand of the Cosmic Clock to sweep through each sign—marking a particular zodiacal Age of human civilization. Technically speaking, the "time" on the Cosmic Clock is marked by the exact point in the eastern sky at which the Sun rises on the morning of the spring equinox. This point changes by about fifty seconds of arc each year, due to the very slow wobbling of the Earth's rotational axis.

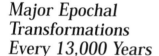

Major Epochal Transformations Every 13,000 Years Currently, we are near the junction point between the Age of Pisces and the Age of Aquarius. This point marks the time for a major epochal transformation in human civilization. This type of major transformation occurs only once every 12,960 years, corresponding to six hours on the Cosmic Clock.

At these special points there is a cosmic "changing of the guard." The old qualities of Cosmic Intelligence that have guided the evolution of human civilization for the previous 13,000 years are replaced by fresh new qualities, marking a new beginning for all of humanity. The new form of human civilization then is guided by the newly emergent qualities of Cosmic Intelligence during the subsequent 13,000 years, until it too grows old and loses its collective memory, and another major epochal transformation must occur.

The transitions that occur every six hours on the Cosmic Clock may be compared on a smaller scale to the transitions that occur every six hours on an ordinary clock. In our daily experience, we have given these times special names. They correspond to dawn (6 A.M.), noon (12 P.M.), sunset (6 P.M.), and midnight (12 A.M.).

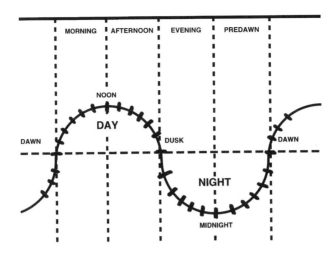

Figure 3—Twenty-Four Hour Cycle of Day and Night

The twenty-four-hour cycle of day and night can be divided into two twelve-hour periods (day and night) and four six-hour watches (morning, afternoon, evening, and predawn). The qualities of natural law manifest in collective awareness during these periods are different, and the transition points between these periods mark the times when the qualities of natural law must undergo profound changes.

These times mark profound transition points in Nature, when the laws of Nature undergo great transformations. During the transitions between these periods the qualified laws of Nature are temporarily suspended, and the unqualified transcendental reality shines through the fabric of Nature. Thus, in ancient cultures the transition points of dawn, noon, dusk, and midnight, were considered the most auspicious times to meditate and offer worship to God.

At each transition point, the qualities of natural law predominant during the previous six hours are replaced by a new set of qualities that predominate during the subsequent six hours. We know from our own personal experience that each six-hour "watch" has its own unique qualities, and feels quite different from the others.

The ordinary twenty-four-hour cycle of day and night thus involves four six-hour watches, and requires the hour hand to make two complete revolutions around the face of the clock. Like this daily cycle, the complete evolutionary cycle of human civilization also consists of twenty-four zodiacal Ages, and is divided into four "watches" comprising six zodiacal Ages each. Thus the hour hand of the Cosmic Clock must make two full revolutions around the twelve signs of the zodiac in order to complete each cycle of epochal Day and Night.

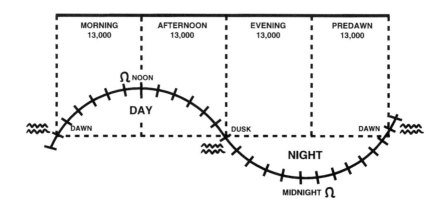

24 AGES, FOUR WATCHES OF EPOCHAL CYCLE
AND TRANSITION POINTS ∿∿∿ AND ♌

Figure 4—52,000 Year Cycle of Epochal Day and Night

The epochal cycle of Day and Night spans a total of twenty-four zodiacal Ages, each of which is approximately 2,160 years in length. Just as the daily cycle is divided into two periods of twelve hours each, so the epochal cycle is divided into two periods consisting of twelve Ages each. These constitute the epochal Day and Night. During the epochal Day the light of pure consciousness shines more brightly in collective awareness than during the epochal Night. Just as the daily cycle is further divided into four six-hour watches, so also the epochal cycle is further divided into four 13,000 year watches, each of which spans six zodiacal Ages. During these four watches the qualities of natural law that manifest in collective awareness are profoundly different. The transition points between watches correspond to epochal Dawn, Noon, Dusk, and Midnight. They occur at the beginnings of the Age of Aquarius and the Age of Leo.

The qualities of human civilization that manifest during the different watches do not repeat themselves in an endless round. Rather, they unfold in an upward evolutionary spiral. At the dawn of each new Day, the human race manifests a higher state of evolutionary development than at the dawn of the previous Day. This is how human life gradually progresses—Day by

Day—towards higher levels of spiritual enlightenment and social responsibility.

During this journey, the most important points correspond to the zodiacal Ages that mark the sixth and twelfth hour on the Cosmic Clock. These correspond to the Age of Aquarius and the Age of Leo, respectively. At the beginning of these two Ages, separated by approximately 13,000 years, major epochal transformations occur in human civilization, and new knowledge is imparted and new qualities are infused into the collective awareness of the human race.

Now that we stand at the threshold of a new Day, we are about to make a huge quantum jump in our collective evolution. The magnitude of this evolutionary jump is completely unprecedented. The sheer number of human beings walking the Earth at this time is unprecedented, and at no previous time in human history have such sophisticated material technologies been available to the masses. These are all important elements in the amazing drama that is about to unfold, as we step into the Light of a new Day of human civilization on Earth.

The entire human race is on the verge of a collective evolutionary transformation that will utterly and irrevocably alter every aspect of our existence in ways that we can only begin to imagine. It is now time to begin preparing for those changes, both individually and collectively, if we are to survive them and behold the Light of a new Day.

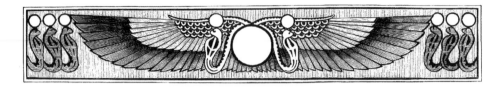

3. THE REVELATION OF JOHN

The epochal cycle of Day and Night described above is not unique to the Earth. It represents a universal cycle that governs the sequential unfoldment of human civilization on all Earth-like planets throughout the Universe.

Just as all individual human beings display certain common stages of developmental growth, so also, the various human civilizations located on different Earth-like planets throughout the Universe display the same or similar stages of evolutionary unfoldment. The specific periods of these cycles vary depending upon the location and nature of each given planet, but the basic structure of the cycle remains the same. The transformation from one stage to another is always governed by the sequential unfoldment of an epochal cycle of Day and Night, consisting of twenty-four zodiacal Ages and four watches. The epochal cycle of Day and Night thus may be understood as a universal archetype that is embedded in the very fabric of Creation itself.

This archetypical pattern is encrypted in many of the cultural myths and esoteric wisdom traditions that have been passed down from generation to generation throughout the Ages. For example, consider the following passage taken from the fourth chapter of the Revelation of John:

> After this I looked, and there before my eyes was a door opened in heaven; and the voice that I had first heard speaking to me like a trumpet said, 'Come up here, and I will show you what must happen hereafter.' At once I was caught up by the Spirit. There in Heaven stood a throne, and on the throne sat one whose appearance was like the gleam of jasper and cornelian; and round the throne was a rainbow, bright as an emerald. In a circle about this throne were twenty-four other thrones, and on them sat twenty-four elders, robed in white and wearing crowns of gold. From the throne went out flashes of lightning and peals of thunder. Burning before the throne

were seven flaming torches, the seven spirits of God, and in front of it stretched what seemed a sea of glass, like a sheet of ice.

In the centre, round the throne itself, were four living creatures, covered with eyes, in front and behind. The first creature was like a lion, the second like an ox, the third had a human face, the fourth was like an eagle in flight. The four living creatures, each of them with six wings, had eyes inside and out. . . .[7]

In the Book of Revelation, this passage sets the stage for the opening of the book or scroll that was sealed with seven seals, and which contained the revelation of the Apocalypse—the end of the current epochal cycle of human civilization.

The scene associated with this revelation is highly symbolic. Certain elements are represented here that specifically relate to the archetypical pattern of the epochal cycle of Day and Night. Let us consider some of these elements.

First, the One seated on the central throne, who lives for ever and ever, and who created all things, clearly represents God, the Creator. As the ultimate architect of time and space, and the Creator of all worlds, he is placed at the center of the circle of twenty-four thrones.

The Divine Messenger

It is said that "round the throne was a rainbow, bright as an emerald." The rainbow symbolizes the bridge, connection, link, or covenant between Heaven and Earth. In all the ancient traditions the link or connection between Heaven and Earth is associated with the Divine Messenger—the celestial being that mediates between the mortals on Earth and the immortals in Heaven.

In the Vedic tradition this celestial being was called Agni; in the Egyptian tradition he was called Thoth; in the Greek tradition he was called Hermes; and in the Roman tradition he was called Mercury. In the Christian tradition this same function was fulfilled by the Holy Spirit. Regardless of the names or forms that were associated with the Divine Messenger at different times and in different cultures, the universal function of the Divine Messenger is the same. He serves as the link between the Creator in Heaven and human beings on Earth.

One of the unique features of the Divine Messenger is that he is identified with the emerald, which embodies his own divine energy. Thus, in astrological traditions, the gemstone of the planet mercury is the emerald. Also, the most celebrated ancient alchemical text, ascribed to Hermes Trismegistus (thrice great Hermes) himself, is called the *Emerald Tablet (Tabula Smaragdina),* supposedly because it was originally inscribed on a tablet of emerald. This characteristic mark also is found in the description of the rainbow in the passage above. It is said that the rainbow was "bright as an emerald." This unmistakably identifies the rainbow around the throne with the Divine Presence of God—which is known as the Holy Spirit or Divine Messenger.

The Wheel of Time   The circle of twenty-four thrones surrounding the central throne may be interpreted as the Universal Wheel of Time that governs the evolution of human civilization on Earth and throughout the Universe. It represents the epochal cycle of Day and Night, consisting of twenty-four zodiacal Ages, which are specifically symbolized by the twenty-four thrones. The zodiacal Ages are represented by thrones because the qualities of divine intelligence that manifest during each Age rule the tendencies of all beings that live during that Age. The twenty-four Ages have immense power, for they literally govern the trends of time during their reign. They govern the birth and death, the rise and fall, of entire civilizations.

Only the Creator, who sits at the center of the Wheel, is not influenced by the power of time. Because he has created and presides over the Wheel of Time, he transcends its influence and thus lives for ever and ever, not experiencing the changes that created beings must endure.

The twenty-four elders who sit on the twenty-four thrones represent the collective consciousness of humanity during each of the twenty-four Ages.

They are represented as "elders" because they are our predecessors—our forefathers and foremothers. They are the ones who have come before us on the Wheel of Time. Having ascended to the celestial regions of Heaven, they observe us from afar, and are adorned in white robes and crowns of gold.

Emanations of
Divine Power

The "flashes of lightning and peals of thunder" that emanate from the central throne represent the emanations of creative power and divine law that are carried by the Divine Messenger to the various regions of the Universe. Just as a thunderstorm, which is filled with flashes of lightning and peals of thunder, serves to balance opposing electrical forces in Nature, so also, the emanations of God serve to balance the opposing spiritual forces that arise in Nature at different times.

These emanations may be understood as luminous vortex filaments of subtle matter-energy. These cosmic filaments have been variously described by the ancient Seers as pillars of fire, columns of fire, tubes of fire, threads of creation, cosmic reeds, branches of the burning bush, branches of the Tree of Life, etc. The ancient Seers often described the same phenomena in many different ways using various metaphors.

However, the metaphorical nature of these intuitive descriptions does not impinge on their precision or accuracy. It should be no surprise to find that a lightning bolt may be described scientifically as an elongated luminous vortex filament composed of charged particles (electrons and ions). The word "vortex" refers to the helical motions of the elementary particles as they propagate along the filament. This motion resembles the circular motion of water in a bathtub whirlpool, or air in a tornado. This same vortex motion also is found in the luminous subtle matter-energy that makes up the lightning-like emanations of the Creator.

God's divine will is symbolized by the peals of thunder associated with the lightning bolts. The will of God is manifest in his divine speech, which resonates like thunder in the fathomless bosom of Heaven. This speech is not audible to ordinary ears. It can be heard only on the level of pure consciousness as primordial sound, or divine speech. Divine speech is pregnant with the organizing power of Nature—natural law. It gives direction and purpose to the emanations of divine power that emanate from the throne of God.

Here on Earth, the emanations of divine power descend from Heaven at periodic intervals. The Divine Messenger comes every 2,160 years to initiate the transformations from one zodiacal Age to another, and he comes every 13,000 years to initiate the transformations from one watch to another. However, there is an especially powerful emanation of divine power that comes every 52,000 years to initiate the transition from one Day to another— and this transition occurs at Dawn. Because the hour hand of our own Cosmic Clock is now approaching 6 A.M., we anticipate that an extremely powerful emanation of divine power will descend upon Earth sometime within the next ten to twenty years. The visions described in the Revelation of John specifically refer to this period of time we are now entering.

The Seven Layers of Universal Life   The next image presented in the passage refers to the "seven flaming torches, the seven spirits of God" that stand before the central throne. These represent the seven layers of universal life that surround the throne of God at the very center of the Universe. These seven layers of universal life are blazing with celestial fire, and collectively constitute the subtle structure of the Universe as a whole.

When perceived on the level of nonlocal intuition, the Universe as a whole displays the structure of a vast luminous Cosmic Egg, composed of seven concentric layers of universal life. Each of these seven layers is filled with billions of worlds and innumerable beings. Seven aspects of God's universal awareness oversee the evolution of these seven groups of worlds; the beings that dwell in them are represented by the seven spirits of God. All emanations of divine power descending from the throne of God must pass through these seven spirits or seven layers of universal life in order to reach the Earth. To clearly envision the structural relationships among these layers, we will need to present a nonlocal map of the Universe as a whole. This subject will be taken up in chapters 6 and 7.

The "sea of glass" or "sheet of ice" that stretches in front of the throne represents the cold and dark metaphysical sea of consciousness that surrounds the luminous structure of the Cosmic Egg on all sides. This sea of consciousness is vast beyond imagining, and may be compared to the transparent embryonic fluid that envelops, nourishes, and protects the golden yoke of the Cosmic Egg. It is perfectly still like a waveless ocean, and resembles a vacuum or void, empty of all manifest forms and phenomena. It is also extremely cold—much colder than anything within the Cosmic Egg. Indeed, it is colder than absolute zero, and represents a field of perfect order and zero entropy.[8] Hence, though it has a fluid character, it is described as a "sheet of ice."

The Four Living Creatures

The four living creatures located around the throne represent the four aspects of God's divine awareness that oversee the transformation of one 13,000 year watch into another.

They are described as "living creatures, covered with eyes, in front and behind" because they are all-seeing modes of divine awareness that comprehend both the past and future course of all things. They witness the activities of human beings and understand the roots of those actions in the ancient past and their consequences in the far distant future.

Each living creature is described as having "six wings." These wings symbolize the six zodiacal Ages associated with each watch. The ancient metaphor *tempis fugit*— "time flies" is employed here. By means of its six wings (or Ages) each watch of 13,000 years flies along its course.

For ordinary mortals caught upon the Wheel of Time, the passage of time crawls slowly through the months, years, centuries, and millennia. On the other hand, for the immortals, continuously immersed in the bliss of God, time revolves smoothly along its course.

The four living creatures are symbolically described as a lion, an ox, a human, and an eagle. These same four symbols had appeared earlier in the

Old Testament, in visions of Ezekiel:

> I saw a storm wind coming from the north, a vast cloud with flashes of fire and brilliant light about it; and within was a radiance like brass, glowing in the heart of the flames. In the fire was the semblance of four living creatures. . . . Each had four faces. . . . all four had the face of a man and the face of a lion . . . the face of an ox and the face of an eagle. . . . The appearance of the creatures was as if fire from burning coals or torches were darting to and fro among them; the fire was radiant and out of the fire came lightning.[9]

These symbols are deeply esoteric. What do they signify? We believe that they are symbols of the four astrological signs that rise together when one 13,000 year watch is being transformed into another. It is at such times that the pillar of celestial fire descends upon the Earth like a lightning bolt from Heaven.

In astrology, the sign of Leo may be symbolized by a lion, the sign of Taurus by an ox, the sign of Aquarius by a human, and the sign of Scorpio by an eagle.[10] Whenever there is a transition from one 13,000 year watch to another, these four signs rise together at the equinoxes and solstices.

Thirteen thousand years ago, when Leo rose in the east on the morning of the spring equinox, then Scorpio rose in the east on the morning of the summer solstice, Aquarius rose in the east on the morning of the autumn equinox, and Taurus rose in the east on the morning of the winter solstice. This is what is meant when it is said that the four signs rise together.

The Greeks had a name for signs or constellations that rise together in this fashion. They were called *paranatellonta*. The four signs called Leo, Taurus, Aquarius, and Scorpio are the paranatellonta of one another. Whenever one of them rises on a solstice or equinox, all the others must rise as well.

Symbolically speaking, the four living creatures thus may be said to preside over the transformation of one 13,000 year watch into another. They manifest themselves at those times when God's celestial fire descends upon our planet in its full glory, and a new Golden Age dawns for all humankind. They thus hold the key to human destiny in their hands.

The Sphinx

It is interesting to note that some ancient traditions associate the four living creatures with the original form of the Sphinx.

> Before the Sphinx was carved into its present configuration, its earlier form, according to ancient Egyptian and Coptic traditions, was that it had the front paws of a lion, the back paws and tail of a bull, and the face of a human. Furthermore, along its sides, where today one can see the remains of stone incendiary boxes, fires were lit at night to give the Sphinx the appearance of having the flaming wings of an eagle.[11]

Is it possible that the Sphinx holds the key to human destiny within its grasp? Many esoteric traditions believe that the Seers of the distant past buried their most profound knowledge in a secret underground chamber or "Hall of Records" beneath the Sphinx. This ancient tradition now has found some modern corroboration. Recent seismic surveys have located a rectangular chamber beneath the paws of the Sphinx, and the opening of this chamber is bound to occur sometime within the next few years. Is this the fabled Hall of Records? Does it contain knowledge and information that is critical to the destiny of mankind?

In their recent book, *The Message of the Sphinx: A Quest for the Hidden Legacy of Mankind,* Graham Hancock and Robert Bauval have attempted to decipher the architectural cryptogram embodied by the Sphinx and the Pyramids of the Giza plateau, using clues from the ancient texts and stellar correlations. They propose that in addition to the rectangular chamber beneath the front paws of the Sphinx, there may be yet another undiscovered chamber, which they call the "Genesis chamber," buried deep beneath the rear paws of the Sphinx.

In addition, their investigations, which are based upon archeological and geologic evidence, as well as celestial correlations, suggest that the Sphinx may be vastly older than is currently believed. They suggest that the Sphinx may date back to around 10,500 B.C.—a time early in the astrological Age of Leo. During that epoch, the four signs Leo, Taurus, Aquarius, and Scorpio also rose at the solstices and equinoxes. Did the Sphinx originally represent a stone embodiment of four living creatures described by the prophet Ezekiel and John? Does it preside over the transition from one world Age to another? Does it hold a secret message for all mankind?

Having set the elaborate scene described above, John then goes on to describe the opening of the sacred scroll, sealed with seven seals. This scroll is said to contain the portents of what is to come hereafter, at the time of the Apocalypse—the end of the present world Age. A detailed exegesis of the seven portents associated with this prophesy lies beyond the scope of this book.

However, we would like to ask the following questions: Why did John go to such lengths to set the scene described above for his revelations? Was he delineating in cryptic terms an esoteric key that would unlock the mystery of the Ages? Was he revealing an ancient secret, passed on among the initiated since time immemorial, concerning the cycle of the Ages—and the ultimate fate of mankind? Was he privy to the secrets of the Sacred Science of the Seers—a science so profound and so powerful that it must be hidden, buried in secret vaults, and veiled in esoteric metaphors, to keep it from being discovered and misused by the worldly powers that rule the general population? Or was he a simple Seer, who cognized in his own pure awareness the Truth concerning the cycle of the Ages, and the monumental events that await us at the end of time?

From the cryptic description given above, it seems clear that John was deeply aware of the fundamental principles of the Sacred Science. It seems he also was aware of the profound implications that those principles had for the whole human race, especially at the present time, which may be understood as the time of Revelation.

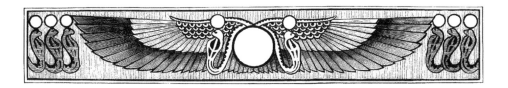

4. THE NATURE OF PURE KNOWLEDGE

The knowledge of the Divine Plan and the cycles of time that govern its unfoldment constitutes only a small portion of a vast body of esoteric knowledge that once was possessed by many ancient cultures and "prehistoric" civilizations around the world. This ancient knowledge, which may be called the *Sacred Science of the Seers,* is the most powerful and mysterious knowledge that ever has been revealed to human awareness.

The Sacred Science is not an ordinary empirical science. It is a spiritual science. Those who discover and develop this knowledge are not ordinary scientists. They are spiritual visionaries or Seers. This means that the Sacred Science comes primarily through spiritual vision and intuitive cognition. It also may be developed on the basis of objective experimentation. But it comes primarily as a self-revealed "gift" of pure knowledge.

Pure Consciousness   Those who receive the gift of pure knowledge are called Seers. They are called Seers because they have developed the ability to see the world through the eye of *pure consciousness.* Although this concept is somewhat abstract, it holds the key to understanding the Sacred Science. Therefore it will be useful to understand what is meant by "pure consciousness" and how the world appears when viewed through it.

In essence, pure consciousness is our own deepest and truest being. Through deep transcendental meditation[12] it may be experienced as the simplest, least excited state of human awareness. But it also is more than that. It is not just a state of human awareness. It is the unbounded field of pure intelligence that underlies all things in Creation. It is the eternal, infinite, nameless, formless, state of pure Being that serves as the very Self of the entire Universe.

The ancient Vedic Seers divided the structure of reality into four main levels of existence which were called (i) gross, (ii) subtle, (iii) causal, and (iv) transcendental. The first three of these levels possess a material nature and exist within the field of Creation. The fourth level transcends all created forms and phenomena, and is identical with the field of pure consciousness that underlies all things.

Levels of Existence	Constituent Substance
Gross	Elementary Particles and Atomic Matter
Subtle	Polarized Subtle Matter-Energy
Causal	Unpolarized Subtle Matter-Energy
Transcendental	Superfluid Pure Consciousness

The Four Levels of Existence

The relationships among these four levels may be explained using a simple analogy. If the fourth or transcendental level is compared to the ground of all existence, then causal phenomena correspond to the seeds planted within that ground, subtle phenomena correspond to the sprouts arising from those seeds, and gross phenomena correspond to the plants and trees that develop from the sprouts. The different levels thus are hierarchically related. Each level of existence provides the basis and support for the emergence of the next grosser level.

For the sake of simplicity, throughout the remainder of this book, the term "subtle" will be used to refer to both the subtle and causal realms of existence, which may be characterized as mental levels of experience. The realm of gross existence, on the other hand, corresponds to the entire field of objective experience.

The field of pure consciousness belongs to neither the mental nor the objective realms of experience. It transcends them both and is completely independent. According to the ancient Seers, the unbounded field of pure consciousness is none other than the Supreme Being who serves as the Universal Knower and Creator of all things. This Universal Being is completely self-sufficient in its ability to know or apprehend reality. It does not need to operate through the mind, intellect, or senses in order to know something. The universal field of pure consciousness can see without eyes, hear without ears, and know without mind.

> He seizes, though he has no hands. He walks, though he has no feet. He sees, though he has no eyes. He hears, though he has no ears. He knows everyone, though Himself is not known by anyone. The wise call Him the primordial Being—the Ancient One.[13]

Nonlocal Intuition

The unique type of comprehension that exists on the level of pure consciousness may be understood as a form of *nonlocal intuition*. The faculty of nonlocal intuition is not available on the levels of the mind, intellect, or senses. It is available only on the level of pure consciousness.

The word "nonlocal" basically means "faster than light." Nonlocal intuition is the type of knowing that enables the enlightened Seers to instantaneously apprehend vast regions of space—regions that may span millions or billions of light-years—within their own unbounded awareness.

The mind, intellect, and senses can function only locally—at the speed of light. Pure consciousness, on the other hand, is nonlocal in its functioning. It instantaneously can embrace vast regions of space that are unimaginable to our limited minds and intellects.

Through the faculty of nonlocal intuition the ancient Seers were able to probe the fathomless bosom of Heaven and discern the divine correspondences that exist between Heaven and Earth. These divine correspondences may be understood as the nonlocal relationships that exist between the macrocosm and the microcosm.

It is these relationships that enable the human soul to reflect the Light of Heaven. It is these relationships that enable the human soul to reflect within itself the image of God. The divine correspondences between Heaven and Earth are the essential keys that are needed to unlock all the secrets of the ancient Sacred Science.

Clearly, the comprehension of these divine correspondences is not ordinary knowledge. It is not something that one can find in a book. It can be known only intuitively on the level of pure consciousness. The ancient Seers called this type of intuitive knowledge *pure knowledge.*

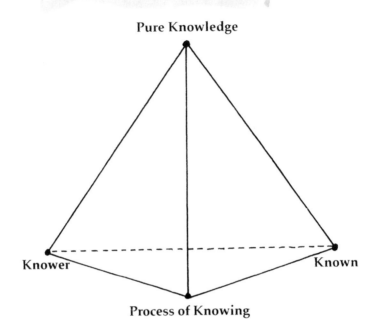

Figure 5—The Three-In-One Structure of Pure Knowledge

If the relationships among the knower, process of knowing and known are symbolically represented as forming a triangle, the unified structure of pure knowledge then may be represented by a single point which unites the three points of the base triangle. The total set of relationships forms a tetrahedron, the simplest Platonic solid, which the Greeks believed symbolized the sacred fire—the fire of pure knowledge.

Simply stated, pure knowledge may be defined as the unified wholeness of the knower, process of knowing, and known.[14] It represents a state of knowledge in which the knower and the object of knowledge are nonlocally connected to form a single unified whole.

On the level of pure knowledge, the very soul of an object is cognized as it exists within itself. The transparent essence of the object stands self-revealed, without any veils to hide it.

This type of experience is completely self-referral in its nature. To experience the nonlocal reality of an object on the level of pure consciousness, one must breathe the very soul of the object and become one with it. Having become one with the object, even from a distance, it ceases to be an object and becomes an aspect of one's own Self. This is how the Seers cognized the deepest essence and truest being of the world around them.

Transparent pure knowledge is the secret essence of Creation. It is secret because it exists only on the level of pure consciousness. It cannot be accessed by mind, intellect, or senses, so it remains hidden or concealed from everyone except the Seers.

The Unmanifest Blueprint of Creation

When the Seers comprehend the structure of pure knowledge within themselves their awareness becomes filled with both primordial sound and light. The sound conveys the spiritual name or identity of the object, while the light conveys the spiritual form of the object. Of these two, the name is more subtle than the form. It precedes the form, and is the very soul of the object.

Through the faculty of nonlocal intuition, the ancient Seers were able to comprehend the spiritual names and forms of all things in Creation. The structure of the Universe as a whole was comprehended in terms of resonant patterns of primordial sound and light. This grand awakening of totality embodied the blueprint of Creation, the very soul of the Universe.

Within the unmanifest blueprint of Creation are the archetypes or ideal forms of all things. These archetypes are embedded in the universal field of pure consciousness as vibratory patterns of primordial sound and light.

The knowledge of the transcendental patterns of primordial sound and light inherent within the blueprint of Creation constitutes the essence of the Sacred Science. Because this knowledge can be gained only by the Seers, it is called the Sacred Science of the Seers. But the Seers did not invent or originate this knowledge. They merely cognized it on the level of pure consciousness.

The Seers may come and go, and the expressions of pure knowledge may wax and wane at different times in human civilization, but the Sacred Science in itself is eternal and will go on forever. It cannot die because it is nonlocally embedded in the very structure of pure consciousness, and may be cognized in each new Age by new Seers.

Anyone who is established in pure consciousness, and who has the requisite power of intuition may re-cognize the sacred knowledge. This can happen at any time, anywhere in Creation.

Expressions of Pure Knowledge

But the mere cognition of the knowledge is not enough. It is one thing to cognize the knowledge, and another to understand it intellectually. The ability to understand and express the knowledge depends upon the functioning of the mind, intellect, and senses. These faculties are profoundly influenced by the vast cycles of time that govern the sequential unfoldment of human civilization on Earth.

This means that the full understanding of the Sacred Science can evolve and take shape only in the minds of the Seers during the Golden Ages of humanity. Although the Seers may cognize the pure knowledge on the level of unbounded pure consciousness, their ability to comprehend the practical implications of that knowledge is conditioned by the times in which they live. When in the cycle of Ages the collective consciousness of humanity as a whole is clouded by ignorance, the Seers also will be impaired in their ability to express and share the knowledge with others.

Different Seers have cognized the Truth at different times, and depending upon the time in which they lived, they have expressed it differently. They naturally used the metaphors, images, and symbols that were consistent with the cultural and linguistic traditions of the regions and times in which they dwelt.

Unfortunately, the Truth is not captured by such relative expressions—it is merely indicated. The real Truth cannot be found in any book or expression of knowledge, no matter how spiritually inspired, scientific, or logical it might be. It can be found only within one's own Self, on the level of pure consciousness.

The true source of the Sacred Science is the eternal, uncreated, and indestructible blueprint of pure knowledge that is embedded within the structure of pure consciousness. All of the manifest expressions of knowledge are designed merely to awaken that blueprint within one's own soul.

Because of the variety souls on Earth, the Seers have employed many different expressions to accomplish this purpose over the ages. What resonates with one person in one time may not resonate with another person in another time—so different systems of philosophy, religion, and science have been promulgated at different times and in different regions to satisfy the needs of the diverse tendencies in human society.

Although it may seem that the world's various traditions of knowledge have arisen in a helter-skelter fashion, driven by forces of chance and opportunity, in truth, all ancient traditions of knowledge have been part of a Divine Plan for the evolution of human society on Earth—a plan that is now rapidly approaching its culmination.

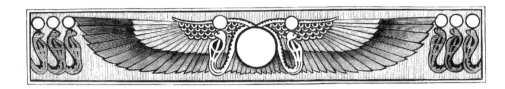

5. THE SACRED SCIENCE OF THE SEERS

The Sacred Science described above is not an abstract spiritual philosophy. It is a real science, which when properly understood has profound practical, technological applications.

The essential teaching of the Sacred Science concerns the relationship between pure consciousness and ordinary atomic matter. All forms of spiritual and material evolution that are relevant to human life depend upon this relationship. Indeed, the relationship between consciousness and matter holds the key to unlock all the treasures in Heaven and Earth.

The technologies associated with the Sacred Science are specifically designed to infuse consciousness into atomic matter. Such technologies are not trivial. They are the most powerful technologies available to human beings anywhere in the Universe. Unlike modern technologies, the subtle technologies are not based upon the principles of ordinary electronics. They are based upon the deepest principles of the Sacred Science, and utilize specific sacred sounds, crystals, precious metals, and currents of subtle matter-energy or celestial fire.[15]

Subtle matter is the finest, most subtle material substance in Creation, and is directly responsible for upholding the relationship between pure consciousness and atomic matter. Because it is composed of tiny charged particles, subtle matter can present a luminous appearance. Our auras and individual spiritual bodies are made out of this luminous material. It is also the stuff out of which the celestial bodies of the gods and angels are made.

As stated previously, the ancient Vedic Seers called this substance chitta (mind stuff).[16] It was called mind stuff because it provides the material basis for the reflection of consciousness in all created beings.

The ancient Taoist masters called this same substance chi, the electromagnetic life force that serves as the link between pure spirit and gross matter.[17] Although chi is a material substance, it is considered responsible for all forms of mental processing, thus displaying properties that are partly subjective and partly objective.

These notions are not unique to the Seers of the East. The western Seers of the ancient Hermetic tradition, which has deep roots in ancient Egypt, concur by saying:

> Mind. . . is the very substance of God, if indeed there is a substance of God.[18]

In general, subtle matter (chitta or chi) may be viewed as the subtle life force that supports all forms of life throughout the Universe. This field of matter-energy is not constituted of electrons, protons, neutrons, or photons. It is composed of charged particles that are extremely subtle, in fact trillions of times smaller than electrons, and thus far too minute to be detected individually by modern instruments.[19]

Experience of Subtle Matter-Energy

Although this life force is extremely subtle, it is not completely beyond perception. On the contrary, it forms an intimate part of our everyday experience. Every object or individual in our environment manifests its own unique field of subtle life force, which pervades and envelops that object or individual on all sides. When we encounter these different objects and individuals, we perceive the different qualities displayed by the fields of life force that surround them. These subtle perceptions spontaneously influence our own field of life force, and we feel differently.

For example, in some places, for no particular reason, our hearts are happy, while in others our hearts are sad. In some places our minds are clear, and in others our minds are dull. These qualitative perceptions are not based just upon the data provided by our five senses. They are based upon perceptions of subtle matter-energy made directly by our hearts and minds.

Almost everyone has had the experience of being with someone who "puts on a happy face," but whose presence nevertheless is heavy and depressing. On the other hand, another person may illumine a room with happiness and brightness by their very presence, without saying or doing anything.

The influence of subtle matter-energy also plays a very important role in sexual attraction. The glow that usually is associated with sexual attraction is not just caused by the sheen on a person's face or the luster of their hair. It is due to the subtle life force that surrounds them on all sides. Because men and women possess opposite "charges" of subtle matter-energy, they attract each other like magnets. This invisible magnetic attraction is an effect of the interactions of the fields of subtle life force that radiate from every pore in our bodies.

The field of subtle life force that radiates from a given person will vary in its strength and quality during the normal course of a day and also over the course of a person's lifetime. It is most strongly influenced by the quality of our thoughts and emotions. In particular, the life-nourishing quality of the life force is powerfully enhanced by the emotions of love, happiness, and contentment, and it is diminished by the emotions of anger, misery, and anxiety.

When we are filled with love, we radiate that love into our environment and we leave an invisible cloud of love hanging in the atmosphere wherever we go. Everything we touch then becomes infused with our nourishing life force, and everyone around us is raised to a higher level of awareness, emotional balance, and health. As we continue to pour our love into the environment, we become channels through which the subtle life force of the Universe may flow in ever more powerful streams.

When the human soul attains the state of spiritual enlightenment, it becomes an inexhaustible source of this nourishing life force. The universal love that surrounds such a soul nourishes the entire Universe and serves as a powerful magnet that attracts all beings. By bathing in the field of universal love that surrounds such an enlightened soul, a large number of unenlightened souls may be spontaneously healed, emotionally balanced, and elevated to higher states of awareness. Just as a single candle may light many candles, or a single seed may produce a plant containing many seeds—so each enlightened soul becomes a powerful source of nourishing life force that can fill an almost unlimited number of empty cups.

Subtle Matter
Technologies

The enlightened Seers, who gained their knowledge by direct spiritual vision and intuitive cognition, directly perceived the currents of subtle matter in themselves and in their environment as luminous streams of celestial fire. This direct knowledge allowed the Seers of ancient times to develop subtle technologies that had many marvelous applications.

In the ancient civilizations that long ago disappeared from our collective memory, the subtle technologies were used to heal and rejuvenate the spiritual body, resulting in extended life and spiritual enlightenment. Through such spiritual healing methods, otherwise incurable mental and physical diseases could be completely reversed, and the body could be filled with spiritual Light and elevated to a state of perfect health. Because these technologies integrated the spiritual and material realms of existence, and awakened the Divine Presence in otherwise unconscious matter, they were considered the most priceless, sacred treasures of entire cultures.

The legends associated with the Ark of the Covenant (chapter 34), for example, give some idea of the profound fascination and worshipful significance that certain spiritualized objects have held for vast numbers of people during the course of recorded history. However, we believe that these stories merely record the last known example of a lost technology that once was possessed by Seers around the world.

During the previous Golden Age the enlightened Seers used their sacred technologies to perform miraculous feats to call down the Light of Heaven onto the Earth. However, over the many thousands of years, there has been a gradual decline of spiritual awareness on our planet. Because of this decline, both the Sacred Science and its subtle technologies have been lost.

Such technologies generally are available only during the Golden Ages of humanity, when the light of pure consciousness shines in the hearts of the people. During the Dark Ages of humanity, they are hidden away, cloaked in mystery, and buried beneath a thick rubble of myth and legend. Now that the Dark Ages of humanity are coming to an end, and a new Golden Age is about to dawn, it is time for the Sacred Science of the Seers and its associated technologies to resurface in human awareness.

The Sacred Science of the Seers should be viewed as a supreme gift, a divine legacy that we have received from the gods. It resembles the Promethian Fire.[20] It is not a toy. It must be used wisely and with great respect, for it has immense power both to create and to destroy.

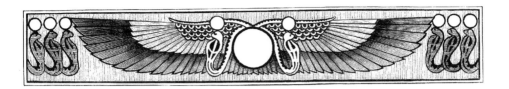

6. THE HOLOGRAPHIC SPECTRUM OF CREATION

Just as our lost memory is restored when we wake up at the beginning of each new Day, in the same manner, our position and role in the scheme of God's Creation also is restored. In order for us to fully understand our role in Creation, we must first become realigned with the overall structure of the Universe.

The physical Universe actually is a much larger and more amazing place than even the most adventuresome astrophysicist might imagine. Using our best telescopes, the farthest that we can see into outer space is only a few billion light-years. Beyond that is the Hubble limit, where the light from the distant galaxies is so red-shifted that it completely disappears from the visible spectrum. It is not possible, even in principle, to see beyond this region using ordinary visible light. The Hubble limit thus forms the boundary of our *local universe.*

But it does not form the boundary of the Universe as a whole. Those who possess the faculty of nonlocal intuition can see beyond this limit, and grasp the total structure of the Universe within their own unbounded pure awareness. Using this inner vision, the ancient Seers compared the structure of the Universe to a divine mansion or castle, filled with many cosmic rooms.

The cosmic rooms within the overall structure of the Universe cannot be seen with telescopes. They can be seen only through the faculty of nonlocal intuition, through the eye of pure consciousness. The cosmic rooms represent the different states of universal knowledge that are experienced by the Seer as his or her awareness expands or contracts through different scales of time and space.

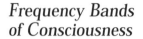

Frequency Bands of Consciousness

Each of these rooms is associated with its own frequencies of consciousness, which are experienced as different qualities of spiritual sound. The universal knowledge inherent in each cosmic room can be experienced by attuning one's awareness to these universal spiritual sounds. This is how the knowledge is received into our individual awareness.

The different qualities of spiritual sound associated with the different cosmic rooms may be understood technically as different frequency bands of consciousness. These frequency bands constitute the holographic spectrum of Creation.

Just as different frequency bands within the electromagnetic spectrum may be used to carry enormous amounts of information, such as various television and radio programs, similarly, the different frequency bands of consciousness that constitute the holographic spectrum of Creation carry vast amounts of universal knowledge.

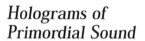

Holograms of Primordial Sound and Light

This knowledge is nonlocally stored within the all-pervading field of subtle matter-energy as interference patterns of primordial sound and light. These interference patterns play the role of vast holograms embedded within the very fabric of space.

An ordinary hologram is an interference pattern of coherent light that is recorded on a piece of photographic film. Once the interference pattern has been recorded, the film may be used to recreate a three-dimensional image of the object. This is accomplished by shining coherent light through the film once again. When this is done, the information about the object that is nonlocally stored within the hologram is spontaneously reassembled, and a waveform is projected into space that recreates the three-dimensional image of the original object.

Similarly, holographic projections can take place within the unbounded awareness of the Seers. In the case of these subjective holograms, the all-pervading field of subtle matter-energy plays the role of the film, and the frequencies of primordial sound within the field of pure consciousness play the role of beams of coherent light.

Just as an ordinary hologram displays its stored images when a beam of coherent light is passed through it, so also, the knowledge stored in the vast holograms of space may be recalled when a particular resonance of primordial sound is awakened in the pure consciousness of the Seer. In some traditions these holograms are called the *akashic records*. They hold the record of every thought, word, and deed projected by every being in Creation since the beginning of time.

More specifically, each frequency band of primordial sound within the holographic spectrum contains its own unique version of the unmanifest blueprint of Creation. It presents its own story of Creation, from beginning to end, as viewed from that scale of time and space. Thus, by attuning one's awareness to the different frequency bands, one can gain access to the different storehouses of pure knowledge and the visions of reality associated with them.

The Mechanics of Creation   This is how the ancient Seers gained knowledge about the mechanics of Creation. They tapped into the frequency bands that exist on the larger scales of time and space and downloaded the knowledge associated with those bands into their own awareness. Because the knowledge stored on the larger scales of time and space is universally the same, different Seers belonging to different cultures and religious traditions have described the mechanics of Creation in similar ways.

The Seers often described the mechanics of Creation using the metaphor of a primordial fluid. This fluid, which resembles a void, is stirred into activity by the Breath or Word of God. Although the details vary slightly from tradition to tradition, a generic version of the Creation myth might go something like the following:

In the beginning, the forms and phenomena of Creation did not exist. The entire Universe was dissolved within the primordial waters, which were quiescent as a waveless sea. At that time the primordial waters were covered in darkness, and resembled a void or abyss. Then, at the inception of Creation, a cosmic wind or breath passed across the face of the deep, and the waters began to stir and move within themselves. This breath carried the Divine Word, which existed before Creation. The Divine Word was identical with the unmanifest blueprint of Creation (or Logos) that has existed since all Eternity within the divine awareness of the Creator. By means of the Word, the cover of darkness was removed and the primordial waters began to flow and swirl within themselves. This caused the Light to become separated from the darkness, the subtle to become separated from the gross. Various gradations of matter and energy thereby evolved within the fathomless bosom of Nature. Through subsequent stages of transformation, these gradations of matter and energy eventually coagulated into the finite form of the Universe as a whole. The Universe then appeared as a luminous Cosmic Egg floating upon the primordial waters. Like the Cosmic Sun rising out of the ocean at dawn, it dispersed the nocturnal gloom and filled the darkness with Light. Having caused the material structure of the Universe to become manifest, the Supreme Being then entered into his Creation by breathing the breath of life, the Divine Word, into it. It is the Divine Word alone that appears as the immortal soul of all beings in Creation.

The ancient Seers were fond of describing the mechanics of Creation in this manner because this is how the process appeared to them on the more universal levels of their own awareness. By expanding their awareness, the Seers thus were able to gain more general knowledge concerning the Universe as a whole, and by contracting their awareness they were able to gain more specific knowledge concerning individual places and things. In this way the entire Universe was open to them like a book—and they read it through the eye of pure consciousness.

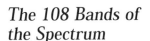

The 108 Bands of the Spectrum

According to the ancient Vedic Seers there are a total of 108 frequency bands of consciousness that constitute the complete holographic spectrum of Creation. This spectrum extends from the largest scale of time and space to the smallest scale of time and space in the field of relative existence. The Transcendental Reality that transcends the entire field of relative existence may be called the Supreme Being.

The Supreme Being lies beyond all names and forms. It is simultaneously bigger than the biggest, and smaller than the smallest wavelengths of consciousness within the field of time and space. Thus, it is characterized by both infinite dynamism and infinite silence, infinite frequency and zero frequency, at the same time.

The 108 frequency bands that lie within the field of relative existence constitute the ancient secret path by which the nonlocal awareness of the Supreme Being simultaneously ascends and descends into the field of Creation. In the process of this cosmic ascent and descent, the Supreme Being simultaneously and sequentially assumes the role of all beings, both sentient and insentient.

The holographic spectrum spans a range of space-time scales that is inconceivably huge. The entire spectrum is divided into two halves—the macroscopic half and the microscopic half. Each of these halves contains exactly fifty-four frequency bands. The structure of experience available in the upper half of the spectrum is increasingly filled with the light of pure knowledge, while the structure of experience available in the lower half is increasingly filled with the darkness of pure ignorance.

Human awareness spans the gap between these two halves. It bridges the gulf between pure knowledge and pure ignorance. It exists on that scale of the holographic spectrum that lies exactly in between the largest and smallest scales in Creation. This is the scale where individual beings, clothed in material Nature, first wake up to their true status and become identified with universal pure consciousness.

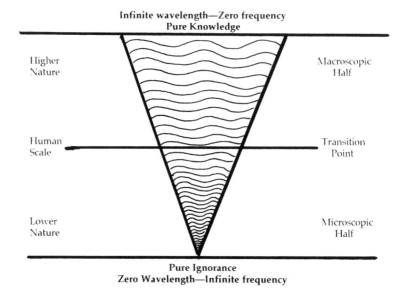

Infinite wavelength—Zero frequency
Pure Knowledge

Higher
Nature

Macroscopic
Half

Human
Scale

Transition
Point

Lower
Nature

Microscopic
Half

Pure Ignorance
Zero Wavelength—Infinite frequency

Figure 6—Holographic Spectrum of Creation

The holographic spectrum of Creation may be compared to the electromagnetic spectrum. However, it is not composed of electromagnetic waves. Rather it is composed of waves of primordial sound or nonlocal impulses of consciousness. The spectrum is divided into two halves—the macroscopic half and the microscopic half. Human awareness spans the gap between these two halves. Human awareness sits at the junction point between the worlds of spiritual Light and the worlds of material darkness that respectively constitute the upper and lower halves of the universal spectrum.

Once the human soul becomes fully identified with universal pure consciousness, it automatically gains the ability to ascend the scales of Creation and cognize the higher spiritual planes of reality. Through such cognitions, the Seers gain access to the blueprint of Creation as it exists on different scales of celestial existence. They gain access to the structure of universal knowledge available in the different cosmic rooms of Creation. Having gained access to this knowledge they then have the responsibility to make it accessible for the betterment of mankind. The Seers do this as part of the Divine Plan, whose ultimate goal is to make every aspect of human life on Earth a perfect reflection of divine life in Heaven.

Ordinary human beings do not have the ability to ascend and descend the scales of Creation. Unlike the Seers, ordinary humans are stuck in their own frequency band—they are locked onto their own channel of experience.

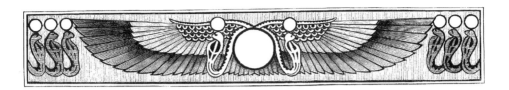

7. THE SEVEN-LAYERED STRUCTURE OF THE UNIVERSE

Ordinary human awareness is locked onto the various forms of matter and energy that exist within our local region of the Universe. According to the nonlocal vision of the ancient Seers, human beings live in the outermost of seven concentric layers of universal life that collectively form the Cosmic Egg. These seven layers of universal life are filled with subtle matter-energy or celestial fire. Because they appear to be blazing with celestial fire, in the Revelation of John they were described as seven flames, and were identified with the seven universal spirits of God.

In the Vedic tradition these seven layers were identified as the seven higher worlds or *Sapta Lokas*. Starting with the outermost layer and progressing towards the innermost layer, these were called *Bhu Loka* (the Galactic World), *Bhuvar Loka* (the Astral or Dream World), *Suvar Loka* (the Shining Heaven), *Mahar Loka* (the World of Great Souls), *Janar Loka* (the World of Divine Beings), *Tapo Loka* (the World of Evolutionary Fire), and *Satya Loka* (the World of Truth).[21]

These seven heavenly regions were directly cognized through the faculty of nonlocal intuition by the great Seers in every ancient tradition. Consider for example, the following passage from the ancient Hermetic texts that traditionally are ascribed to the Divine Messenger (Hermes Trismegistus), and which present the mechanics of Creation:

> And the fiery substance became self-organized, with the gods therein; *and Heaven appeared, with its Seven Spheres,* and the gods, made visible in starry forms, with all of their constellations. And Heaven revolved, and began to run its circling course. [emphasis added] [22]

The seven luminous spheres that constitute the Cosmic Egg are the abodes of all created beings in the Universe. Each of the seven layers is filled with billions of worlds and countless individual beings of different types.

To oversee and administer the evolution of the various worlds and beings within these seven layers, the Creator, remaining one and undivided, has as if divided his awareness into a seven-fold aura or halo of Divine Presence, symbolized in the Revelation of John by the rainbow surrounding the throne of divine power. The seven aspects of this halo of Divine Presence are the seven spirits of God, which collectively constitute the Holy Spirit or Divine Messenger.

The Holy Spirit or Divine Messenger is nothing other than the extended presence of the Creator within the field of Creation. It is through the Holy Spirit, divided into seven different aspects, one for each layer of universal life, that the Creator expresses his divine will and administers the Universe. In various traditions, these seven aspects of God's divine all-seeing awareness are called the seven administrators, the seven spirits, the seven sages, or the seven Seers.

The outermost of the seven layers of universal life, which itself spans an enormous distance (estimated at over 100 trillion light-years across), is filled with galaxies like our own, primarily composed of gross matter. The galaxies within the outermost layer thus consist of ordinary elementary particles, atoms, and molecules. Human beings, possessing gross bodies similar to our own, dwell in this region. In this outermost (or lowest) of the seven luminous spheres, the density of subtle matter is comparatively low.

The Inner Celestial Regions

The other six cosmic regions, which are nested one within the other like the layers of an onion, have diameters that are smaller than our own region. As a general rule, each subsequent inner region appears to be approximately ten times smaller in linear dimension than the previous outer region.

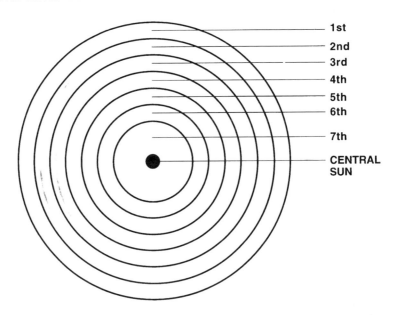

Figure 7—The Cosmic Egg and Seven Spheres of Universal Life

When the ancient Seers grasped the totality of the Universe within their awareness, they found that it resembles a Cosmic Egg, consisting of seven concentric layers of universal life. Each of these layers is incredibly vast and contains numerous galaxies and worlds. The outermost, first layer is the region in which our own galaxy is found. The six inner layers consist of progressively more subtle or celestial worlds. At the heart of the Seventh Heaven is the Central Sun, which is the seat of Supreme Intelligence for the entire Universe. It should be noted that the diagram above is not drawn to scale. Each layer actually is ten times larger or smaller than the previous depending upon whether one is ascending (towards the center) or descending (towards the periphery).

Even though the volume of space occupied by the inner celestial regions is less than that occupied by the outer regions, the beings that dwell in the inner regions resonate with higher bands of universal consciousness than ordinary human beings. Consequently, they are endowed with an intuitive vision that enables them to embrace much larger regions of universal life within their awareness. Compared to the outer worlds, the inner regions thus are experienced as more expanded or universal worlds, even though their physical dimensions are increasingly compact towards the center of the Universe.

Even so, these inner regions are not small. They are vast enough to be filled with many celestial galaxies similar in size to the galaxies in our own region of the Universe. Although the celestial galaxies may be similar in size to our own, their constituent material is different. The galaxies of the six inner celestial regions are composed, as one moves towards the innermost cosmic region, of progressively subtler and yet more dense gradations of matter-energy. Because of the presence of this subtle matter, these regions are filled with a spiritual Light and glory that is beyond description. They appear to be blazing with celestial fire.

However, if we were able to photograph these regions with our Earth tele-scopes and cameras, we would see nothing but dark empty space. This is because the subtle light that is emitted from the different grades of subtle matter does not interact with gross elementary particles and atoms. Rather, it is a form of subtle energy that interacts only with its own grade of subtle matter.[23] All ordinary mortal eyes are blind to this light. Thus, the sublime spiritual forms and phenomena that abide in the six inner regions of the Universe can be seen only by the subtle eyes of the Seers.

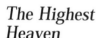

The Highest Heaven   At the very center of the innermost region is the Central Galaxy of the Universe, which is about the same size and shape as our own galaxy. The Central Galaxy in different traditions is variously called the Isle of Paradise, the Isle of Flame, the Island of Jewels, the Seventh Heaven, or the Highest Heaven.

It is called the Isle of Paradise because it is incomparably beautiful and radiant in its celestial glory. It is the permanent home of the universal gods and ascended Seers who are continuously immersed in Heavenly Bliss. The Central Galaxy is called the Isle of Flame because the density of celestial fire in this region is greater than anywhere else in the entire Universe. It is liter-ally on fire with the blazing glory of God. Compared to our own cold dark region of the Universe, the warm spiritual effulgence of the central Isle of Flame is totally inconceivable. It is called the Island of Jewels because the star systems that compose it resemble so many lustrous, shining jewels, sparkling with different colors and nested in the bosom of Heaven.

Collectively, the star systems that compose the Central Galaxy constitute the Seventh Heaven. It is called the Seventh Heaven because it is the innermost of the seven spheres of universal life. It also is called the Highest Heaven because it is located on the very peak of the cosmic mountain—at the luminous heart of the Universe.

The Highest Heaven serves as the divine abode of the universal gods and ascended Seers, who collectively constitute the Divine Universal Government. These celestial beings, who rule the destiny of all things in the Universe, do not possess gross bodies made up of ordinary atoms and molecules. They possess luminous divine bodies that are composed of pure crystallized subtle matter.

The unique feature of this type of matter is that it is infinitely correlated with everything that exists in the Universe. This most evolved type of subtle matter cannot be found in our region of the Universe. It exists only in the Highest Heaven.

The divine beings whose bodies are composed of this crystallized subtle matter possess so much spiritual vision and power that they are more or less omniscient and omnipotent. They rule the Universe not by force and coercion, but by the power of universal love and divine will.

Because of the nonlocal comprehension of these divine beings, they immediately are aware of all the evolutionary developments that occur within the far-flung worlds under their jurisdiction, and periodically send out rays or emanations of their own soul essence to regulate, facilitate, and nourish these developments.

Regarding these exalted beings the ancient Vedic texts proclaim:

> The gods (devas), the never-slumbering beholders of mankind, who are entitled (to their share of the immortal nectar), have obtained great immortality; conveyed in chariots (or bodies) of light, possessed of unsurpassable wisdom, devoid of sin, they inhabit the exalted station of heaven for the well-being (of the world).[24]

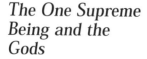

The One Supreme Being and the Gods Although any one of these divine beings would appear as a god to us, all of these beings are emanations of the one Supreme Being who transcends the entire Creation and abides in the immortal transcendental regions that are nameless and formless, beyond all considerations of time and space.

The ancient Seers unanimously have declared that the transcendental wholeness of the Supreme Being is eternal, unborn, unchanging, and immovable. Nevertheless, through the agency of the Divine Word, which is the creative power of God, the Supreme Being appears to enter into Creation and assume the form of all beings.

Each individual soul may be understood as a reflection of the Supreme Being within the field of Creation. The purity and clarity of this reflection depends upon the density and purity of the material out of which the subtle body is fashioned. The enlightened human soul is the lowest category of soul that can reflect universal divine awareness. All souls below the status of an enlightened human being can reflect only individual values of awareness.

The various types of divine beings that dwell in the six celestial regions of the Universe possess subtle bodies that generally display much higher degrees of subtle matter density and purity than that of the average human being. As a result, these beings reflect the light of consciousness more intensely, and possess divine powers that lie beyond the reach of the ordinary human nervous system.

On a cosmic scale, the term "gods" represents the different systems of celestial fire out of which the subtle body of the Universe as a whole is formed. Some of these beings possess brilliant egg-shaped bodies, and dwell in the luminous orbs of the Sun and stars. Others possess subtle bodies that resemble our own. Still others possess galactic and universal forms that resemble filamentary clouds of celestial fire, spanning billions of light-years.

The gods serve many purposes in Creation. Most importantly, they serve as the direct manifestations of the Creator on different scales of Creation, and are the agencies through which the Creator administers Creation.

Although the gods are more elevated on the hierarchy of spiritual manifestation than ordinary human beings, we should never think that we are lowly creatures. Human beings possess a unique position in God's Creation. We are the only beings who can embrace the total spectrum of the holographic Universe within our awareness. This is because enlightened human beings possess both a mortal and a divine nature. Regarding such enlightened Seers, Hermes Trismegistus states:[25]

> For man is a being of divine nature; he is comparable, not to the other living creatures upon Earth, but to the gods in Heaven. Nay, if we are to speak the truth without fear, he who is indeed a man is even above the gods of Heaven, or at any rate he equals them in power. None of the gods in Heaven will ever quit Heaven, and pass its boundary, and come down to Earth; but man ascends even to Heaven, and measures it; and what is more than all beside, he mounts to Heaven without even quitting the Earth; to so vast a distance can he put forth his power.

Nevertheless, in the natural hierarchy of the structure of God's Creation, the gods lie above human beings. This hierarchy may be understood in terms of the natural communion or controlling influence that one soul exerts upon another.

> There is a communion between soul and soul. The souls of the gods are in communion with those of men, and the souls of men with those of the creatures without reason. The higher have the lower in their charge; gods take care of men, and men take care of creatures without reason. And God takes care of all; for He is higher than all.

Luminous subtle matter (or mind stuff) is the divine substance through which the will of God is administered. It the substance that connects or unites the various souls within the spiritual hierarchy of God's kingdom. Regarding this most potent substance, it is said:

All things are dependent on the being of God alone, and are administered by means of mind [luminous subtle matter] alone. There is nothing more divine than mind, nothing more potent in its operation, and nothing more apt to unite men to gods and gods to men. . . . Blessed is the soul that is filled with mind, and ill-fated is the soul that is devoid of it.

The souls that are filled with mind or luminous subtle matter are blessed because they are filled with the administrative power of God—a power that is capable of uniting men to gods and gods to men.

The Universal Being

Within the field of Creation there is one unique soul that is more abundantly filled with mind than any other. It is the oldest, purest, and most perfect soul in the Universe. This soul is known as the Universal Being. He is the Creator of all beings. Because the Creator possesses a superabundance of mind, he presents the most complete and perfect reflection of the Supreme Being within the field of time and space.

In the Sacred Science, there are two aspects to God—one of which is infinite and the other of which is finite. The infinite aspect of God corresponds to the Supreme Being—the infinite, eternal state of pure being that lies beyond the largest and smallest scales of time and space. The finite God, on the other hand, represents that aspect of the Supreme Being that is identified with the finite Universe. This finite aspect of God is called the Universal Being.

Although the Universal Being dwells within the finite field of time and space, he cannot be adequately described, for he encompasses all things within the Universe. He not only encompasses all things, but he also is the Creator and maintainer of all things. He is the ultimate emanator of all mortal souls, the Father of all gods, and the Creator of all worlds. All the gods constitute his agencies of administration, all souls constitute his agencies of perception and enjoyment, and all worlds constitute his Universal Body. He is the very soul of all created things.

Nevertheless, the Universal Being does not act independently. He is just one aspect of the Supreme Being, who oversees the activities of an infinite number of similar Creators or Universal Beings that abide in an infinite number of Cosmic Eggs.[26] The Supreme Being is the ultimate ruler and controller of all of the Universal Beings, who are nothing more than His own self-referral reflections within the field of time and space.

The Hermetic texts are clear about the hierarchical relationship between the Supreme Being and the Universal Being:

> He whom we name God Supreme, a God apprehensible by intuitive thought [pure consciousness] alone, is the ruler and director of that god [the Creator or Universal Being] perceptible by sense, who embraces within himself all substances and all matter, and all things without exception that have to do with birth and production.[27]

Although the Universal Being encompasses all things, and therefore can be located anywhere in the Universe, the permanent seat of his omniscient, omnipotent, and omnipresent awareness is located at the heart of the Central Sun of the Central Galaxy, which is his own special divine Abode of Light. This is the central throne referred to in the Revelation of John. It also is the peak of the cosmic mountain. From this vantage point the Creator or Universal Being oversees and administers all things in Creation, including the evolutionary unfoldment of human civilization on Earth.

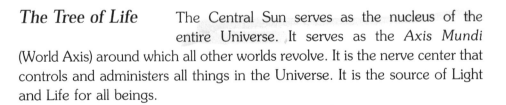

The Tree of Life

The Central Sun serves as the nucleus of the entire Universe. It serves as the *Axis Mundi* (World Axis) around which all other worlds revolve. It is the nerve center that controls and administers all things in the Universe. It is the source of Light and Life for all beings.

Vast numbers of elemental souls continuously emanate from the Central Sun like clouds of sparks rising up from a blazing fire. These elemental souls correspond to particles of chitta, or luminous soul essence. Having emanated from the heart of the Central Sun, these elemental souls are incorporated into the bodies of the gods and dispatched to various regions of the Universe, where they are used to nourish and enrich evolving souls.

The soul streams emanating from the Central Sun resemble brilliantly shining rays or pillars of celestial fire. These streams may be viewed as so many forms of the Divine Messenger. They constitute the luminous body of the Holy Spirit.

The pillars of celestial fire that emanate from the Central Sun are used to carry the Divine Presence of the Creator to every region of the Universe. Each planet, star, and galaxy in the entire Universe is ultimately connected with the Central Sun through these branching rays of celestial fire.

This many branched network of celestial fire constitutes the Tree of Life. According to the Book of Genesis, the divine Tree of Life is rooted at the center of Paradise, from where the four main streams or rivers of celestial life emerge.[28]

The blazing Tree of Life may be understood as the celestial embodiment of the Holy Spirit or Divine Messenger. It is responsible for carrying the Divine Presence of God from the Highest Heaven all the way down to the outermost regions of the Cosmic Egg, where there are trillions of ordinary galaxies like our own. Its roots thus are said to be "above," while its branches are "below." This celestial Tree is clearly described in the ancient Bhagavad Gita:

> High the root, below the branch,
> The eternal Ashvattha Tree,
> Of which they say the leaves are the (Vedic) hymns.
> He who knows this is a knower of the Veda.[29]

The word "Ashvattha" indicates a species of fig tree used by the Vedic Seers to kindle their sacrificial fires. This particular tree was used because it has a divine correspondence to the celestial Tree. Each piece of fruit hanging on the branches of the fig tree contains myriad seeds, each of which can become the source of a new tree. The figs hanging on the tree thus correspond to the galaxies scattered throughout the sky. Each galaxy contains billions of stars, each of which may be viewed as the source of trillions of celestial rays, which branch out to all parts of the Universe.

However, this is only the surface meaning of the word. On a deeper level of consideration, the word "Ashvattha" is derived from *ashva stha,* which means "where the horses are tied." However, the word "ashva" not only means "horse," but it also indicates a star or galaxy. In the Shatapatha Brahmana, a part of the Vedic literature that deals with the divine correspondences between the Vedic rituals and the structure of the Universe, it is said that the word "ashva" has a secret esoteric meaning. It is said to signify the *ashru* (tear drop) "that flowed together in the beginning." These tear drops are none other than the stars and galaxies that flowed together at the beginning of Creation from the intergalactic and interstellar subtle matter fields. The stars and galaxies are called "horses" because they serve as the celestial vehicles by which the gods move about within the field of Creation.

The Ashvattha Tree thus may be understood as the celestial hitching post of the ashvas—the celestial horses of the gods. It is the celestial tether to which all the restlessly moving stars and galaxies are tied, moored, and anchored.

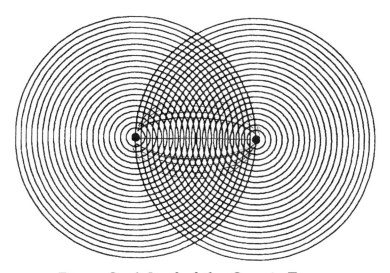

Figure 8—A Leaf of the Cosmic Tree

The leaves of this divine Tree are equated with the hymns *(chandamsi)* of the Veda. More precisely, the word "chandamsi" indicates the Vedic "meters" by which the nonlocal impulses of primordial sound are measured out. When the nonlocal impulses of primordial sound are reflected in the rays and streams of celestial fire that connect the various stars and galaxies, they generate interference patterns within the subtle matter fields. When viewed through the faculty of nonlocal intuition, these interference patterns resemble the petals of a lotus or the leaves of a tree, both of which are signified by the word *parnani* (leaf, petal).

These leaves or petals are filled with primordial sound. They are filled with the impulses of cosmic life force that uphold the organic unity of the entire Creation. Because the blazing Tree of Life reflects the nonlocal impulses of primordial sound within its many branched structure, it may be said to be the celestial embodiment of the Veda, the unmanifest blueprint of Creation.

The celestial embodiment of the Veda contains within itself the highest secret wisdom concerning the Creation. This secret wisdom is not available through ordinary perception or intellect. It cannot be seen by those whose awareness is locked onto the ordinary forms of matter and energy out of which our small planet is fashioned. The Bhagavad Gita thus states:

> Its form is not perceptible here in this world,
> Nor its end, nor its beginning, nor its staying.[30]

The secret wisdom inherent in the Tree of Life cannot be known by ordinary humans. It can be known by the enlightened Seers alone. However, it is especially possessed by the Divine Messenger, variously known as Agni, Thoth, or Hermes. He is specifically identified as the "wisdom-god" because his divine body is none other than the blazing Tree of Life itself.

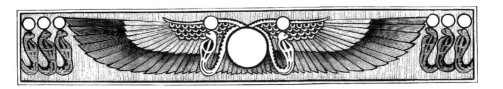

8. THE MILKY WAY GALAXY

Within the outermost layer of the Cosmic Egg there are trillions of ordinary galaxies like our own, most of which are filled with many millions of star systems that support human life. Except for the fact that we are located within it, our own galaxy, the Milky Way, is nothing special. It is a typical spiral galaxy nested among billions of other similar galaxies that are scattered like glowing sparks throughout our local region of the Universe.

Using powerful telescopes, the different galaxies within this outermost region have begun to be examined and catalogued by modern astrophysicists. Based upon their observations of the general forms that the galaxies display, they have identified three main types of galaxies: (i) elliptical galaxies, which resemble an egg-shaped ball of stars and luminous gas; (ii) spiral galaxies, which have a well-defined structure involving a luminous disk and spiral arms; and (iii) irregular galaxies, which appear as a random assortment of stars and interstellar gas.

These three main types of galaxies represent different developmental stages in galactic life. During the early stages of its development, a galaxy displays an elliptical form, resembling a luminous egg-shaped ball of stars and interstellar gas. As the galaxy approaches maturity it assumes a well-defined spiral shape. This spiral form represents the most mature state of a galaxy. It occurs about midway through the galactic life cycle. When the galaxy is in its old age, its center falls apart, and the well-defined structure of the galaxy dissipates into an irregular cloud of stars and gas.

It should be pointed out that this view is not consistent with currently accepted astrophysical theories. It soon will be discovered that the modern astrophysical theories concerning the origins of the universe, the galaxies, and stars are based upon a number of false assumptions. These false assumptions, among other things, make modern estimates of the ages of stars and galaxies incorrect. A full discussion of these problems is beyond the scope of this book, but they are very significant. In our opinion a whole new model of cosmogenesis is deeply needed that takes into account the existence of subtle matter-energy and its influence on the process of Creation.

Although conventional wisdom holds that distant galaxies were discovered only recently through the use of modern telescopes, the enlightened Seers have known of such galaxies since time immemorial. The enlightened Seers did not need telescopes to behold the structure of the Universe; they could observe it directly through the faculty of nonlocal intuition.

When observed through the faculty of nonlocal intuition, one learns a great deal more about the structure of the galaxies than their characteristic forms and distributions in space. One learns about their inner nature, their spiritual history, and divine personality.

Based upon their nonlocal intuition, the ancient Seers viewed the galaxies as miniature universes, or miniature cosmic eggs, each one of which is presided over by a great celestial being, who serves as the "creator" of the galaxy. The gross form of the galaxy represents the cosmic body of this celestial being.

Cosmic Life Spans According to the Vedic Seers, the life cycle of the Universe as a whole spans a period of about 311.04 trillion years.[31] This represents the life span of the Universal Being, known as the Creator.

The life span of the Galactic Being, on the other hand, is much shorter. It spans a period of only 4.32 billion human years. The ancient Seers called this period a *kalpa*. At the beginning of each kalpa, the galaxy, which may be compared to a "cosmic sun," is churned out of the Milky Ocean of intergalactic subtle matter, and at the end of each kalpa it dissolves back into this field. After remaining unmanifest for an equal period of time, the galaxy is churned out of the Milky Ocean once again, and a new cycle of galactic Creation begins.

The rising and setting of the galactic sun thus was considered to represent a daily cycle of Creation. The period when the galactic sun appears and shines within the Milky Ocean represents a Day of Creation, and the period when the galactic sun disappears back into the Milky Ocean represents a Night of Creation.

The life span of the Universe as a whole then was conceived in units of these daily cycles. There were 360 days and nights within a Year of Creation, and 100 years in the full life span. This comes to around 311.04 trillion years.

According to the Vedic tradition, we are currently in the first Day of the fifty-first Year of Creation. This means that our present Creation has been in existence for over 155.5 trillion years!

The tradition further claims that in the current Day of Creation, it is about 1 P.M. in the afternoon. This means that our own galaxy, the Milky Way, is in its most mature phase, being a little over halfway through its current life cycle. Because it is in its mature phase, it is natural for the Milky Way to display a well-defined spiral form.

In quantitative terms, these intuitive conclusions specify that the Milky Way first emerged from the Milky Ocean of intergalactic space about 2.52 billion years ago. These figures do not accord with modern estimates of the age of the Universe (which is hotly disputed by different theorists), or the age of the galaxy. Indeed, modern estimates place the Earth at about 4 billion years old.

The figures given above are not based upon the objective theories and calculations of modern scientists. They are based upon our interpretation of the nonlocal intuitions of the ancient Seers. According to this interpretation, the Universe is much older than any modern estimate, and the galaxy is much younger than any modern estimate. Only time will tell which of these understandings is more accurate.

The Subtle Body of the Galactic Being   As mentioned previously, when the enlightened Seers beheld the structure of the Milky Way through their nonlocal intuition, they saw not only the gross forms of the stars and interstellar clouds of gas scattered throughout space, but also the subtle body and personality of the Galactic Being. When the vast subtle body of the galaxy is observed through the eye of pure consciousness, it resembles a nebulous cloud of subtle matter-energy filled with filamentary currents of celestial fire. These filaments of celestial fire resemble so many bolts of lightning hidden in the bowels of a cosmic thundercloud. The subtle body of the galaxy is thus glorious beyond imagination. It pervades the gross visible structure of the Milky Way and further extends beyond it on all sides by a distance that is about ten times the dimension of its visible form.

To use a bit of poetic license, it can be said that the luminous form of the galaxy is nested in the belly of the cosmic thundercloud like a lion roaring in a cave. The continuous roars of the galactic lion echo through the fathomless bosom of space like rolling thunder emanating from the heart of God.

With respect to the Milky Way, the "heart of God" is located at the center of the galaxy, at the very peak of the galactic mountain. The peak of the galactic mountain represents that point in the galaxy where the subtle matter density is highest. From that point, one's nonlocal intuition is completely unobstructed, and one can see into the bosom of Infinity.

The galactic mountain is a local reflection of the universal mountain, whose peak lies at the heart of the Universe as a whole. Whereas the peak of the universal mountain corresponds to the Central Sun of the Universe, the peak of the galactic mountain corresponds to the central star of the galaxy.

* * *

The Central Star of the Galactic Being

Although the central star of the galaxy cannot be observed using ordinary telescopes, it can be observed by using radio and infrared telescopes, which can penetrate the thick veil of stars and interstellar dust that surround it. Using these techniques, modern astronomers have located this star, and named it Sagittarius A* ("Sagittarius ay star"). It is named Sagittarius because it lies in that portion of the sky ruled by the sign of Sagittarius.

Sagittarius A* is a unique object in the galaxy. Based upon modern observations, Sagittarius A* is located at the galaxy's central point. It is the one object around which everything else orbits. In addition, Sagittarius A* is by far the most luminous and energetic object in the galaxy. It emits about five times as much energy at radio wavelengths as the Sun does at visible ones.[32] At infrared wavelengths, the output of the galactic center is about twenty million times that of the Sun.[33]

Not only is it a source of intense light, but it also is a tremendous source of matter. The galactic center is known to emit an intense *galactic wind* consisting of ionized hydrogen and helium gas. The galactic wind streams away from the center of the galaxy in a manner similar to the solar wind emitted by the Sun. However, the galactic wind is much denser than the solar wind. It has been estimated that the galactic wind emits about one solar mass from the galactic center every century. This means that if our own Sun were to emit as much matter as the central star of the galaxy, it would be entirely dissipated in 100 years! No one has yet been able to explain the mysterious ability of the galactic center to emit such profusions of matter and energy.

Although some scientists have tried to explain the mysterious properties of the galactic center by invoking the theory of a black hole, there is no real evidence that this theory is accurate.

> There is little evidence that gas is moving inward toward Sgr A*, as the black hole theory requires. As far out as ten thousand lightyears from the galactic center, gas is instead moving radially outward. Such outflow challenges standard astronomy. For if Sgr A* is losing one solar mass of material per century, unless this material is replenished at its center its entire mass would be dissipated within less than 100 million years. [34]

The central mother star of the Milky Way thus appears to play a similar role in the galaxy as does the Central Sun for the Universe as a whole. The central star of the Milky Way serves as the creative heart of the Galactic Being.[35] To use another analogy, it may be compared to the fecund nipple of the cosmic breast. As such, it issues forth a continuous stream of milk, in the form of subtle matter-energy, to nourish all the stars that have been conceived within the womb of the great Galactic Being.

It sends forth not only subtle matter-energy, but also hydrogen and helium ions, which may be viewed as the seeds of future stars. These hydrogen and helium ions represent newly created elements, generated within the heart of the central star. They are not remnants of the Big Bang. They have been newly evolved within the high density fields of subtle matter-energy that constitute the heart of the Galactic Being.

The Worlds of Light at the Galactic Center   Although the galactic center is a prodigious source of matter and energy, it is not alone. Within 1.3 light-years of Sagittarius A*, a total of 340 individual stars have been detected, all of which orbit the central star at very high velocities.[36] These stars also appear to be emitting large quantities of energy and matter. Within ten light-years, there are many thousands of other similar stars. All of these secondary stars appear to be hovering around the galactic center like a swarm of luminous bees hovering around their queen. From the vantage point of the central star, the sky would thus appear to be blazing with the effulgence of a thousand suns.

This reminds us of the celebrated passage in the Bhagavad Gita in which the celestial form of God is described:

> If a thousand suns were to rise all at once in the sky, such splendor would resemble the splendor of that Great Being. There the entire Universe, standing as one, though divided in many ways. . . was beheld in the body of the God of Gods.[37]

Surrounding the galactic center is the luminous bulge of the galaxy. The bulge of the galaxy consists of a swarm of about ten billion stars that are significantly older than the stars like our own, which lie in the spiral arms of the galactic disk. In addition to being older, these stars are known to have a higher metallicity than those in the disk. This factor is very important. The metallicity of a star is a measure of the percentage of heavy metals, such as iron, silver, nickel, platinum, gold, lead, etc., contained in the solar mass. The stars at the center of the galaxy have a higher metallicity than those in the luminous disk because they are older and more evolved. They also are more abundant generators of subtle matter-energy.

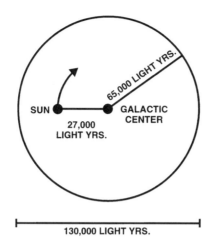

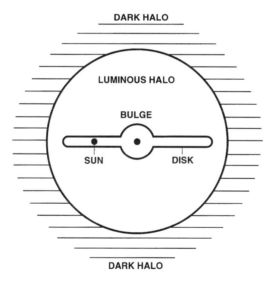

Figure 9—The Milky Way and Our Solar System

Our solar system is located within the flat luminous disk of the galaxy about 27,000 light-years from the galactic center, or about 40 percent of the distance from the center to the disk's edge. As one moves towards the center of the galaxy, the metallicity of the stars increases. Those stars with higher metallicity are both older and more evolved than those with lower metallicity.

The correlation between the subtle matter production of a star and its metal-licity is an alchemical secret. It is based upon the esoteric fact that the atomic nuclei of the heavy metals can, under certain circumstances, become the most concentrated sources of celestial fire in the Universe. In order to do so, the nuclei must become fully spiritualized. We will discuss the nature of this alchemical transformation in chapter 31.

Galactic Civilization

The ancient and highly evolved star systems that exist within the luminous bulge of the Galaxy contain millions of planets that support human life. Because these worlds are immersed continuously in the high density field of luminous subtle matter that exists at the center of the galaxy, they may be understood as permanent Worlds of Light. These glorious Worlds of Light are inhabited by highly evolved races of human beings who are so filled with the Light of God that they resemble celestial gods. However, they possess gross physical bodies similar in many ways to our own. Indeed, the ancient Seers considered these beings to be our spiritual ancestors.[38]

The permanent Worlds of Light that exist at the center of the galaxy may be understood as forming the very heart and soul of the Galactic civilization. The Galactic civilization is exceedingly ancient. It existed long before any human beings ever set foot on our planet. In fact, the Galactic civilization was considered by the ancient Seers to be the true Earth World, of which our own planet is just a small part.

Through their nonlocal vision, the ancient Seers understood that the struc-ture of the Milky Way galaxy and of our own planet are linked together by various divine correspondences. Similar correspondences link the structure of the Milky Way galaxy with the Central Galaxy of the Universe as a whole. In accordance with these divine correspondences, the ancient Seers assigned the spiritual names of the different celestial regions that they beheld through their nonlocal intuition to the various rivers, mountains, and regions of the Earth that they beheld with their physical eyes. There is thus a profound sense of dual correspondences inherent in all of the ancient teachings and scriptures.

When one reads the texts passed down by the ancient traditions, one must keep this duality of meaning in mind at all times. References to events, places, and things on Earth have a direct correspondence to spiritually similar events, places, and things in the Galactic world, and in the Universe as a whole. The ancient texts, which were almost always verbal in their nature, were designed to weave these different layers of reality together in the mind of the reciter and listener, thereby invoking the presence of Heaven on Earth.

The civilizations that exist within the Worlds of Light of the central bulge are far more advanced spiritually and technologically than any of the human civilizations that have existed so far on Earth. They possess both the spiritual and technological means to travel from world to world over vast interstellar distances, and they have the ability to transmute any form of matter into any other form. In effect, they possess complete mastery over Nature.

However, because these civilizations are suffused with the Light of God, they coexist harmoniously with one another, and are organically organized into a single Galactic civilization. This Galactic civilization is charged with overseeing and assisting the physical and spiritual evolution of human beings throughout the galaxy.

Over the last two billion years, spiritual expeditions of human beings have continuously emanated from these central Worlds of Light to fertilize evolving planets throughout the far-flung regions of the galaxy. These expeditions are not undertaken casually. They are carefully organized and orchestrated in accordance with the Divine Plan for each evolving planet.

In general, the human population on a given planet is left alone to evolve its own unique form of civilization through its own inner processes of development. However, when a planet like the Earth enters into a Golden Age, various enlightened representatives from the Galactic civilization descend upon the planet to assist in the reorganization and revitalization of every phase of life and living. We believe that such a descent is destined to take place on Earth sometime soon. However, no one really knows exactly when, where, or how this event will occur. It is a highly secret part of the Divine Plan.

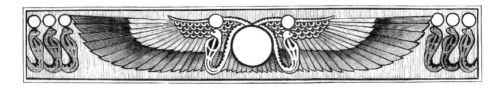

9. THE DIVINE KA

The billions of stars that populate the Milky Way galaxy may be viewed as the enlightened offspring of the Galactic Being. It embraces them all within its spiral arms and nourishes them with the celestial fire overflowing from its luminous heart. Our own Sun is one of its beloved star-children. It is filled with the same light of universal pure consciousness that illumines the souls of all the celestial beings throughout the Universe, including that of the Creator in Heaven.

Throughout history, human beings have worshipped and honored the Sun as the source of Light and Life for our planet. Without the warmth and light provided by the Sun, no organic life could survive on the surface of the Earth and the oceans would remain frozen in their beds. However, the Sun is much more than just a source of physical warmth and light. It is a great celestial being whose cosmic awareness oversees and administers the spiritual evolution of all things within our solar system.

The idea that the Sun is a great cosmic being may be hard to accept for those who have been indoctrinated into the religion of objective science, but this is understandable. When the Sun is viewed through our earth-bound telescopes it appears to be nothing more than a huge hot ball of gas floating all alone in the vastness of the sky. But the enlightened Seers know the Sun as much more than this.

The Universal Song of Divine Love   The stars that populate the galaxy may appear to be isolated islands of light floating in the sky, separated from one another by the incomprehensible silence of interstellar and intergalactic space, but this is a profound illusion. The stars are fully enlightened souls who are filled with a cosmic knowledge and a blissful exuberance that is beyond mortal comprehension. Although each star may appear to be floating alone in a vast void, it does not experience any sense of loneliness or separation. Because they possess an exalted faculty of nonlocal intuition, the celestial luminaries experience a deep oneness with one another and with the Universe as a whole. They experience themselves as lovingly embraced by the One Eternal Supreme Being who is the very Self of the entire Creation.

The Supreme Being is infinite in its comprehension and compassion. It is infinitely filled with divine Love. The divine Love of the Supreme Being knows no boundaries. It experiences no separation. It marks no time. God's universal Love may be compared to a nonlocal breeze that flows through all things and eternally sings the glory of the Absolute. This timeless universal song of divine Love serves as the very glue of the Universe. It is that which unites all things, and allows all things to breathe together as one.

The stars and galaxies that shine in the vastness of the sky are great celestial beings continuously singing the song of universal love to one another. They are the mouthpieces through which the song of God is sung. Like a vast swarm of luminous bees humming in the night, they whisper the transcendental song of God, and become inebriated on the honey-like nectar of divine Love.

It is only when one's awareness becomes as silent and profound as the fathomless depths of intergalactic space, that one can begin to hear the murmur of this celestial song. This song is the proverbial *music of the spheres.* Upon hearing the celestial harmony of this music within one's awareness, all the air issues from one's lips and one's heart stops beating. At that moment, one falls into the arms of Eternity and tastes the divine nectar that continuously thrills and invigorates the gods. This divine nectar is pure Love. It is nothing other than pure Love.

The nectar of divine Love flows along the subtle rays of luminous life force that connect star with star, and galaxy with galaxy throughout the Universe. These rays are also connected to the Earth, and can be experienced by the enlightened awareness of the Seers. The Egyptian Seers represented their awareness of these celestial rays in their shrines, tombs, and temples.

Figure 10—Divine Knowledge of the Stars

This figure is taken from the second golden shrine in the Tomb of Tutankhamen. It indicates the rays of celestial fire that connect the stars with human consciousness. Through these rays the ancient Egyptian Seers obtained divine knowledge of the stars and the cosmos.

To use an analogy, the galaxies scattered throughout the Universe may be compared to cells in the Universal Body. Similarly, the stars scattered throughout each galaxy may be compared to cells in the galactic body. The cosmic body of the Universe thus contains many hierarchically structured layers of cells, one embedded within the other. Within this vast glowing structure of celestial reality, every cell is connected to every other cell by luminous rays of celestial fire. These rays form the subtle nervous system within the body of God. Through this complex system of celestial rays, all the cells in the body of God are conversing with one another. They are all singing the song of universal harmony and rejoicing in wholeness.

Although the Universe contains trillions and trillions of celestial bodies within itself, all of these bodies are nonlocally coordinated and connected to form a single undivided whole. This reveals the true meaning of the word "Universe," which may be interpreted as "unity-in-diversity."

Just as each cell and organ in the human body somehow knows its specific role in the context of the whole, so also, the various solar and galactic beings know their specific roles in the context of the Universe. Their awareness is both universal and individual, nonlocal and local, simultaneously.

The great soul that resides in the luminous orb of the Sun is thus fully aware of its specific role in the overall Divine Plan of the Universe. It is aware not only of the bigger picture, but it also comprehends in great detail everything that occurs within the solar system. In this light it sends out various types of spiritual and physical emanations to administer the worlds and beings under its immediate care.

The Crystalline Heart of the Sun

The solar being is a very ancient soul who has been continuously engaged in profound meditation for over a billion years. The intense heat and light of the Sun has been generated through this meditation.

The focus of this meditation is a small egg-shaped cocoon of luminous subtle matter that lies at the center of the solar orb. This ball of celestial fire is so filled with spiritual power that it resembles a shining crystal or radiant diamond. It may be understood as the crystalline heart of the Sun.

The crystalline heart of the Sun is composed of the most concentrated form of subtle matter-energy possible in our solar system. As a result, it reflects an extraordinarily high level of universal pure consciousness. Although the consciousness of the Sun is much higher than that of a human being, there are certain divine correspondences between solar and human consciousness that link us together.

The Divine Ka in the Human Heart

The simplest of these correspondences concerns the size and shape of the luminous egg of celestial fire that lies at the heart of the Sun. The luminous egg that lies at the heart of the Sun is more or less identical in size and shape to the luminous egg that is nested in the human heart. Surprising as it may seem, they are both about the size and shape of the pad at the end of an adult human thumb.

This thumb-sized egg of celestial fire is known as the Divine Ka. There is a Divine Ka at the heart of every celestial being in the Universe. All the planets, stars, and galaxies have their own Divine Kas. There is even a Divine Ka for the Universe as a whole. It is seated at the very heart of the Central Sun. The Universal Divine Ka is the supreme seat of the Universal Soul. It is the divine archetype towards which all other souls aspire.

This includes all human souls as well. Every human heart contains a Divine Ka that serves as the seat of the human soul. In the hearts of the unenlightened, the Divine Ka is too small and too weak to reflect the light of pure consciousness and resonate with the music of the spheres. In order to do so, the Divine Ka must be nourished with celestial fire. When it has been properly nourished, the Divine Ka grows and develops into a blazing thumb-sized cocoon of celestial fire residing within the heart. When the Divine Ka thus becomes awakened, the human soul becomes enlightened, and begins to sing the song of divine Love.

Although the Divine Kas at the heart of different enlightened beings generally are composed of different gradations of celestial fire, the size and shape of all Divine Kas throughout the Universe are similar. This holds true in spite of the fact that as the soul becomes more and more enlightened, the Divine Ka may become enveloped by additional layers of celestial fire. No matter how many celestial robes may eventually envelop the enlightened soul, the Divine Ka retains its original diminutive form through which it first gained enlightenment. However, as it becomes enveloped by additional layers of celestial fire, the original seed does grow more and more dense and self-organized.

This knowledge of the Divine Ka is not new. It has been known to enlightened Seers around the world from the beginning. To cite two examples, it can be found in the ancient texts of both the Vedic and Egyptian traditions.

The Vedic Tradition   In the Vedic tradition, the sound *ka* is the first consonant of the Sanskrit alphabet and literally means "who." Regarding this there is the following ancient myth.

When the Supreme Being first incarnated into a created form at the beginning of Creation, it assumed the form of an egg-shaped person the size of a thumb *(angushta-matra purusha)*. This was its most diminutive form. This thumb-sized person was lying all alone on a cosmic lotus floating on the primordial waters.

When the Universal Being first awakened and found itself floating all alone in the midst of the primordial ocean he cried out "Ka?" ("Who am I?"). This was the first primordial sound uttered or experienced by the awareness of the Creator. Having broadcast this primordial question to the Supreme Being (his own higher Self), the Creator was given knowledge of his own immortal nature, and became enlightened. He then ceased to be afraid, and assumed lordship over the entire Creation. He became the Universal Being, the Father of created beings.

In the Vedic tradition, the Creator of the Universe, the Father of all beings, is called *Brahma* (the all-encompassing one). He also is called *Svayambhuva* (the self-developed one), and *Padma-Bhavam* (the one born at the center of the cosmic lotus).

By meditating on the Supreme Being for a very long time, the Creator, in the form of a small luminous egg, expanded and grew. Eventually he developed into all seven layers of universal life and assumed the form of the Cosmic Egg of the Universe as a whole. The entire Universe thus may be viewed as the Cosmic Body of the Creator.

Because the Creator first cognized his own eternal Self by uttering the sound "ka," this was taken to be his secret spiritual name. According to the ancient Seers, it is this same Divine Ka, the very Self of the Universe, that resides within the heart of all beings.

There is an entire hymn from the Rig Veda devoted to this concept of the Universal Being. A few verses from that hymn are given below.

> The luminous golden egg was present at the beginning; when born, he was the sole lord of created beings; he upheld this Earth and Heaven—let us offer worship with an oblation to the Divine Ka.
>
> (To him) who is the giver of soul, the giver of strength, whose commands all (beings), even the gods, obey, whose shadow is immortality, whose (shadow) is death—let us offer worship with an oblation to the Divine Ka.
>
> Through whose greatness these snow-clad (galaxies exist), whose property men call the (celestial) ocean with the (celestial) rivers, whose are these quarters of space, whose are the two arms—let us offer worship with an oblation to the Divine Ka.
>
> Whom heaven and earth established by his protection, and, shining brightly, regarded with their mind, in whom the risen sun shines forth—let us offer worship with an oblation to the Divine Ka.
>
> When the vast waters overspread the universe containing the (luminous) egg and giving birth to Agni (the Celestial Fire), then was produced the one breath of the gods—let us offer worship with an oblation to the Divine Ka.[39]

The Divine Ka at the heart of the Universe may be understood as the seat of the Universal Soul. It is the divine archetype in whose image all the Divine Kas throughout the Universe are fashioned.

Regardless of the appearance of the gross or subtle body of each enlightened being, within its heart resides a Divine Ka, which is similar to the Divine Ka at the heart of the Universe. Because of the similarity of the Divine Kas, the souls of all of the enlightened ones throughout the Universe are able to nonlocally resonate with one another. This resonance takes place on the level of pure consciousness. It takes place on the level of primordial sound. The resonant frequency of the Divine Ka is the first awakening note of the song of divine Love. It is the high-pitched limit of the Cosmic Hum that is continuously hummed by all the celestial beings. It is continuously hummed so that all things in the Universe will cohere together as a single whole. This hum is the fundamental tone on the basis of which the celestial music of the spheres gradually unfolds within one's soul like a vibrant flower.[40]

The Egyptian Tradition

The concept of the Divine Ka is not unique to the Vedic tradition. The ancient Egyptian Seers used the same syllable *ka* to denote the celestial form of the human soul.

Ka is the ancient Egyptian term for a spiritual essence, which existed alongside human form and yet maintained individuality. The ka was an astral [celestial] being, and yet it was also considered the guiding force for all human life. The Egyptians recognized the 'double' aspect of the ka, and in some statues the kings were depicted as having an identical image at their side. While existing within the human being during his or her mortal life, the ka was the superior power in the realms beyond the grave. The term for death was 'Going to one's ka' or Going to one's ka in the sky'.

Kas resided in divine beings as well, and pious Egyptians placated the kas of the gods in order to receive favors. They served as the guardians of places at the same time. Osiris was always called the ka of the Pyramids. The ka entered eternity before its human host, having served its function by walking at the human's side to urge kindness, quietude, honor, and compassion. Throughout the life of the human, the ka was the conscience, the guardian, the guide. After death, however, the ka became supreme. . . . The ka was also viewed as a part of the divine essence that nurtured all existence in the universe.[41]

The similarity of the Vedic and Egyptian traditions with respect to the Divine Ka is not a mere coincidence. The ancient Seers belonging to these two great spiritual cultures literally "saw" the same reality, and understood the principles of the Sacred Science in similar ways.

To further illustrate this, there is an ancient creation myth in the Egyptian tradition, dating back to the Old Kingdom, that closely parallels the myth of the Divine Ka in the Vedic tradition. The Egyptian version of the myth is used to explain the birth of the Creator in the form of the sun-god—Atum-Re—who also is known as the "child" who dwells in the Isle of Flame. As stated previously, the Isle of Flame may be understood as the Central Galaxy of the Universe, which is blazing with celestial fire. The sun-god or child that dwells within that blazing Isle of Flame is none other than the Creator. The Egyptians conceived of the Creator as the sun-god Atum-Re, because he dwells there in the form of the Central Sun.

According to the Egyptian myth, the sun-god Atum-Re gave birth to himself. Like Lord Brahma, he also was self-developed. He developed himself from the primordial ocean, called Nu or Nun. This ocean represents the primordial waters that existed prior to the emergence of any form or phenomenon. In the creation myth, the first thing to arise out of the primordial waters was a cosmic lotus. The lotus arose along with the emergence of the "primeval mound," which lay at the very heart of the lotus. Our intuition tells us that this primeval mound represents the small luminous egg of subtle matter-energy that first formed at the center of the Universe, and eventually would become the highest peak of the universal mountain. From this egg-shaped lump or mound of celestial fire, the sun-god Atum-Re developed. The ancient Egyptian Seers thus conceived of the birth of the Creator in much the same manner as the Vedic Seers.

The primordial mound from which the sun-god Atum-Re developed may be understood as the Divine Ka of the Universe. The Egyptians specifically identified this primordial mound with the sacred *benben*, a mysterious stone that symbolized the principle of rebirth, resurrection, and immortality. According to authorities on the subject, the original stone was worshipped in the temple of the sun-god at Heliopolis, while its replicas were placed on the sacred mounds or holy sites all over ancient Egypt. Why were they distributed in this manner? It was to reflect the Light of Heaven on Earth. The benben stones were placed at various holy spots on Earth to reflect the distribution of Divine Kas scattered throughout the Heavens.

However, for the purpose of individual evolution, the Divine Ka does not need to be located externally in a stone. It may be found within one's own heart. The awakening of the Divine Ka within one's heart is the first step towards attaining full knowledge of God. When the Divine Ka is realized in one's own heart, the Divine Presence is no longer found outside oneself at a distance. From that time forward, God is experienced as being both far and near at the same time. He dwells not only in the heart of the Sun, the Milky Way, and the Universe, but also within one's own heart. Regarding the presence of the Divine Ka within the heart it is said:

> The dweller in the body is the size of the thumb. He is the inner spirit. He has his seat in the heart of men.[42]

> He is [both] far and near. The seers see him in the cavity of their hearts.[43]

> He is all-knowing and all-pervading. His glory rises from Earth to Heaven. He resides in the celestial abode of God within the heart.[44]

The thumb-sized cocoon of celestial fire within the human heart is the abode of God. It is the place where God dwells in the human body. When one realizes the Divine Ka within one's heart, and begins to experience the sequential expansion of consciousness, one gradually comes to see that the entire Universe is reflected within one's soul. The cocoon of celestial fire within the heart then appears as though it were a miniature Cosmic Egg. As this realization becomes more and more profound, the correspondence between the individual human soul on Earth and the universal soul of the Creator in Heaven becomes more and more perfect.

According to the Sacred Science, the ultimate goal of life is that every part of the Universe should reflect the whole as perfectly as possible. In order to fulfill this goal, the divine correspondences between Heaven and Earth must be fully enlivened within every human heart. When this is accomplished, the Light of God shines forth within one's individual soul, and it becomes a reflection of the soul of the Universe. The represents the completion of the *Magnum Opus*—the "Great Work" that has been set before us, and it also represents the beginning of Eternal Life.

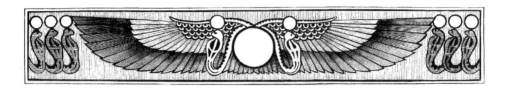

10. THE MORTAL SOUL

To prepare for the coming global Illumination we must begin, individually and collectively, to enrich and purify the subtle matter concentrations within our own bodies and within the body of our planet as a whole. By charging our bodies with increasing levels of subtle matter-energy, the Divine Ka within our hearts becomes nourished, like an embryo in the womb, and gradually grows towards its ultimate awakening in the light of pure consciousness.

To understand how to nourish the Divine Ka within our hearts, we first must examine in more detail the nature of subtle matter, its organization within the body, and how it connects us with the environment. This basic understanding also will illumine certain fundamental principles of the Sacred Science.

The subtle body of each individual system, whether of a planet, a human being, an ant, or an atom, fundamentally is composed of subtle electro-magnetic particles organized into a hierarchically structured field. There are billions of these subtle particles in every cubic centimeter of so-called empty space, but within the subtle body of natural systems the density of these particles is much higher. It is as if each natural system is pervaded by and enveloped in its own high density cloud or aura of subtle particles. This cloud of subtle particles is alive. It is vibrantly filled with cosmic life force and is capable of reflecting consciousness.

---◆---

***Subtle Matter
Metabolism*** The cloud of subtle particles associated with each natural system does not exist in isolation. It is constantly exchanging matter and energy with its environment. The subtle body is a living, breathing entity that inhales subtle matter-energy from its environment, metabolizes it, and then exhales it back

into the environment. This inhalation and exhalation takes place through every pore, cell, molecule, and atom of all natural systems.

When subtle matter is absorbed into the subtle body of a particular system, it becomes impressed by the innate tendencies and qualities associated with that system, and then takes on those qualities. When this subtle matter eventually is passed from the body, those same qualities are translated to the environment. This is how the unseen presence of an individual is conveyed into the atmosphere.

Each natural system automatically exudes its subtle presence wherever it goes, and this presence lingers in the air and in its surroundings, and is absorbed by other objects in the environment even after it has gone. For example, if an individual is angry, then that anger is automatically impressed upon the subtle matter that is inhaled into its body. When this subtle matter is exhaled into the environment, it will carry that angry influence with it. When this "angry" subtle matter later is absorbed into another system, it will introduce this angry influence into the new system. In this manner, we constantly exchange the subtle presence of our personality with everything and everyone around us. There is no way to avoid this. It is just the way things are.

Subtle Matter Generation

However, subtle matter-energy is not incorporated just from the environment. Large quantities of subtle particles spontaneously are generated or created within our bodies all the time. These particles do not appear by magic. A nuclear mechanism is responsible for their generation, which we will discuss in more detail in chapters 30 and 31. Suffice it to say for now that subtle particles are continuously generated within our bodies by the whirling motions of nucleons (protons and neutrons) within the nucleus of every atom. Every individual being who possesses a gross body thus produces enormous quantities of subtle particles within its own physiology.

The secret of spiritual evolution is to increase the production of subtle particles within the body to the point where one becomes a self-sufficient source of celestial fire. Upon attaining this state of self-sufficiency, one becomes completely independent of the subtle matter fields in the environment. In addition, one's own subtle body grows rapidly in density, and becomes able to permanently reflect pure consciousness. The subtle emanations of such individuals carry a powerful spiritual influence that automatically nourishes and assists the spiritual evolution of everything in their environment.

Polarized Subtle Matter

As stated previously, the subtle particles are polarized into two types. One type possesses a masculine charge *(yang)* and the other type possesses a feminine charge *(yin)*. Female beings typically generate more of the subtle particles possessing feminine charge, and male beings typically generate more of the subtle particles possessing masculine charge. These different values of subtle charge are responsible for creating the invisible yet tangible sexual attraction between male and female beings. Sexual energy, which the ancients generally symbolized by coiling snakes, is just the polarized form of subtle matter-energy.

The neutral or balanced form of subtle matter-energy, which includes an equal abundance of both masculine and feminine energy, is the nonsexual spiritual power that is capable of reflecting pure consciousness. The ancients generally symbolized this neutral form of subtle matter-energy by a straight column of light or celestial fire, around which the polarized currents of subtle energy are wound like coiling snakes.

Although either the masculine or feminine charge typically predominates in subtle bodies of male and female beings, the subtle bodies of the celestial beings and enlightened Seers generally are composed of more or less neutral, balanced currents of subtle matter-energy. The subtle bodies of such beings thus are asexual and are powerful reflectors of pure consciousness. They possess a balanced coexistence of masculine and feminine energies within themselves.

Ordinary human beings, on the other hand, possess subtle bodies that are either masculine or feminine in preponderance and organization. The subtle body composed of the polarized form of subtle matter constitutes what the ancient Seers called the *mortal soul* or *lower self*. In some traditions, it was also called the "breathing self."[45]

The mortal soul of a human being is not essentially different from the mortal soul of any other creature or organism. In general, it may be described as an individuated field of polarized subtle matter-energy that reflects at least some degree of consciousness and may encode within its structure millions of years of physical evolution. The mortal soul is thus identical with the subtle body of the individual.

Condensed Subtle Matter   The subtle body of each human being consists of myriad streams of subtle matter. These streams not only weave the fabric of the subtle body, but they also interact with the "bound streams" of subtle matter that are tied up in the form of gross matter.

According to the ancient Seers, all forms of gross matter, including all the elementary particles and atoms, are nothing more than coagulated forms of subtle matter. Each such particle may be viewed as a nexus composed of various streams of subtle matter-energy bound up together into a tiny "knot."

The atomic elements thus represent condensed knots of subtle matter-energy. These knots are continuously fed and nourished by the subtle streams of life force flowing through them.

When the gross body composed of gross atoms and molecules ceases to function, the subtle body, composed of the currents of subtle matter, separates itself from its attachments to the gross body, and floats free with the mind fully intact. We then exist in a subtle, spiritual form, which is capable of reflecting consciousness, and which encodes the blueprint of our previous gross body and our entire evolutionary history within itself. This information is encoded within the structure of the subtle body as a set of mental impressions. These impressions constitute the memory possessed by the mortal soul.

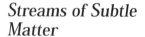

Streams of Subtle Matter   As long as the mortal soul dwells within the gross body, it feeds the gross body with subtle life force and causes various currents of subtle matter to circulate through each individual atom, molecule, and cell. The subtle currents carry nourishment and spiritual power from one atom to another, and from one region of the body to another. These are the channels through which the vibrating life force *(prana)* flows. It is by means of this subtle life force that we reflect consciousness and perform all of our mental processing.

The Taoist Masters used their knowledge of these subtle streams to develop the art of acupuncture. By placing needles made of metal at the energy centers where these subtle streams intersect, they stimulate the flow of subtle energy or chi throughout the system.

The Vedic Seers called these subtle currents *nadis* (streams), and counted 72,000 of them in the human physiology. However, these are just the major streams. There are literally trillions of subtle streams that weave the fabric of our subtle and gross bodies.

Because the subtle particles that flow within these streams carry electric charge, the filamentary streams of subtle matter appear luminous. They radiate photons. However, these photons are not quantized into the discrete packets that are absorbed and emitted by atoms. They display a subquantum, continuous spectrum that cannot be observed by objective instruments. Nor can this spectrum be observed by the gross human eye. It can be observed only by the spiritual eye which itself is composed of subtle particles.[46]

The ability to see with the spiritual eye depends upon the density of the subtle body. The higher the density of the subtle body, the more evolved is the soul and the more powerful are the subtle senses.

The maximum concentration of subtle matter-energy within the subtle body resides in the luminous thumb-sized egg of subtle matter within the heart, the Divine Ka. This is the seat of universal consciousness in the human being, the archetypical form of the human soul. This is the source for all the branching rays of subtle matter-energy that course throughout the body. One whose subtle body is dense enough to see the Divine Ka, or drop of subtle matter in the heart, as well as the luminous currents of subtle matter that radiate out from it, may be called a Seer.

Just as a drop of crystal clear water hanging from the tip of a leaf can reflect the brilliance of the Sun, similarly, the thumb-sized drop of subtle matter nested in the heart of a human being can evolve to the point where it fully reflects the light of pure consciousness. When this occurs, the Divine Ka awakens, the mortal soul becomes immortal, and one becomes enlightened. Although this marks the end of one's evolutionary history on Earth, it also marks the first step in the most amazing cosmic adventure that one can possibly imagine.

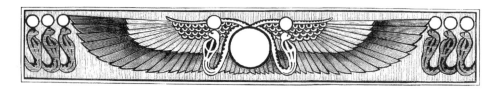

11. THE THEORY OF MORPHIC FIELDS

As stated before, the subtle body is a hierarchically structured field of subtle matter-energy that contains the complete history of the individual within itself. However, this history is not restricted to just the individual system. The evolutionary history of each individual system is intimately and nonlocally connected with the evolutionary history of all other similar systems that exist now, or that ever have existed in the past. In modern terminology, the subtle matter field that carries the collective history of a class of systems may be understood as a *morphic field*.

A morphic field is a subtle matter field that nonlocally resonates with a particular type of natural system, stores information regarding past generations of such systems, and actively participates in their natural evolution. Such fields were first hypothesized by Rupert Sheldrake in the early 1980s and the evidence supporting the existence of such fields has been growing ever since.

> According to this hypothesis, the nature of things depends on fields, called morphic fields. Each kind of natural system has its own kind of field; there is an insulin field, a beech field, a swallow field, and so on. Such fields shape all the different kinds of atoms, molecules, crystals, living organisms, societies, customs, and habits of mind.[47]

Each morphic field is envisioned as carrying a kind of collective memory that plays an active role in shaping the habits and tendencies of individual systems. Sheldrake suggests that

> natural systems, such as termite colonies, or pigeons, or orchid plants, or insulin molecules, inherit a collective memory from all previous things of their kind, however far away they were and however long ago they existed. Because of this cumulative memory, through repetition the nature of things becomes increasingly habitual.[48]

**Morphic
Resonance**
Sheldrake postulates that morphic fields influence other morphic fields through a process called *morphic resonance*. This process is believed to take place on the basis of similarity.

> The more similar an organism is to previous organisms, the greater their influence on it by morphic resonance. And the more such organisms there have been, the more powerful their cumulative influence.[49]

Although the process of morphic resonance was conceived to explain the influence of past generations of natural systems upon present generations, it is similar to the process of divine correspondence that was deemed so important by the ancient Seers. In our view, these two processes are deeply related. They both are nonlocal in their nature[50] and based upon the principle of similarity.

According to Sheldrake, morphic resonance may be understood as a nonlocal transfer of information or knowledge between an individual system and a delocalized field that encodes or carries the collective memory pertaining to all similar systems in the Universe. Sheldrake acknowledges that this transfer of knowledge or information cannot occur on the basis of any of the known physical force fields. To account for this transfer he has had to postulate the existence of morphic fields.

However, Sheldrake's concept of a morphic field is rather vague and general. In addition, the actual mechanics by which information or knowledge is nonlocally transferred from one region of the Universe to another is not well understood.

**Subtle Matter as
Morphic Fields**
To clarify our understanding of these mechanics we must be precise about the nature of a morphic field. In our view, a morphic field may be defined as the local field, cloud, or aura of subtle matter-energy associated with a

particular natural system. Such fields pervade and surround each individual system in the Universe. A star, a planet, a human being, a dog, a termite, an amoeba, an insulin molecule, or a hydrogen atom—each individual natural system has its own morphic field.

Morphic fields also are associated with collective systems as well. This not only applies to things like termite colonies and flocks of pigeons, but also to forests, rivers, mountains, families, cities, cultures, and nations. Every type of collective or individual system that exists in the vast hierarchy of Creation has its own unique morphic field that oversees the activities of that system, preserves its cumulative history, actively participates in its evolution, and resonates with similar fields throughout the Universe.

Although we have made a distinction between individual and collective fields, in truth, all morphic fields are collective fields. They always contain a *fine structure* of increasingly smaller fields within themselves. The fields that exist on each scale of fine structure are organized into networks of similar fields, all of which are connected together by rays of subtle matter-energy.

This analysis is completely general. Even the most elementary morphic field, such as that associated with an individual electron, is believed to contain layer upon layer of increasingly fine structure within itself. Although there is no limit, at least in principle, to the subtlety of structure within a morphic field, at a certain point the consideration of subtler fields ceases to be meaningful in any practical sense.

Subtle Beings as Morphic Fields   In spite of the fact that we have described the structure of morphic fields using analytical concepts, it must be understood that morphic fields are not mechanical fields of matter and energy that unconsciously interact with one another. From a spiritual point of view, they are conscious entities that participate actively in the evolution of the system.

To the ancient Seers, the various morphic fields were not postulates of some hypothetical theory. One reason the Seers were called Seers was because they were able to see these fields with their subtle perception. To the ancient Seers, the morphic fields existing on different levels of Creation were perceived directly as different types of subtle beings. Every natural system thus was perceived as having both a gross physical body and a subtle spiritual body. The subtle body was seen as a spiritual being that consciously participated in the evolution of the system, even if the natural system itself was more or less unconscious—as in the case of a mountain or a tree.

We should not be alarmed by this. The subtle beings that pervade the fabric of Nature are not foreign or alien to us. They are part of our own breath. They manifest the inner presence associated with all things.

Such subtle beings are tied intimately to the systems, individual or collective, with which they are associated. In fact, their subtle energy is continuously being generated and replenished by the very life-breath of these systems. The morphic field associated with a particular system may be understood as the soul or subtle body of that system.

The subtle beings observed by the ancient Seers on different scales of Creation were given different names in different cultures. These subtle beings manifested differently in different regions and climates, and so were represented as having different forms and correspondences. In general, it can be said that these subtle beings constituted the religious pantheons of many ancient cultures.

Three Types of Subtle Beings

If we take the liberty of making a broad generalization, we can categorize the different types of subtle beings or morphic fields into three main categories, which we can call (i) *nature spirits,* (ii) *terrestrial gods,* and (iii) *celestial gods.* In truth, there are many shades and variations that lie between these categories, but for the time being, these should suffice.[51]

To make these categories more concrete, let us define nature spirits as those morphic fields associated with the different collections of minerals, plants, and animals. These are the spiritual agencies of Mother Nature.

The terrestrial gods, on the other hand, may be understood as those morphic fields associated with ordinary (unenlightened) groups, cultures, and nations of human beings. The "spirit" of a team, tribe, clan, city, state, or nation is not just a vacant euphemism. It represents the tangible subtle presence that actively participates in and oversees the activities of the group with which it is associated. Whenever one hears about the god of this nation, or the god of that people, one can be sure that a terrestrial god is being referred to. In ancient times, such divine beings were worshipped and supplicated to receive favor and support for a particular activity. The celestial gods, on the other hand, are universal, and do not belong to any nation, tribe, or people.

The term terrestrial god also can be applied to the collective soul of our planet as a whole. In general, it applies to the soul or collective consciousness of any planet, prior to the attainment of planetary enlightenment.

The morphic fields associated with enlightened societies, nations, and planets may be referred to as celestial gods. Such fields are considered celestial because they are filled with the Light of Heaven. However, the term celestial god applies especially to the celestial luminaries—the stars and galaxies. In general, every individual star, collection of stars, individual galaxy, and collection of galaxies throughout the Universe possesses its own unique morphic field. All of these morphic fields may be understood as celestial gods.

Among other things, this means that the celestial gods, by their very nature, tend to overlap one another in all kinds of ways. Thus, in ancient cultures, different celestial gods are described as sharing many of the same cosmic functions and divine attributes. This makes the boundaries between such gods appear ill-defined. However, the reason for this is simple: the subtle bodies of the celestial gods are interpenetratingly distributed throughout the cosmos. So it is natural for them to share in their qualities and responsibilities. This has perplexed modern scholars, who typically assume that the ancient Seers were imprecise or naive in their thinking.

Mechanics of
Morphic Resonance

Now that we have defined the nature of a morphic field, and categorized their different types, we need to consider the mechanism by which similar morphic fields, separated by vast distances, communicate with one another and share knowledge about their history and evolutionary development. As stated above, Sheldrake calls this transfer mechanism morphic resonance.

To be systematic, we will consider morphic resonances on two levels: (i) local, and (ii) nonlocal. A local morphic resonance represents an exchange of matter, energy, or information that occurs at a subluminal (slower than light) speed, while a nonlocal morphic resonance occurs at a superluminal (faster than light) speed.

Generally speaking, all forms of morphic resonance are supported by currents, rays, or streams of subtle matter-energy that flow among the fields. In particular, local morphic resonances are upheld by polarized currents of subtle matter-energy, while nonlocal resonances are upheld by unpolarized currents.

In both cases, these resonances are supported by longitudinal density waves or impulses that flow along the rays. When these impulses propagate at subluminal speeds, they may be understood as waves of prana, or cosmic life-breath. On the other hand, when they propagate at superluminal speeds they may be understood as waves of primordial sound.

Both types of impulse coexist in every morphic field. Morphic resonance thus occurs both locally and nonlocally for all fields. However, in any given field the influence of one type of resonance generally will predominate. The distinguishing factor is the attainment of the state of enlightenment.

Prior to the attainment of enlightenment, the soul of the system is affected primarily by local influences carried by impulses of prana—impulses that come from similar fields in the nearby environment. After enlightenment, the soul becomes affected primarily by nonlocal influences. These nonlocal influences are carried by the impulses of primordial sound that come from similar fields scattered throughout the Universe.

In both instances, the influences are carried from field to field through a process of resonance. Resonance is a common physical phenomenon. It is well known that if two guitar strings, for example, are placed side by side (though not touching each other), and are of the same thickness, length, and tautness, then when one of them is plucked, they will both vibrate together. This phenomenon, involving a transfer of energy from one string to another, is called spontaneous resonance.

Resonance phenomena require three elements: (i) a transmitter that sends the vibration, (ii) a medium that conveys the vibration through space, and (iii) a receiver that receives the vibration. Regardless of the medium involved, in order for resonance to occur, the transmitter and the receiver must be attuned to one another, that is, they must be qualitatively similar in their material structure.

In the case of morphic resonance, the role of the transmitter and receiver are played by similar morphic fields, and the medium that conveys the resonance is the rays of celestial fire that connect the fields.

The ability of subtle matter fields to convey a local influence is not too difficult to understand. But how is it possible for subtle matter fields to transfer matter, energy, and information from one region to another at superluminal speeds? On the surface, this would seem to contradict the laws of physics. Is there a gap in our understanding of the laws of physics that would allow such an exchange?

Superluminal Transfers of Matter, Energy, and Information

According to Einstein's Theory of General Relativity, if a physical object is accelerated towards the speed of light, as it approaches light speed it becomes harder and harder to make it go any faster. In effect, the object appears to become heavier and heavier, and thus harder to accelerate. As it approaches light speed, the object, no matter how small in mass originally, appears to develop an infinite mass, and thus requires an infinite amount of energy to accelerate further.

Physicists call this type of apparent mass the inertial mass of the object. This is the same type of mass that we feel when we put our foot on the accelerator of our car and suddenly speed forward. When we do so, we are suddenly pulled back against the car seat by a mysterious force. This force is called the inertial force—a force that is formally equivalent to the gravitational force. Just as ordinary mass is acted upon by the gravitational force, so inertial mass is acted upon by the inertial force. Unlike gravity, which pulls us towards the center of the Earth, the inertial force pulls us in the opposite direction of our acceleration.

Einstein's theory predicts that if one's car were to continuously accelerate towards the speed of light, as it approached light speed, the inertial mass of the car would approach an infinite value. More than likely, this means that the car and everything in it would be squashed flat and annihilated. Any information contained in the car would be destroyed, and thus would never reach its destination.

This scenario seems to be pretty accurate. By accelerating elementary particles, such as electrons, towards the speed of light, scientists have observed the powerful effect of the inertial force upon them, and this effect matches the theory nicely. If this is true, then how is it possible for impulses of matter, energy, and information to propagate at superluminal speeds along the unpolarized rays of celestial fire?

Exotic Matter

The answer may lie in a new mechanism that is just beginning to be discussed in the physics literature.[52] This mechanism involves a new, yet undiscovered, type of matter called *exotic matter* —a form of matter that has a negative mass-energy density.[53]

The importance of this type of matter is simple. It is the key to manifesting an antigravitational or *levitational force*. In general, any form of matter that has a negative mass-energy density will experience a repulsive, rather than an attractive force within a gravitational field, and thus will appear to levitate.

This levitational force would be the symmetric inverse of both the gravitational and the inertial forces. This means that levitating systems would experience the symmetric inverse of free fall. It is well known that when systems are in free fall they do not experience any "Gs" or inertial forces. Hence, it has been postulated that if it were possible to create and manipulate a field of exotic matter around a physical system, the levitational force so generated could be used to make the field (as well as the system within it) accelerate to superluminal speeds. Because the inertial force would not apply during such acceleration, the system would not experience any stress or strain, and would appear to be weightless. To use a popular term, it has been proposed that such a mechanism could be used to accelerate the physical system to "warp speed."

Unfortunately, physicists have never observed exotic matter; they have never produced it in their laboratories; and they don't even know if it really exists at all. However, there may be a reason for this. What if exotic matter were very subtle, and almost impossible to detect using ordinary objective instruments? In addition, what if there were very little of it in our region of the Universe?

This leads to our main question: What if exotic matter and unpolarized subtle matter are one and the same thing? Could the chariots of the gods, which are enveloped in a blaze of celestial fire, actually be enveloped in a field of exotic matter?

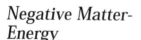

Negative Matter-Energy

The key to this proposed identity between exotic matter and unpolarized subtle matter lies in the concept of negative (or minus) mass-energy. What does *negative mass-energy* mean? What type of matter has minus mass and minus energy? It seems to be a contradiction in terms. In all ordinary matter the mass-energy of the system always has a positive value. So what type of matter can possibly have a negative mass-energy? The physicist's answer is "exotic matter." Our answer is "unpolarized celestial fire." But there is an important twist to this answer.

In our view, negative mass-energy is not a form of matter at all. It is a form of unmanifest pure consciousness. We propose that this is the type of mass-energy that is carried by the impulses of primordial sound. To the degree that the field of unpolarized subtle matter-energy can reflect the impulses of pure consciousness within itself, to that same degree will it possess a negative mass-energy density.

As discussed previously, the ability of the field of unpolarized subtle matter-energy to reflect pure consciousness varies with the particle density of the field. As the particle density increases, the reflection of pure consciousness increases. If we equate pure consciousness with negative mass-energy, then we also may equate unpolarized subtle matter with exotic matter. By so doing, we simultaneously illumine a mechanism by which the negative mass-energy density of a particular field may be increased. It can be increased by increasing the particle density of the field.

This directly impacts the speed at which transfers of matter, energy, and information might occur within a given field of unpolarized subtle matter. The higher the density of the field and its associated rays, the more pure consciousness will be reflected, and the greater will be the transfer speed. In principle, the transfers may take place at any speed, including superluminal ones.

This explains how enlightened souls and the celestial gods send out rays of their own soul essence to various parts of the Universe, and communicate with one another over vast distances. The speed of this communication depends upon the level of pure consciousness reflected by the soul. The greater the reflection of pure consciousness, the higher the speed, and the more efficient is the transfer of matter, energy, or information.

To use a modern analogy, the enlightened beings scattered throughout the Universe may be viewed as "cosmic computers" that are all nonlocally linked by rays of celestial fire, resembling fiber optic cables. The power of each being to process information within itself and to communicate quickly, clearly, and efficiently with similar beings throughout Creation depends upon the density and purity of the subtle matter-energy out of which it is composed. The key to such communication lies in the ability to generate a high density field of unpolarized celestial fire, which can then transmit and receive impulses of primordial sound.

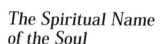

The Spiritual Name of the Soul   The nonlocal communication that takes place between morphic fields occurs through the power of divine speech. Divine speech represents the silent whisper of the soul on the level of pure consciousness.

Every soul, no matter how low, is innately endowed with the power of divine speech. This nonlocal power may be hidden or covered over by our ordinary "life-breath," but it is still there deep within the soul. As our soul becomes more enlightened, this power grows and develops. We eventually develop the ability to consciously send and receive impulses of primordial sound throughout the Universe.

This is how enlightened human beings, as well as the celestial gods, communicate with one another over vast cosmological distances, spanning millions, billions, and even trillions of light-years. They do so through the power of divine speech invested in their soul. It is this divine speech that carries the information or knowledge that is transferred between morphic fields.

Generally speaking, every ray of celestial fire within a given morphic field may be used to carry both impulses of prana and impulses of primordial sound. Given the fine structure that exists within every field, the collection of such impulses can present a complicated frequency signature.

This frequency signature plays an important role in the process of morphic resonance. Every morphic field in Creation, whether that of an electron or a galaxy, naturally generates a frequency signature or sonic blueprint that constitutes its own unique *spiritual name*. This name cannot be heard by the gross ears. It can only be heard on the level of pure consciousness.

Nevertheless, it is an extremely important element. The spiritual name of the soul is the secret code that links it with other similar souls throughout the Universe. In general, systems that possess similar spiritual names automatically are linked together through the process of morphic resonance. Stated in another way, the degree of morphic resonance between two systems depends upon the degree of similarity of their spiritual names. This principle is one of the most important keys to the Sacred Science of the Seers. It can be used to unlock all the treasures of Nature.

The Concept of Spiritual Purity

The ancient Seers developed their knowledge of the divine correspondences between Heaven and Earth based upon their cognitions of the sacred names of things. They cognized the names of things in Heaven and they cognized the names of things on Earth and then they compared the two sets of names. Those things that possess similar spiritual names are deemed to correspond to one another, regardless of how different their outer forms may appear.

This is how the ancient Seers were able to determine the spiritual purity or impurity of any system in Nature. In essence, the Seers compared the spiritual name of the natural system on Earth with the spiritual name of the divine counterpart of that system in the Highest Heaven. The purity of the natural system then was measured or determined by the degree of similarity or dissimilarity between it and its divine counterpart.

This may sound complicated, but it doesn't require much intellection to determine if two names are similar. It is a completely intuitive process.

The ability to determine the purity or impurity of a system played an essential role in the Sacred Science of the Seers. Using their natural intuitive discrimination, the ancient Seers designed methods, processes, and technologies to enhance the spiritual purity of any natural system and thereby to increase the degree of correspondence between the system and its divine counterpart in Heaven. By doing so, the ancient Seers spontaneously increased the power of the morphic resonance between Heaven and Earth, and thus invoked the Light of God to descend on our planet. This is how the ancient Seers used the principle of divine correspondence to enhance the evolutionary development of all beings on Earth.

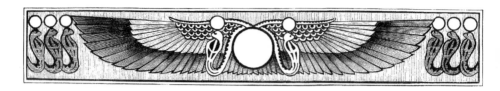

12. THE PRINCIPLE OF DIVINE CORRESPONDENCE

The process of morphic resonance may be understood as the basic force of evolution responsible for guiding the destiny of all things. It may be understood as the divine agency or creative power of God. Although this power resides to some degree in the soul of every creature, it is found most abundantly in the souls of the enlightened Seers and celestial gods throughout the Universe. They are the principal agencies through which the creative power of God is expressed on various scales of time and space within the field of Creation.

The all-powerful force of evolution is like a great river that spontaneously flows to the sea. It is completely automatic and spontaneous in its operation. Nevertheless, the ancient Seers understood how to use and apply this force for the benefit of all beings. They applied this force not only in their meditations and sacred rituals, but also in their sacred technologies. In fact, the force of evolution was the ultimate source of power for all the sacred technologies of the ancient Seers. It is used even today to power the miraculous technologies that exist on Worlds of Light throughout the galaxy. It will thus be worthwhile to examine the basic principles that the Seers employed to harness this force.

———————— · ◦◦◆◦◦ · ————————

"As Above, So Below" In order to manipulate and apply the force of evolution to achieve practical goals, one must have a deep understanding of the principle of divine correspondence. This one principle is capable of revealing all the practical applications of the Sacred Science.

In essence, the principle of divine correspondence states that "what is above is like what is below, and what is below is like what is above."[54] Even more simply, it may be stated: "As above, so below."

What exactly does this aphorism mean? And how does it relate to the force of evolution?

The terms "above" and "below" as used here do not relate to relative height or altitude. Rather, they indicate different levels of density of subtle matter-energy. That which is "above" corresponds to any region where the density of subtle matter is higher than some other region, which then is called "below."

Let us give an example. In the Universe as a whole, the regions that lie above correspond to the celestial regions at the center of the Cosmic Egg. Conversely, the regions "below" correspond to the earthly regions that constitute the outer shell of the Cosmic Egg, in which we are located. The celestial regions lie above the earthly regions because the density of celestial fire is much higher towards the center of the Universe than towards the periphery. This same type of centralized organization is true in every type of natural system, including atoms, cells, planets, star systems, and galaxies.

The principle of divine correspondence may be interpreted as follows: the things that exist in the higher, more celestial regions of the Universe are not essentially different in form or structure from the things that exist in the lower, more earthly regions—except for the fact that the density of subtle matter-energy in these two regions is different.

For example, we have already seen that the Central Galaxy of the Universe is about the same size and shape as an ordinary spiral galaxy in our own region of the Universe.[55] It may be composed of much higher and subtler grades of matter and energy than the galaxies in our region, but it is still a galaxy. Like any ordinary galaxy, it contains billions of star systems, planets, and individual beings who live on these planets.

Of course, the celestial planets are not ordinary planets, and the beings that live upon them are not ordinary beings—they are extraordinary and divine in all respects. But nevertheless some of the planets there resemble our own planet. This resemblance is far from perfect, because our own planet is not nearly as evolved as those in Heaven, but the resemblance is unmistakable.

What does this mean? We suspect that it means something unbelievably marvelous. We believe that the only real difference between the celestial worlds that lie above and the terrestrial worlds that lie below is the density of celestial fire that pervades these different regions.

A Hypothetical Journey

To make this point clear, let us imagine a hypothetical situation. Let us imagine that we could nonlocally transport our entire solar system from its present location in the outer shell of the Universe to a new location within the Central Galaxy. But let's not do this too fast. Let's take a few hundred years, so that we have time to adjust to the dramatic changes that must occur as we proceed on our journey.

During the first part of the journey we will traverse the outer shell, a region that spans over 100 trillion light-years. As we mentioned earlier, because each layer of the Cosmic Egg is approximately ten times the expanse of the next inner layer, if we travel at a constant speed, up to 90 percent of our journey could be taken up traversing this outer layer. Although we will experience a gradual increase in the ambient levels of celestial fire as we move through this region, we will find that the basic structure of our world remains the same—everything will just gradually become more enlightened.

Eventually, we will come to the subtle energy barrier that separates our layer from the next higher layer of celestial life. This barrier is not imaginary. It has an actual location in physical space. It resembles an invisible cosmic wall, composed of laminar currents of subtle matter-energy. In the language of physics, such invisible walls in space are called *current sheaths*. These walls serve as barriers to separate adjacent layers of universal life, and preserve the integrity of the different subtle matter densities that exist in them.

During our hypothetical journey we must pass through these cosmic walls in order to enter into the next layers of celestial life. These are likely to be dramatic events. When we pass through a cosmic wall, our solar system will experience a sudden quantum jump in its evolution. Everything on Earth will be elevated rapidly to a higher level of spiritual evolution, and the material structure of our bodies and the planet as a whole will be radically altered.

This means that our own physiologies and the physiologies of all the plants and animals will undergo profound chemical and structural changes.

Similar dramatic evolutionary transformations will occur every time we pass through one of the cosmic walls and enter into a new layer of universal life. After six such transformations, we will finally arrive at the Central Galaxy.

By the time we arrive at our destination in the Central Galaxy our physical bodies will remain similar in form (i.e., the same number of limbs, eyes, ears, etc.) but the internal structure and organization of the body will be radically different.

Because of the high density fields of celestial fire in the Highest Heaven, the atoms within our bodies will become completely spiritualized. They will reflect a high degree of pure consciousness, and will display a negative mass-energy density.

Our bodies, composed of such *enlightened atoms,* will seem completely weightless. Being fully spiritualized, our bodies will respond instantly to our slightest desire. We will be able to expand or shrink our bodies, or change our forms at will. We will be able to fly unaided at superluminal speeds to any location throughout the entire Universe. In effect, our bodies will be transformed into divine bodies, composed of an exotic type of matter that within our region of the Universe does not naturally evolve, and cannot be created artificially in a stable form.

Although this is a purely hypothetical situation, it contains a profound truth. The truth is this: the only difference between our world and the celestial worlds is the density of celestial fire in which they are embedded.

The Seed and the Tree

This can be elaborated further by another analogy. When an acorn is planted in the ground and then properly nourished and watered, it gradually develops from a seed, to a sprout, to a sapling, to a full grown oak tree. Although these objects possess vastly different forms, we do not consider them to be different types of beings. We recognize them as different stages of growth of the same entity. At one end of the growth spectrum the entity is called an acorn and at the other an oak tree. But they are the same being.

In a similar manner, human beings on Earth and the celestial beings in Heaven may be viewed as two different stages in the spiritual evolution of the same type of soul. The human soul is like the acorn and the celestial soul is like the oak tree. Just as the acorn will spontaneously grow into the oak tree if it is given proper nourishment and time, so also, the human soul will spontaneously develop into a celestial soul if it given proper nourishment and time.

The principle of divine correspondence thus teaches us that whatever exists up above in the Highest Heaven already exists in seed form down below in our own world. All of the knowledge and wisdom possessed by the greatest of the Seers is present within every human soul; all of the divine powers of the gods in Heaven is latent in the human physiology, and all of the celestial beauty of Paradise is inherent within the Earth. All that we have to do is awaken these potentials.

How can we do this? By increasing the density of luminous subtle matter-energy in our minds and bodies, and in the body of the Earth.

When the density of subtle matter-energy is increased within our physiologies the most marvelous things begin to occur. Miracles begin to happen. Why is this? Because we begin to resonate nonlocally with more and more highly evolved beings. As the density of our soul increases, we resonate more powerfully with the celestial fields that connect us with our celestial guardians and overseers. These celestial beings are then able to provide more and more help and spiritual guidance for us on our path.

Eventually this culminates in the experience of enlightenment. When one becomes enlightened, the Divine Ka becomes awake, and one begins to resonate with all the Divine Kas that exist now or that ever have existed since the beginning of Creation. This marks the first real awakening of the soul to its true identity and place in the Universe.

Upon attaining the state of enlightenment, the soul realizes that its own higher Self is truly immortal, and that it has been enlightened since before the emergence of Creation. With that realization, the entire evolutionary history of the soul, which may span millions of years of physical evolution, appears to be little more than a dream in the night. The soul then becomes liberated from its deep-seated illusions about life and death, and becomes totally free.

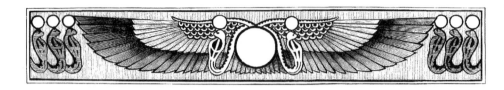

13. THE IMMORTAL SOUL

The development of a fully enlightened human soul involves much more than simply material evolution. There is an even longer process of spiritual evolution that both precedes and accompanies the process of material evolution. This spiritual evolution does not take place on Earth. It occurs in the celestial regions that lie towards the center of the Universe.

To fully understand the origins of human existence, we must expand our vision beyond the realm of our own small planet. We must grasp the idea that the human soul represents a unique union of the local and the nonlocal, the mortal and the immortal, the material and the spiritual sides of existence.

We have already discussed the nature of the mortal soul—the form of the soul that exists prior to enlightenment, and that encodes millions of years of evolutionary development within itself. This form of the soul is bound by local physical forces. Because it is composed primarily of polarized subtle matter-energy, it is unable to reflect the light of pure consciousness, and therefore its awareness is restricted to the functioning of the ego, intellect, mind and ordinary senses.

For the mortal soul to become enlightened, the Divine Ka within the heart must be nourished and awakened. It must evolve to the point where it becomes indistinguishable from the Divine Ka possessed by the higher Self *(atman)*.

The Higher Self

The relationship between the lower self and the higher Self is a deep and profound mystery. The higher Self may be understood as an eternal, birthless, formless mode of unbounded pure consciousness that serves as the Divine Archetype of the individual soul. It is a nonlocal, uncreated spiritual emanation of the Supreme Being. Although we may use the plural number "higher Selves" when discussing such emanations, this is somewhat misleading for there is no sense of multiplicity among them at all.[56]

To use a simple analogy, the higher Selves may be compared to the harmonic modes superposed within a single musical tone. Theoretically any musical tone is composed of an infinite number of harmonic modes; however, we experience the tone as only a single sound. The harmonic modes within the sound do not cry out to be heard as individual tones. Rather, they merge themselves into one another to produce the experience of interpenetrating harmonic unity. In the same manner, the higher Selves do not seek to disassociate themselves from the Being of God. They remain forever submerged within the Transcendental Wholeness of the Supreme Being, even when they appear to play the role of individual beings within the field of Creation.

Regarding these birthless souls, it is said:

> All the souls should be known as naturally analogous to space and as eternal. There is no plurality among them anywhere, not at all. All the souls are, by their very nature, illumined from the very beginning, and their characteristics are well determined. . . . They are, from the very beginning tranquil, unborn, and by their very nature unattached, equal, and non-different. . . . The souls never came under any veil. They are by nature pure as well as illumined from the very beginning. Thus, being endowed with the power (of knowledge), they are said to know.[57]

The original word translated in the above excerpt as "souls" is *dharmah,* which can also be translated as "divine laws." The collection of divine laws that govern the evolution of all things in the Universe are inherent in the uncreated and indestructible blueprint of Creation that permanently resides in the Being of God, in the field of pure consciousness.

The divine laws are identical with the Divine Word—the impulses of primordial sound that reside in the unbounded ocean of consciousness. The dharmah thus may be understood as immortal modes of primordial sound. They are uncreated modes of pure consciousness. It is these transcendental modes of primordial sound that appear as the higher Selves.

We wish to emphasize that each immortal soul is identical with a particular mode of primordial sound—a particular Divine Word. This Divine Word resides eternally within the Being of God. It constitutes the spiritual name and very being of the higher Self.

The point of enlightenment arrives when the spiritual name of the lower self (or *jiva*) and the spiritual name of the higher Self (atman) become indistinguishable. At that point, the lower self merges with the higher Self, and falls into the fathomless bosom of Eternity.

Unlike the mortal soul, which has evolved and taken shape over millions of years, the higher Self or immortal soul has existed in a state of perfection and enlightenment since the beginning of time. It was with God before the Creation, and it will be with God after the dissolution of Creation. It is never really born and it cannot die. It is truly immortal.

Being one with the Divine Word and illumined with spiritual Light, each immortal soul enters into the field of time and space by passing through the blazing effulgence of the Central Sun, which may be understood as the "Mouth of God."

The Mouth of God is the bidirectional portal or gateway to immortality. In order to enter the immortal regions of the Supreme Being, the individual soul must enter into the blazing glory of the Central Sun. It must enter into the Mouth of God and be stripped of all mortal vestments. It must be totally consumed by divinity.

The Sons and Daughters of Immortality

On the other hand, for the immortal soul to enter into the field of Creation, it must first emerge as divine speech from the Mouth of God. As the immortal souls, who are one with the Divine Word, pass through the blazing glory of the Central Sun and emerge from the Mouth of God, they become clothed in robes of celestial light. These robes constitute the celestial bodies that have been prepared for them by the Creator. This is how the bodiless Divine Word becomes clothed in celestial matter and is given subtle luminous form.

The subtle luminous form of the higher Self is that of the Divine Ka. Each higher Self is fashioned in the image of the Creator. It is fashioned in the image of the Divine Ka of the Universe as a whole. The Divine Ka thus is the celestial body of the higher Self. It is the celestial vehicle by which the higher Self travels throughout the field of time and space and experiences the wonders of God's Creation.

Upon entering into these celestial bodies, the higher Selves, remaining birth-less and immortal, are conceived as the offspring of God. They are conceived as *amritasya putra*—the sons and daughters of immortality .

Although they become adorned in celestial robes, the sons and daughters of immortality are never really born. They existed before the Creation appeared, and they will exist after it has disappeared.

Having become clothed in celestial light, the higher Selves descend gradu-ally through the various layers of celestial life towards our physical plane of existence. As they descend, they gain more and more concrete knowledge about Creation along the way. Although they are permanently illumined—and possess innate pure knowledge—their knowledge is spiritual in its content. They are wise in the ways of the spirit, but ignorant in the ways of the world. They enter into the field of Creation to learn about the lower material side of their own immortal nature.

Eventually, the higher Selves descend into the outermost of the seven layers of universal life, which is filled with galaxies similar to our own. Entering into a particular galaxy, they initially take up residence in one of the permanent Worlds of Light located in the center of the galaxy.

While abiding within the glorious Worlds of Light at the center of the galaxy, the higher Selves gain experience about the ideal forms of human existence that serve as archetypes for human civilization throughout the galaxy. After experiencing these central worlds for a long period, the higher Selves then descend further and take up residence on a World of Light somewhere within the luminous disk of the galaxy. There the higher Selves learn about the ideal modes of human behavior that exist within the luminous disk, which the ancient Seers called *kurukshetra*—the "field of action."[58]

After experiencing these ideal physical worlds, the higher Selves finally descend into an evolving solar system like our own. Compared to the Worlds of Light from which they have descended, such physical worlds appear completely shrouded in spiritual darkness.

When the higher Selves first descend into such an evolving solar system, they do not venture onto planets such as the Earth. Rather, they initially take up residence in the luminous orb of the system's Sun, where the subtle matter density is greatest. The luminous orb of the Sun serves as a safe haven for these beings. There the Divine Kas feel at home. Within the blazing spiritual glory of the Sun, the higher Selves can rest and witness the activities of their own lower selves on Earth, watching their evolution from a distance. The higher Self thus is sometimes called the *Witness*. Collectively they are called the *Watchers*. Watching over us at all times, they may be understood as our guardian angels, our spiritual guides, and our best friends in time of need.[59]

------------◆◆◆------------

The Marriage of Heaven and Earth

It should be a comfort to know that each mortal soul on Earth, however insignificant, has its own higher Self. The higher Self and the lower self are like twin flames. They were breathed into existence by the same nonlocal act of God, which took place simultaneously on Earth and in Heaven. And they have not evolved separately. Their activities and evolution have been coordinated and nonlocally correlated since the very beginning by the Divine Messenger.

Even though they may have been separated by distances spanning trillions of light-years, the development of the lower material self always has been in the awareness of the higher spiritual Self. The higher Self has nonlocally overseen and witnessed the development of its own lower self through its inherent power of nonlocal intuition. It has observed the evolution of its own lower self without interfering. This is possible because the higher Self is already illumined, fulfilled, and unattached. It knows the outcome of the evolutionary course upon which its lower self is engaged—and it has no need to hurry it up. The higher Self simply allows the will of God to take its course.

The material soul, on the other hand, is shrouded in ignorance and has no real knowledge of who it is, where it is going, or for what reason it was created. This ignorance is primordial. It is beginningless. It has covered the lower self since its inception in the womb of primordial Nature, and it has continued over the course of millions of years.

Furthermore, the lower self is attached to the body and the fruits of its actions, while the higher Self is not. The higher Self is eternally free, unattached, and enlightened. It is the master of its own destiny. The lower self, on the other hand, has no real knowledge of its own higher Self, and remains veiled in ignorance. It is buffeted about by the winds of destiny until it becomes enlightened.

At that point, it finally attains equality with its own higher Self, and merges with it. It is only then that the lower self achieves victory over death. Having received the Light of God within itself, it becomes free from the influence of the local, terrestrial morphic fields that are based primarily upon past events. Only then does the soul become liberated from the influence of its own past action *(karma),* and become totally free.

The higher and lower self thus may be viewed as complementary aspects of the same one being. When they finally come together, they are not strangers to one another. They have shared a divine (nonlocal) correspondence with one another since the beginning of time. The nonlocal correspondence that connects the mortal and immortal soul may be compared to a branch on the eternal Tree of Life. Regarding this there are the following verses:

> There are two birds (souls) with beautiful plumage, who are associated with each other as friends. They roost on the same tree (or branch). One eats the sweet fruits of the tree; while the other abstains from eating, and merely looks on (as a witness). (Though

it sits) on the same tree (as the higher Self), the lower self remains as if drowned (in misery) and so it moans, being worried by its impotence. When it (finally) sees the other, i.e., the lord (or higher Self) and his (transcendent) glory, then it becomes free from sorrow. When the seer (finally) sees the (higher) person—(its own) self-effulgent creator and lord, who is the source of all divine speech, then the illumined (lower self) shakes off both virtue and vice, becomes stainless, and attains absolute equality (with the higher Self). This one (the higher Self) is verily the vital force (prana, breath of God) that shines variously through all beings. Knowing this, the illumined one does not engage in much discourse. He disports in the Self, delights in the Self, and becomes absorbed in (spiritual) effort (to obtain the Light). Such a one is a great knower of Brahman (Supreme Being).[60]

The relationship between the higher and lower self has been described in different ways throughout the ages. In some ancient traditions, the lower self has been compared to the "bride," while the higher Self has been compared to the "bridegroom." These two lovers have been longing for each other since the beginning of time. In order for the two lovers to consummate their desire for sacred union, the bride (lower self) must first prepare herself. The bride prepares herself by entering into the bridal chamber (i.e., the human body). When the bride becomes fully prepared, that is, when the mortal soul reaches the proper level of purity and development, the groom (higher Self) approaches the bride (its own lower self) and briefly unites with her.

This marks the beginning of a beautiful courtship. Once the bride has tasted the lips of her spiritual lover, that is, once the lower self has experienced the ineffable bliss of spiritual union with its own higher Self, it develops an ardent longing for permanent union. Over time, periods of spiritual union are followed by periods of spiritual separation. During this divine courtship, the spiritual vibration of the lower self gradually is raised to a level of equality with the higher Self. Once this equality of vibration is achieved, there is a true marriage of souls, where the lower self (bride) and the higher Self (groom) become a single enlightened being, and from that point forward are never separated. This permanent marriage of the higher and lower self occurs at the point of spiritual enlightenment, and eventually gives complete mastery over both spiritual and material realms.

The love affair of the higher and lower self is continuously played out on all levels of Nature over and over again. Yet its true meaning generally has remained a deep esoteric secret. This esoteric secret is beautifully expressed in the following text:

> And Mind, the Father of all, he who is Life and Light, gave birth to man [the higher Self], a being like to himself. . . And God delivered over to man [the higher Self] all things that had been made. . . and the [seven] Administrators took delight in him, and each of them gave him a share of his own nature.

> And having understood the being of the [seven] Administrators, and having received a share of their nature, he [the higher Self] willed to break through the bounding circle of their orbits, and he looked down through the structure of the heavens. Having broken through the [lowest] sphere, he showed to downward-tending [material] Nature the beautiful [celestial] form of God [that was invested in himself]. And Nature, seeing [in the higher Self] the beauty of the form of God, smiled with insatiate love of man, showing the reflection of that most beautiful form in the water, and its shadow on the Earth. And he [the higher Self], . . .willed to dwell there [in that form]. And the deed followed close on the design; and he took up his abode in matter devoid of reason [or pure awareness]. And Nature, when she had got him with whom she was in love, wrapped him in her clasp, and they were mingled as one; for they were in love with one another. And that is why man, unlike all other living creatures upon Earth is twofold. He is mortal by reason of his [mortal] body; he is immortal by reason of the man of eternal substance. He is immortal, and has all things in his power [by reason of his higher Self]; and he suffers the lot of a mortal, being subject to Destiny [by reason of his lower self].[61]

Polarized and Unpolarized Subtle Matter—Chitta and Chitta-Vritti

From a technical point of view, it should be understood that the subtle body of the lower self is composed of a different grade of subtle matter-energy than the celestial body of the higher Self. The subtle body of the higher Self is composed of unmodified or unpolarized subtle matter, which is capable of reflecting pure consciousness. The subtle body of the lower self, on the other hand, is composed of the polarized modifications of subtle matter. In the technical language of the Vedic Seers, unmodified subtle matter was simply called chitta, while the modifications of chitta were called *chitta vrittis*—literally "vortical modifications of chitta."[62]

The vortical modifications of chitta are composite entities. They consist of trillions of subtle particles dynamically bound together by physical forces to form a single entity, resembling a whirlpool or vortex. Because of the composite nature of these entities, under the proper conditions they can be dissolved back into their elementary constituents. The vortical modifications of chitta are thus perishable. Because the subtle body of the lower self is composed of such modifications, it is deemed to be perishable.

This perishability has another connotation as well. When the lower self evolves from one state of evolution or self-organization to the next, the previous state must be dissolved in order to make way for the new state. Thus all change or evolution on the level of the perishable subtle body inevitably involves some form of dissolution.

The celestial body of the higher Self, on the other hand, is composed of particles of pure chitta.[63] These particles are not composite entities. Furthermore, they are relatively immortal. Once they are churned out of the vacuum, they endure for the entire period of Creation, after which they dissolve back into the vacuum once again. Compared to the perishable subtle body of the lower self, the subtle body of the higher Self thus is relatively immortal.

When the particles of pure chitta are aggregated to form a celestial body, they do so under the guiding influence of pure consciousness. They are not held together by local physical forces. Their relationships are mediated by nonlocal pure consciousness alone. As a result, the celestial body can undergo change and assume various forms, without requiring the action of physical forces. There is no dissolution involved in such changes, because there is no composite physical form that must be dissolved.

The Hermetic texts clearly discuss this subject. They state:

> Immortal bodies undergo change without dissolution, but the changes of mortal bodies are accompanied by dissolution; that is the difference between immortals and mortals.[64]

In the body of an enlightened Seer, the celestial body of the higher Self appears as the egg-shaped cocoon of light called the Divine Ka, which we discussed earlier. This is the chariot of light or celestial vehicle by which the higher Self travels nonlocally throughout the cosmos,[65] dwells within the luminous orb of the Sun, and eventually becomes nested within the human heart.

Although the Divine Ka consists of unmodified chitta, and resembles a cocoon of light nested in the heart, it is capable of extending itself in the form of numberless rays of celestial fire.

> Numberless are the rays of the luminous one who dwells in the heart and shines like a lamp. They are white, green, tawny, golden, and light red.[66]

The rays of celestial fire emanating from the Divine Ka in the heart resemble so many petals of a flower, or the beautiful plumage of a divine bird. The immortal Divine Ka thus may be understood as the true Phoenix, that rises from the ashes of its own mortal soul. The rays of the Divine Ka consist of unmodified pure chitta, and also are capable of reflecting pure consciousness. Because of these rays, the Divine Ka can assume the form of a person that looks just like a luminous human being. Indeed, when a person becomes enlightened, the polarized rays of subtle matter that pervade the mortal subtle body become transformed into unpolarized rays, and the Divine Ka then manifests itself as the enlightened spiritual double of the gross body.

However, the unpolarized luminous subtle body of the Divine Ka is not itself the higher Self; it is merely the celestial robe of the higher Self. Similarly, the cocoon of light within the heart is not the higher Self. It is merely the chariot of light that is possessed by the higher Self.

The higher Self should not be confused with any of its subtle bodies (and it may possess many at the same time). In truth, the higher Self is a bodiless mode of unbounded pure consciousness that is formless and nonlocal in its structure. It resembles pure space, is filled with primordial sound, and cannot be seen as an object, even with the subtle eyes. It cannot be seen as an object because it itself is the Seer. However, it is not unknowable. It can be known through self-referral pure consciousness. If one wishes to know the higher Self, one must become the higher Self. The Self is known by the Self alone. There is no other way.

14. THE COSMIC NETWORK OF CELESTIAL RAYS

The enlightened Seers not only saw the subtle currents in their own bodies and in their immediate environment, but through their nonlocal intuition, they saw the subtle body of the galaxy and of the Universe as a whole. Thus, to the Seers, the Universe appeared to be filled with a vast network of countless filaments of celestial fire.

The streams of celestial fire in the Heavens are similar to the streams of luminous subtle matter in the human physiology. There are trillions upon trillions of such streams throughout the Universe. These branching streams of celestial fire course through the depths of interstellar and intergalactic space like so many bolts of cosmic lightning. They are the celestial highways of the gods.[67] They are the cosmic channels of communication and transportation within the celestial body of God. Their purpose is to carry the life-breath of the Creator from the Central Sun of the Universe to all the galaxies, stars, and worlds that shine like fiery diamonds sprinkled throughout Creation.

The shining streams of celestial fire not only connect each galaxy, star, and planet to the Central Sun of the Universe, but they also connect galaxy with galaxy, star with star, and planet with planet. Every celestial body in the Universe both receives and radiates emanations of celestial fire to every other celestial body in the Universe.

The rays of celestial fire are thus bidirectional in their nature. They carry both the inhalations and exhalations of the gods. Because of the helical motions of the polarized charged particles that flow around them, the celestial rays stretched out by the gods resemble so many spiraling filaments or threads of golden light. In the Greek tradition, this cosmic network of golden filaments was referred to as a "golden fleece."

Similarly, in the Vedic tradition, the cosmic network of golden filaments was conceived of as the woolen filter *(avi)* through which the Soma, or Nectar of Immortality, was strained or poured. By flowing through the woolen filter, symbolically composed of "sheep hairs," the Soma became purified and was made fit for drinking by the celestial gods.[68] Because the spiraling rays of celestial fire begin and end on celestial bodies, such as stars and galaxies, the streams of celestial fire were conceived of as nourishing the bodies of the gods and giving them sustenance and immortal life.

In the Egyptian tradition, the network of celestial rays was symbolized as the divine Field of Reeds. The Field of Reeds did not exist on Earth. It existed in the divine celestial regions of Heaven. It was the domain of Osiris, the lord of rebirth, resurrection, and immortality. In fact, passing through the Field of Reeds was the Egyptian metaphor for death. Why? Because when the mortal soul passes out of the gross body at the time of physical death, it enters into a celestial ray, resembling a hollow reed or tube of light. This ray, which is filled with unmodified pure chitta, and reflects pure consciousness, carries the soul at nonlocal speeds to the heart of a particular celestial being, who then reviews the karma of the soul, and either assigns it to a new world, or returns it back to Earth.

Many individuals who have had "near-death" experiences, have reported such journeys. The experience is that of traveling at tremendous speeds through a tube that is filled with darkness. After some time, however, one becomes aware of a glorious light shining "at the end of the tunnel." As one approaches this light, one finds that it is alive. It is conscious. Upon entering into the presence of this light, the soul intuitively realizes that it is in the presence of a divine being, who is filled with overwhelming wisdom, love, and compassion.

Such journeys are not imaginary. While passing through the "tunnel" the mortal soul is literally traveling at nonlocal speeds over enormous distances. The ancient Egyptians envisioned these celestial "tunnels" as hollow reeds.[69] That is why it was said that to ascend to Heaven and attain immortality, one must pass through the Field of Reeds.

The celestial rays serve not only as highways to carry souls from place to place in the Universe. They also are used by celestial beings to regulate the evolution of the worlds and beings under their care. They administer these worlds by sending out emanations of their own soul essence, which flow as impulses of cosmic life force or waves of celestial fire along the cosmic rays. Among other things, these impulses of celestial fire play a critical role in regulating the cycles of time that govern the patterns of evolution on our planet.

All of the major cycles and natural rhythms of our planet, including the cycles of day and night, of the moon, of the seasons, of the zodiacal Ages, and of epochal Day and Night, are regulated by the impulses of cosmic life force that connect our small planet with the rest of the Universe. The relationships between planetary cycles and cosmic rhythms are not based upon purely mechanical interactions. They are based upon a morphic resonance that nonlocally links our planet with other similar planets throughout the Universe.

The Science of Astrology

The rays of celestial fire connecting our planet with the rest of the Universe also play a critical role in the science of astrology. In the Vedic tradition, the science of astrology is called *Jyotish*, which means "celestial light." This is not the harsh light seen by the gross eyes. It is the soft luminous glow (resembling moonlight) associated with the streams or rays of celestial fire that crisscross the Heavens.

Each celestial ray that converges onto the Earth from the Heavens carries its own unique set of qualities and correspondences. These qualities are derived from the particular celestial body with which that ray is associated. In order to comprehend the enormous number of rays converging onto the Earth from all directions in the Heavens, the ancient Seers divided the sky into twelve equal divisions of thirty degrees each. In western astrology these divisions are called "signs." In the Vedic system of astrology, or Jyotish, these divisions are called *Rashis*, which means a "heap of rays."

It turns out that the same symbols and meanings were assigned to these twelve astrological divisions by Seers all around the world. This was not due to any astrological convention. It was because the Seers everywhere cognized through their nonlocal intuition the same basic qualities in the twelve divisions of the sky. The Seers associated each astrological division with a particular symbol or set of symbols that reflected the qualities and divine correspondences inherent in the "heap of rays" converging onto the Earth through those divisions.

Such astrological considerations were extremely important in virtually all ancient cultures around the world. In ancient times, the science of astrology was not considered to be frivolous or unrealistic. On the contrary, it was considered an extremely important aspect of the Sacred Science. This is because the Seers of every culture recognized the vitally important influence that the celestial rays have upon every phase of life and living on the Earth.

Astrology is not an exact physical science. It is an intuitive subtle science. Its purpose is to align the life of the individual with the life of the Universe as a whole. It does so through a deep knowledge of the divine correspondences between Heaven and Earth. These correspondences are carried by the rays of celestial fire that connect the Earth with every other celestial body in the Universe.

The science of divine correspondences is not trivial. It is very deep. To discern the correspondences between one thing and another requires a profound and penetrating vision. These correspondences are not obvious on the surface. They are registered in the soul. They are encoded in the spiritual names of things, and not in their gross physical forms.

The Three Main Celestial Rays

Although our planet is connected with the rest of the Universe through billions and billions of celestial rays, there are three main rays that play a more important role than any others. These are the rays that connect the Earth with the Sun, with the center of the Milky Way, and with the center of the Universe. These three rays may be called the solar ray, the galactic ray, and the universal ray, respectively. They are filled with masculine, feminine, and neutral energies, respectively.

Through the solar ray the Earth receives an abundance of masculine (yang) energy. This energy stimulates the active nature of all things and governs the day-to-day evolution of the Planetary Being.

The galactic ray, on the other hand, carries an abundance of feminine (yin) energy. This ray brings the passive nourishing influence of the Galactic Center to our planet. The main purpose of this ray is to uphold the natural evolution of the minerals, plants, and animals and ensure that they provide a proper foundation for human existence. The cycles of time regulated by the galactic ray are thus more long range in their scope than those regulated by the solar ray.

In particular, the galactic ray serves to initiate the zodiacal Ages, which change every 2,160 years. At the beginning of each zodiacal Age, a wave of celestial fire descends from the heart of the Galaxy to our planet, temporarily elevating the spiritual awareness of all beings, and infusing new qualities and knowledge into our collective consciousness. These periodic infusions of cosmic life force are not enough to initiate a true Golden Age, but they do serve to clear out obstacles and keep the stream of evolution on course.

In the administrative scheme of the Universe, there are two stages of development for a planet like the Earth. During the first stage, it comes under the jurisdiction of the Galactic Being.

To nurture the planet and embryonic souls under its care, the Galactic Being sends out a nourishing ray of celestial fire that continuously provides subtle life force for their sustenance and development. Periodically, every 2,160 years, it nudges them along by giving them an extra little boost. The soothing, passive influence coming from the Galactic Being helps to balance the more active, dynamic influence coming from the solar being. Their combined and balanced influences are essential to the progressive evolution of life on our planet.

The ray of celestial fire that connects our Earth to the heart of the Galactic Being lies in the direction of Sagittarius—towards the center of the Milky Way Galaxy. The quality of Cosmic Intelligence associated with the galactic ray thus is symbolized by the centaur, the mythical being who is half man, half beast, and who aims his arrow at the stars.[70] The centaur represents the various processes in Nature that govern the transformation of elemental and animalistic souls into Divine Kas, who aim their consciousness towards the stars and Heavens—towards the Light.

Figure 11—Sagittarius—The Centaur

The Egyptian astrological symbol for Sagittarius is a centaur. It represents the dual nature of the human condition, as part animal, part divine. The hind feet of this mythical creature are placed on the ground of the Earth, while its forelegs are raised above the celestial ark or heavenly ship, which delivers the soul to Heaven. The wings on its back symbolize its ability to ascend into the heavens. The straight arrow drawn on the bow represents the unpolarized subtle energy vital to the evolutionary unfoldment of life on Earth. The dual nature of the human condition is further depicted by the two faces on one head. The animal face looks back towards its roots in the Earth, while the human face looks forward to its divine future in Heaven. The centaur thus symbolizes the process of human transformation from its lower animalistic nature to its higher divine nature.

As soon as evolving souls reach the human stage of development, and are initiated into the light of pure consciousness, the primary responsibility for their evolution comes under the jurisdiction of the Universal Being, the Creator—who administers the evolution of human civilization from his permanent abode at the heart of the Universe.

After the Dawn of human civilization, the Galactic Being continues to carry out its functions overseeing the natural evolution of the planetary environment, including the plants and animals. It continues to initiate new zodiacal Ages each 2,160 years. However, from that time forward, the influence of the Creator, which is carried by the ray or pillar of celestial fire connecting the Earth with the center of the Universe, far outweighs the influence from the center of the galaxy.

From the Dawn of the first Day of human civilization on Earth, the Universal Being presides over the subsequent evolution of human civilization through its various epochal cycles of evolutionary unfoldment. He does so through the agency of the Divine Messenger.

Rather than delivering an abundance of either masculine or feminine energy, the universal ray that descends from the Creator delivers a flood of pure chitta, or unpolarized celestial fire, which reflects a high level of pure consciousness.

Although this form of celestial fire is capable of awakening the light of pure consciousness in all things, it is sent especially to enlighten the human beings that have prepared themselves to receive it. The Creator takes a special interest in enlightened human souls because they are deemed his own children—the sons and daughters of immortality. Indeed, newly enlightened human souls may be viewed as newborn celestial beings.

The word "enlightenment" signifies a major phase transition in the journey of life. To the ancient Seers it marked the end of mortality and the beginning of immortality. However, there are many different shades and variations of enlightenment. Not all enlightened souls are equal in their knowledge, vision, or power.

The Two Paths of Enlightenment

Without going into too much detail, it should be stated that once the soul becomes enlightened, it must choose between two paths—(i) the path of knowledge, and (ii) the path of action.

119

Those who embark upon the path of knowledge must direct all of their attention towards transcending the entire Creation altogether. Their goal is to expand their awareness beyond the seven luminous layers of the Cosmic Egg, and beyond the cold dark sea (or causal ocean) that surrounds the Cosmic Egg. Coming to the limit of the causal ocean, they must then break through the Enclosing Serpent that forms the boundary of that ocean. Upon emerging on the other side of the Enclosing Serpent, and finding themselves at the heart of the Cosmic Lotus, they must then expand beyond the Cosmic Lotus, beyond the Metaphysical Cubic Cell of our own Universe, and through the infinite crystalline lattice of Universes to finally and ultimately merge into the Transcendental Wholeness of the Supreme Being. Those enlightened souls who embark upon this great and final journey, which is the journey back "Home," generally adopt a secluded quiet life away from society. Theirs is the path of renunciation.[71]

Those who embark upon the path of action, on the other hand, become enlisted in the service of the Creator. Such souls are continuously educated by the Creator and his celestial agencies, the gods, so that they may assume more and more divine responsibility while remaining within the field of Creation. While continuously engaged in service to the Creator over millions, billions, and even trillions of years, such enlightened souls may sequentially assume the role of celestial beings on higher and higher levels of universal life. However, throughout this long period of divine service, regardless of the glorious celestial forms that these souls may assume, they retain the same Divine Ka through which they first achieved enlightenment as human beings. At the end of a complete cycle of Creation spanning 311.04 trillion years, these enlightened souls will merge themselves, along with the Creator, back into the Transcendental Wholeness of the Supreme Being from which they originally came. In this manner, all enlightened human souls, regardless of the path that they choose, ultimately are destined to attain true immortality in the transcendental bosom of God.

The progressive education of enlightened souls who have chosen the path of action is the unique responsibility of the Creator, and is accomplished in many marvelous ways. On Earth-like planets, it is accomplished primarily through the agency of the Divine Messenger, who regulates the cycles of time that unfold over an epochal Day and Night. On Earth, these cycles are designed to infuse new qualities and new knowledge into human awareness every 13,000 years.

The waves of divine life force that are delivered to the Earth by the Divine Messenger may be understood as the cosmic life-breath of God. They come with clock-like precision every 13,000 years to mark the halfway point in the 26,000 year precessional cycle. This is no coincidence. The periodic wobbling motion of the Earth on its axis (which is responsible for the phenomena of precession) is directly and powerfully influenced by the periodic waves of celestial fire that come from the center of the Universe. These two phenomena are in resonance with one another.

Figure 12—Taurus, the Bull

The Egyptian astrological symbol for Taurus is a bull with a solar disk placed upon its back. The bull is the ancient symbol for masculine virility and creative or seminal power among ordinary creatures. The solar disk is the symbol of creative power in the Universe as a whole. It symbolizes the creative power of Atum—the sun-god, who is the Creator of the Cosmic Egg and all its contents.

Later we will see that when the wave of celestial fire washes over our planet, it can cause major magnetic and gravitational disturbances in the body of the Earth. These disturbances sometimes initiate a shift in the magnetic and geographic poles of the Earth. But more generally, they provide the driving force that regulates the precessional wobble of the Earth on its axis. That is why the ancient Seers were so attentive to the precessional cycle—because it is tied directly to the periodic descent of celestial fire onto the Earth.

The waves of cosmic life force that regulate the precessional cycle do not descend upon our planet from all directions. They flow along the universal ray of celestial fire that lies in the direction of the Pleiades constellation in the sign of Taurus. This is the general direction of the Central Galaxy of the Universe. The immense creative power of this distant region is symbolized by a bull (Taurus), the archetypical symbol of virility and seminal power.

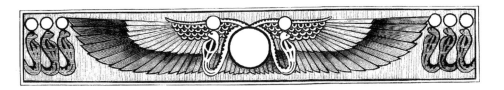

15. ERIDANUS—
THE RIVER OF CELESTIAL FIRE

In ancient Greek mythology, the universal stream that descends to Earth from the Highest Heaven was known as Eridanus—the river of celestial fire. The story of the Eridanus is conveyed in the myth of Phaethon.

In Greek mythology, Phaethon was the son of Helios—the sun-god. It is said that Helios once took an oath to fulfill any wish of his young son. When the young boy asked to drive the chariot of the Sun across the sky, Helios intuitively knew that the outcome would be unfortunate, and tried to dissuade Phaethon from such a dangerous undertaking. But after Helios realized that nothing could change his son's mind, and in order to remain faithful to his vow, he handed the reins of the solar chariot to his young child. As feared, the chariot of the Sun fell off its proper path.

The result was catastrophic. The Heavens became filled with blazing fire, and Atlas (the father of the seven Pleiades) almost failed to balance the world's axis on his shoulders. The Greek writer Nonnos states:

> There was tumult in the sky shaking the joints of the immovable universe; the very axle which runs through the middle of the revolving heavens was bent.[72]

Because of this upsetting of the cosmic order, Zeus (the Creator) had to intervene. He hurled his thunderbolt at Phaethon, who fell in flames into the river Eridanus, which thereafter became known as the burning river.

The Phaethon story is not just a fanciful mythical tale. It presents deep esoteric knowledge pertaining to the transition from one world Age to another. During such transitions, the movement of the Sun and of all the stars in the sky may be altered as seen from Earth. This dislocation of the celestial orbs is caused by a shift in the geographic poles, a subject that we will examine more closely in chapter 24.

This general picture is confirmed by Plato, who gives his own understanding of the Phaethon myth in his *Timaeus*. In this dialogue, the Greek historian Solon is conversing with an Egyptian high priest, who informs Solon that the legend of Phaethon

> has the air of a fable; but the truth behind it is a deviation [paral-laxis] of the (celestial) bodies that revolve in Heaven around the Earth, and a destruction, occurring at long intervals, of things on Earth by a great conflagration.[73]

Although Phaethon fell into the Eridanus, he was not totally destroyed. According to Nonnos, he was taken up to Mount Olympus (the Central Galaxy). The river into which he fell also was elevated to divine or celestial status. It is said that

> The fire-scorched river also came up to the vault of the stars with the consent of Zeus, and in the starry circle rolls the meandering stream of the burning Eridanus.[74]

The word "meandering" used in the translation above is a loose translation of *helissetai*, which means "helixing"—i.e., moving in a spiral pattern like a whirlpool. The Eridanus thus may be compared to a river of celestial fire that moves like a cosmic whirlpool or luminous vortex filament within the starry Heavens.

Although this knowledge has been passed on to us in a form deeply cloaked in mythic images and metaphors, we believe that the Eridanus is none other than the stream of celestial fire that descends upon the Earth from the center of the Universe at the time of epochal transitions. When it comes, the axis of the Earth becomes "bent," and the movements of the Sun and the stars in the Heavens are changed in their course.

When does this descent occur? It occurs when the four living creatures—the lion, the ox, the human, and the eagle—descend from Heaven in their blazing chariot of celestial fire. It occurs when the four cardinal signs Leo, Taurus, Aquarius, and Scorpio rise together during the equinoxes and solstices.

It is thus no coincidence that Eridanus—the spiraling river of celestial fire—was considered to be a paranatellonta of Aquarius. It makes its appearance when the sign of Aquarius rises at the spring or autumn equinox. In accordance with this understanding, the Eridanus, the blazing river of celestial fire, was considered the "gush" from the urn of Aquarius—a gush that came from the direction of Taurus.[75]

According to some scholars, the stream poured from Aquarius's urn was supposed to join another mysterious stream lying in the southern hemisphere. Apparently this ancient knowledge was passed on since time immemorial in certain astrological traditions.[76]

What is the nature of this other celestial stream that joins with the stream flowing from Aquarius's urn? Could this be a reference to the galactic stream that flows from the heart of the Galactic Being? As we have seen, the galactic stream of celestial fire lies in sign of Sagittarius, in a part of the sky that can be seem most clearly in the southern hemisphere.

The two streams of celestial fire are thus uniquely associated with the northern and southern hemispheres of the Earth. The universal stream, which comes from the center of the Universe, can be seen most clearly from the northern hemisphere, and the galactic stream, which comes from the center of the Milky Way galaxy, can be seen most clearly from the southern hemisphere. At the transition point between Ages, these two streams meet and mix their celestial beams—thus uniting the northern and southern hemispheres into a single planetary awareness.

At such a time, the universal ray predominates over the galactic and solar rays. When the universal ray of celestial fire meets the galactic ray, then it takes over the function of that ray, and dominates the evolutionary unfoldment of all things on Earth for thousands of years. The celestial influence of the universal ray remains strong for the duration of the Golden Age that follows its descent. Afterwards, as the power of the universal ray gradually wanes, the regulatory influence of the galactic ray gradually reasserts itself.

Although the cosmic breath of the Creator flows through the universal ray or pillar of celestial fire in a wave-like manner every 13,000 years, the cosmic life force that propagates along this ray does not display a sine wave pattern. It displays itself as a sharply defined impulse, resembling a wave crashing on a beach. More accurately, these waves resemble shock waves, spaced about 13,000 years apart. This means that the density of celestial fire within the ray increases rapidly at the beginning of a Golden Age, and then gradually declines over a long period of time. This pattern is illustrated graphically below.

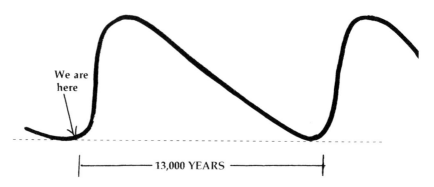

Figure 13—Shock Waves of Cosmic Breath

The wavelike emanations of celestial fire that radiate from the Central Sun may be conceived of as the Cosmic Breath of the Creator. Although these waves are regular and periodic, they do not display a sine wave pattern. Rather, they display a wave pattern typical of a shock wave—a wave that displays a sharp wave front followed by a tail. In the illustration above, our position on the periodic wave cycle is marked by the arrow.

When the Creator emanates his own life force to awaken and initiate a new group of human souls, the ambient subtle matter density in the space surrounding the Earth increases dramatically and suddenly, and the subtle body of every atom, molecule, cell, and organic being on our planet becomes nourished and refreshed.

Because the cosmic life-breath of the Creator is infused into every grain of matter on our planet, the entire world becomes filled with subtle spiritual Light, and a much higher level of consciousness is enjoyed by all beings. The Earth as a whole wakes up as a Planetary Being and assumes its proper role in the cosmic order of the Universe.

When this occurs, the floodgates of knowledge are opened to human awareness, and an Age of Light, a Golden Age, dawns on Earth. The Earth then is transformed, almost overnight, into a Heavenly Paradise, a veritable Garden of Eden. We are extremely fortunate to live at a time when such a dramatic phase transition is about to occur. And it is imperative that we begin to prepare for this event that is unprecedented in our recorded history.

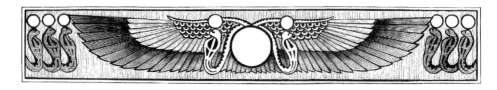

16. COOKING WITH CELESTIAL FIRE

The coming flood of celestial fire represents a phenomenon that will have important implications for every aspect of our lives. To properly understand this phenomenon and its implications, we need to further examine the interaction between subtle matter and ordinary atomic matter.

At the time of the global Illumination, there will be an enormous infusion of subtle matter into every atom on our planet. This "in-fusion" of subtle matter literally represents a *subtle fusion process.*[77] In effect, the subtle matter that descends into our midst will become fused into the nuclei of every atom on our planet.

This type of subtle fusion should not be confused with thermonuclear fusion. In thermonuclear fusion, protons or neutrons are captured by the nucleus of an atom, and this capture results in the formation of a new atomic element. Such reactions can be initiated only in the presence of incredibly high temperatures, such as those at the heart of the Sun. In addition, they generate enormous quantities of heat and deadly gamma radiation as their by-products.

———————·———◆———·———————

**Subtle Fusion
or Tapas**
In a subtle fusion reaction, on the other hand, the atomic nucleus captures subtle particles, each of which has a mass that is trillions of times less than that of a nucleon. These captured subtle particles then are incorporated into the internal structure of the nucleus, which changes by degrees until a new stable state is reached. An atom undergoing this gradual fusion process may be said to be *cooked by celestial fire.* At the time of Illumination, every atom, molecule, and cell on Earth will be slowly cooked from within by celestial fire.

As a result of this comparatively gentle, slow-cooking process, heat energy or infrared radiation is released from the atomic nucleus, but there is no gamma ray production. The ancient Vedic Seers called this type of slow-cooking process *tapas* (evolutionary heat). Tapas may be understood as the fundamental process by which everything in Creation gradually evolves—including all the elementary particles and atoms.

Systems experiencing an intense process of tapas tend to display an abundance of *sattva* (physical lightness and spiritual light). Because of the influence of this sattva, such systems may temporarily lose some of their mass or levitate—an effect that is, at least in principle, empirically testable and measurable.[78]

This atomic process of evolution also is replicated on larger scales of self-organization in Nature. Not only are the subtle bodies of inorganic atoms nourished and evolved in this way, but the subtle bodies of all organic beings also are nourished and evolved in the presence of subtle matter.

As the body absorbs more subtle matter, it spontaneously evolves to a higher level of self-organization. New pathways of subtle energy are forged in the body to handle higher levels of spiritual power, and the structure and chemistry of the gross body adapts to reflect this new pattern of subtle energy flow.

Although these rearrangements temporarily may disrupt the smooth functioning of the system, and cause some discomfort or disorientation, once the fusion process is complete, and a new level of self-organization has been stabilized, the subtle body becomes much more powerful and coherent, and a higher level of consciousness and spiritual bliss is enjoyed by the individual. Those who practice meditation and other spiritual practices already are familiar with these aspects of the evolutionary process.

The Judgment Day   At the time of global Illumination, a sudden rapid infusion of subtle matter occurs throughout the planet. At that time, those who have prepared themselves for this Illumination by gradually evolving their subtle bodies to the point where they can handle this sudden influx of subtle energy, will experience only increased cosmic awareness and surges of spiritual power and bliss.

On the other hand, those who have depleted their subtle energies and weakened the channels of spiritual power within their systems by focusing their energies on the pursuit of gross physical enjoyments, will experience a radical overload of spiritual power. Their subtle bodies will go through such rapid and dramatic evolution that their gross bodies will not have time to adapt. The higher levels of spiritual power coursing through their weakened channels will cause various short-circuits to occur, and as a result, such individuals no longer will be able to hold on to their gross bodies. In effect, they will be consumed by celestial fire.

Those who persist in their desire to cling to darkness up until the time of transition, and take no steps to prepare themselves as abodes of light, will have a much lower spiritual resonance than the incoming subtle energy, and will not be able to sustain the rapid transformations to which they will be subject. As a result, their physical existence on our planet may end. Even before the actual day of Illumination, as the spiritual Light begins to increase more and more rapidly, those souls that cling to a lower spiritual resonance may lose their physical bodies through disease, calamity, or violence.

Of course, the souls themselves do not perish. Even though its gross physical body may die, the human soul still possesses its subtle spiritual body. However, such mortal souls may have a hard time reincarnating on the Earth. In order to reincarnate, a soul must be able to resonate with the spiritual energies of its parents. As the Earth's spiritual vibration grows more pure, and the human population becomes more spiritually evolved, the opportunities for souls with a lower spiritual resonance to reincarnate will be fewer and fewer.

For the time being then, these souls will be escorted by Cosmic Intelligence to a new temporary home in the outer rim of the galaxy that is more suitable for their level of spiritual evolution. Other souls who are not quite so dark will be escorted to nearby star systems within the luminous disk of the galaxy that are in a different phase of their epochal unfoldment than Earth.

There, these souls may continue their development without having to wait thousands of years for an opportunity to reincarnate on Earth. Those who are able to resonate with the Earth's new spiritual energy will await their opportunity to reincarnate in a suitable womb on Earth in accordance with their own spiritual vibrations.

This critical time, when the souls are separated into two groups (those who stay and those who are escorted away) has been called the Judgment Day. But it is not really a judgment at all. Individuals are allowed to choose their own paths and are given the opportunity to fulfill their desires along the paths that they have chosen. Cosmic Intelligence simply is there to help us fulfill our own desires. The souls that are escorted elsewhere will be given new opportunities to evolve towards the Light in their new homes.

In spite of what we have been taught throughout the Dark Ages of humanity, there is no such thing in God's Divine Kingdom as eternal damnation. We live in a dynamic self-determined Universe, where we must live with our own choices and accept responsibility for our own actions. Eventually, by making choices and experiencing the consequences, we learn to ascend the ladder of evolution towards the Light, developing higher levels of consciousness, spiritual responsibility, and bliss along the way. However, the length of time it takes to ascend the ladder of evolution depends largely upon the choices that we make at each stage.

It is only at critical times like the coming transition, that a highway of evolution is opened up for all those who would like to ascend rapidly. This is the real reason why the Earth's population has grown so large in the last 200 years. Many, many souls are being given a chance to take advantage of this enormous opportunity for rapid evolution. Those souls who have consciously made the choice to seek the Light, and have nourished and evolved their subtle bodies to the point where they can handle the influx of spiritual power at the time of Illumination, will enjoy the blessings of an Earthly Paradise.

It doesn't matter whether one is in gross bodily form or not at the time of Illumination. It doesn't matter if one dies just before the Illumination occurs or during it. Everything has been taken into account by Cosmic Intelligence.

If one has developed one's spiritual resonance to the proper level, then one will reincarnate into an appropriate womb at the appropriate time, and be initiated into the light of pure consciousness by an enlightened master.

Many enlightened masters will walk the Earth over the next few thousand years. Although it may seem inconceivable given the current condition of the human race, it will not be long before the Earth is transformed into a World of Light, filled with rapidly evolving and enlightened souls.

The infusion of subtle matter at the time of Illumination will affect not only human life, but also will have a powerful evolutionary effect upon all the other beings on our planet. The plants will undergo such rapid evolution that new species will quickly emerge, more beautiful and fruitful than anything with which we are familiar. The herbs and minerals will become super-charged in their medicinal properties, and the atmosphere, which will be filled with subtle matter and thus endowed with conscious properties, will cause the seasons to be mild and come in time. The animals will also display more consciousness and will experience less misery, animosity, and fear. Human beings will treat each other, the Earth, and all of its creatures with honor and respect, and the very thought of war will seem incomprehensible. The Earth thus will be transformed into a Heavenly Paradise, a shining jewel in the sky, filled with wondrous forms of natural beauty and spiritual Light. This is not a fantasy. According to the ancient Seers, it is our collective destiny.

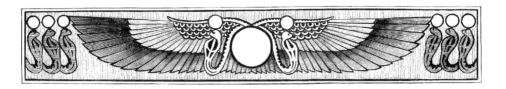

17. THE DIVINE MESSENGER

When the new Golden Age dawns on Earth, our collective awareness will expand and begin to embrace much larger regions of time and space than we have known for thousands of years. We will begin to commune nonlocally with the celestial beings that have nourished and protected us like loving parents since the beginning of time. Although we will walk with our feet on the Earth, our hearts will be filled with the Light of Heaven.

To prepare us for this divine reunion, when the Light of Heaven will descend once again upon the Earth, the gods have sent the Divine Messenger to communicate with us prior to their arrival. The Divine Messenger is known as the Herald of the Dawn. He is not a stranger to us. He has come here before. He is the Holy Spirit that has guided the human race since the Dawn of our first Day on Earth.

For those who are spiritually awake, the Holy Spirit comes just prior to the dawn of every day to awaken us and give us new knowledge.[79] But he comes especially with all of his spiritual power and glory at the dawn of each new Day for all humanity. He comes riding on a cloud of celestial fire from the direction of the Pleiades. His purpose is to heal us from the sorrow of the Night and to awaken us to the joy of a new Day.

The Divine Messenger is not a myth. He is very real. Already we are bathing in his aura. His first faint breath is here now, awakening the collective awareness of mankind, and rekindling the fire of pure knowledge in our hearts.

The Greeks called him Hermes. The Egyptians called him Thoth or Tehuti. The Romans called him Mercury. To the Vedic Seers he was Agni, the divine fire. In the Christian tradition he is referred to as the Holy Spirit.

Although the Divine Messenger has been understood variously by different

Seers and been given different names in different traditions, we should not allow this to confuse us. There is an ancient Vedic aphorism that states: "The Truth is only One, but the wise call it by many names."

Whatever name we might give to the Divine Messenger, his nature and function will remain the same. The Divine Messenger is a universal being. Each star system and planet throughout the entire Universe has its own pillar of celestial fire or universal ray that connects it with the omniscient awareness of the Creator in the Highest Heaven. Each of these pillars of celestial fire is an expression of the Divine Presence of the Creator. It is through such universal rays that the Divine Presence is extended throughout Creation.

Although the Greeks and Romans depicted the Divine Messenger as a youth, this is only one of many appearances. In the Egyptian tradition, Thoth was often represented as a divine being having the body of a man and the head of a sacred ibis—a bird resembling a stork or heron.

Figure 14—Hermes, or Mercury

All such anthropomorphic or iconographic depictions of the Divine Messenger are nothing more than symbolic representations. The Divine Messenger actually is a cosmic being that has a vast and glorious subtle body resembling a pillar of celestial fire. This pillar of celestial fire serves as the communication link between human awareness on Earth and the omniscient awareness of the Creator that abides in the Central Galaxy at the heart of the Universe. It serves to deliver the sacred teachings to humanity at the Dawn of each new Golden Age.

Figure 15—Thoth, the Ibis-Headed God

The Egyptians conceived the Divine Messenger as Thoth—the scribe of the gods. In accordance with their symbolic traditions, they represented him as having the head of a sacred bird, the ibis. This signified his ability to ascend and descend the scales of Creation.

When the Divine Messenger imparts the sacred teachings to humanity at the beginning of each new Golden Age, he does not need to take a human form.[80] Although he is capable of doing so, the Divine Messenger does not need to physically incarnate on the Earth to convey his message. The sacred teachings generally are transmitted silently and invisibly directly into the hearts and souls of all those who are awake, and who are willing to use this knowledge for the benefit of humanity. They are transmitted as impulses of primordial sound along the pillar of celestial fire, which is filled with pure consciousness.

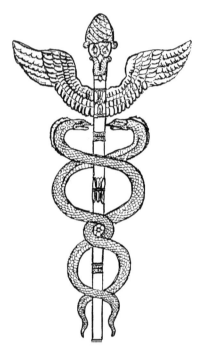

Figure 16—The Caduceus

In the ancient western traditions of knowledge, the pillar of celestial fire was symbolized by the Caduceus, the sign or standard of the Divine Messenger. In ancient times, all heralds were required to carry this standard to signify that they were messengers.

The serpents that are coiled in a double-helix formation around the winged staff symbolize the polarized masculine and feminine currents of subtle matter, while the straight rod itself symbolizes the balanced neutral current, which reflects the highest spiritual awareness and constitutes the Pillar of Divine Fire itself. The wings at the top symbolize the ability of the highest spiritual awareness (pure consciousness) to ascend and descend the scales of Creation, like a divine bird that can ascend into the celestial regions of the sky and descend back to the Earth.

Today we are familiar with the Caduceus as the symbol of the medical profession. The healing profession adopted the Caduceus as its symbol because the ancient Seers understood that subtle energy is the key to all healing processes. Because Hermes, Thoth, or Mercury represented the essence of this subtle energy, he presided over the healing arts.

In ancient times, the double-helix formation was a more universal symbol, commonly used on both sides of the globe to connote the presence of divine energy. Such symbols can be found going back to the earliest cultures all around the world. For example, they have been found associated with the ancient Sumerian culture of southern Iraq as well as the ancient Aztec culture of South America.

Figure 17—Sumerian Sculpture

This illustration presents a sculpture from ancient Sumeria, a civilization in Mesopotamia that predates the first dynasty of Egyptian pharaohs. The serpents coiled around the central rod are a symbolic precursor of the Caduceus. Note the winged attendants on either side, who control or contain the serpent energy.

Figure 18—Aztec Serpents

This illustration is taken from an Aztec temple relief. It depicts an attendant offering worship to the coiled serpent, symbolic of the polarized subtle energies. Although the winged bird symbol is absent from this depiction, the concept of the Feathered Serpent (Quetzalcoatl) was prevalent throughout Mesoamerica, and was worshipped as the divine being who brought the light of civilization and sacred wisdom to the people in ancient times.

Figure 19—The Tree of Knowledge of Good and Evil

In the Judeo-Christian tradition, these same symbols are utilized to convey the story of Adam and Eve. The Fall of Adam and Eve occurred when they tasted the fruit of the Tree of Knowledge of Good and Evil offered by the serpent.

The story of the Fall can be interpreted as follows: as long as one's awareness remains unpolarized, one will remain in the presence of God, that is, in the Garden of Eden. One will be sheltered by the Tree of Knowledge. But as soon as one is tempted by the serpent to enter into the realm of polarized energies, and partake of the fruit of the Tree, then one automatically falls out of "grace." One falls out of God's unified presence and into the realm of duality, that is, the field of good and evil, with all of its implications for conflict, competition, strife, and struggle. This illustrates how the ancient Seers used different symbols to express the same set of ideas.

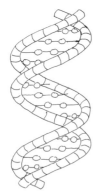

Figure 20—The Double Helix of the DNA Molecule

Modern scientists now know that the double-helix pattern is deeply related to the basis of biological life—the DNA molecule. The DNA molecule, which contains the genetic blueprint of life, consists of two chains of molecules displaying the form of a double helix.

Do the two currents of subtle energy that flow along these two chains of molecules carry the masculine and feminine energies? Is there a neutral current of celestial fire that flows along the axis of the double helix? Is the similarity between the DNA and the Caduceus a mere coincidence, or did the ancient Seers intuitively realize that the double-helix pattern is fundamental to all of life?

It should be no surprise to find that the pillar of celestial fire, which consists of both polarized and unpolarized energies, has both a universal manifestation for the Earth as a whole, and an individual manifestation within each human physiology. In the human body the pillar of fire is manifest as the three main *nadis* (streams) of subtle matter-energy that flow along the spine.

Figure 21—The Uraeus

In the Vedic tradition, these three currents of subtle energy constitute the *kundalini shakti*—the energy coiled at the base of the spine like a snake in a hole. The word "kunda" literally means a "pot" or "fire pit." The word "lini" signifies the coiled shape of the subtle energy within the kunda. Thus, the word "kundalini" refers to the coiled subtle energy in the pot or fire pit at the base of the spine. When this energy is awakened, it rises up along the spine like a snake raising its head to strike. In the Egyptian tradition, the uraeus or cobra that is attached to the front of the pharaoh's crown symbolized the fully awakened kundalini energy flashing forth from the third or spiritual eye.

In the Vedic tradition, the subtle serpentine energy of the kundalini has three forms, which are called the *ida, pingala,* and *sushumna*. The stream of subtle energy that goes to the right eye, and the left hemisphere of the brain, represents the solar stream (pingala), while the stream of subtle energy that goes to the left eye, and the right hemisphere of the brain, represents the lunar stream (ida).

Figure 21—Kundalini Energy

In addition to these two polarized streams, there is a third neutral stream called the sushumna, which is fiery *(agneya)* in its nature. The sushumna is the unpolarized spiritual current that proceeds directly from the base of the spine through the heart, to the third or spiritual eye, and then to the crown of the head. These three streams taken together form the kundalini shakti or serpent power, which is deeply related to the process of spiritual awakening.

The three streams of celestial fire within the human physiology bear a divine correspondence to the three celestial rays, discussed in chapter 14, that regulate the cycles of evolution for the planet as a whole. In particular, the solar ray corresponds to the pingala, the galactic ray corresponds to the ida, and the universal ray corresponds to the sushumna.

When the spiritual current of the sushumna is enlivened within the human physiology, it acts like a fountain of spiritual energy that fills the head with celestial fire. When the subtle fire in the head reaches a certain critical density, it becomes capable of reflecting unbounded pure consciousness. At that point, the luminous spiritual current emerges through the crown of the head and assumes the form of a glorious spiraling column of light. The presence of this spiraling column of luminous subtle energy has been traditionally represented as a "halo."

Those who possess the divine halo and are established in the state of pure consciousness may be considered enlightened. They automatically have Agni (the Divine Messenger) as a "guest in their house." The Holy Spirit abides in their body in the form of a glorious column of divine fire. Such enlightened souls may be understood as earthly embodiments of the Divine Messenger.

As an earthly embodiment of the Holy Spirit, or Divine Messenger, one may ascend or descend the scales of Creation like a divine bird. That is why the Holy Spirit is symbolized in the Christian tradition by a white dove. The same Holy Spirit also is represented by the two wings attached to the top of the Caduceus. The representation of the Divine Messenger or Holy Spirit as a divine bird is very ancient. It is deeply connected with the myth of the phoenix—the divine bird that is reborn again from its own ashes at the beginning of each new world Age.

Figure 23—The Phoenix

According to the Greek tradition:

> Only one such bird existed at any time, and it was always male. It had brilliant gold and reddish purple feathers, and was as large or larger than an eagle. . . . At the end of each life cycle, the phoenix burned itself on a funeral pyre. Another phoenix then rose from the ashes with renewed youth and beauty. The young phoenix, after rising from the ashes, carried the remains of its father [consisting of sacred ash] to the altar of the sun god in the Egyptian city of Heliopolis [City of the Sun]. The long life of the phoenix, and its dramatic rebirth from its own ashes, made it a symbol of immortality and rebirth.[81]

In the Heliopolitan tradition of ancient Egypt, the concept of the phoenix was embodied in the form of the *bennu* bird—a water bird that resembled an ibis. The word "bennu" means "to rise in brilliance." At Heliopolis, the bennu bird was considered to be a divine manifestation of the sun-god, whose rising and setting governed the cycles of time.

Figure 24—The Bennu Bird

The bennu bird is the Egyptian version of the phoenix. Like the sacred ibis, it was a water bird. In Egyptian mythology, one must cross a great body of water on a celestial ark or ship in order to get to Heaven. Thus, in Egyptian art, the bennus are often standing in the celestial ship or watching over it. In the figure to the right, the celestial ship is perched on a sacred pillar and appears to carry a stairway to heaven within itself. We believe this symbolizes the pillar of celestial fire that carries the soul to Heaven. The bennus, which preside over all forms of resurrection and ascension, are watching over this scene.

Within the Heliopolitan tradition, the periodic renewal of the world was tied directly to the return (or periodic rising) of the bennu. Ancient sources have indicated lengths of time for this period ranging from 500 years to over 90,000 years. But in one authoritative study a figure of 12,954 years is given.[82] This is remarkably close to the 12,960 years corresponding to a half-period of the precessional cycle. In effect, the return of the bennu or phoenix symbolized the advent of a new 13,000 year watch, when a new Golden Age would dawn, and the gods once again would rule the Earth.

The concept of the divine bird or phoenix is not unique to the western traditions of Greece and Egypt. It is also tied deeply into the ancient Vedic wisdom. In the Vedic tradition, the divine hawk (shyena) is identified as Agni—the Divine Messenger. It was the responsibility of the divine hawk to ascend to Heaven and acquire the Soma, or Nectar of Immortality. Having acquired the Nectar of Immortality from the gods, it was the job of Agni, in the form of the divine hawk, to bring this Nectar back to Earth for the rejuvenation and revitalization of all things.[83] This is just another version of the phoenix myth. It symbolizes the revival of the world that takes place at the beginning of each new Golden Age.

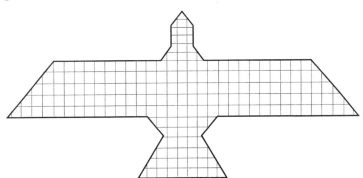

Figure 25—Agni in the Form of the Divine Hawk

This presents a diagrammatic view of the sacred fire altar employed in the performance of the Agni Chayana—"the building up of Agni in layers of bricks." The altar is constructed in the form of a huge hawk (shyena) or divine bird and literally is called "Agni."

The Vedic Seers also used the symbolism of the divine hawk in some of their most sacred and elaborate rituals. One such ritual, called the *Agni Chayana*, was centered around the construction of a huge fire altar, the "Agni," made out of specially shaped clay bricks. These bricks were stacked in layers to form the image of a divine hawk.

The divine hawk symbolizes the very essence of Agni—the divine fire. After the completion of the ritual, which lasted for more than an entire year, the altar and all the sacrificial implements used to construct it were set on fire. After the blazing conflagration died down, only the ashes of the ritual performance and the baked bricks of the altar, built in the form of the divine bird, remained. The influence of the ritual performance, designed to bring peace and coherence to the world, was said to last for as long as the altar of clay bricks remained standing on the Earth.

In Vedic mythology, the divine bird responsible for delivering the Soma also sometimes was identified as Garuda—the divine eagle that serves as the celestial vehicle for the Supreme Being. Garuda's exploits in capturing the Soma, or Nectar of Immortality, and bringing it back to Earth are described in a number of the Puranas, which constitute the sacred mythological lore of the Vedic tradition.

According to some mythological accounts, Garuda was related by birth to the race of divine serpents, the Nagas. The Nagas were associated with the hot fiery regions of the nether worlds, while Garuda was associated with the cool celestial regions of Heaven. Although they were related by birth, they were bitter enemies. Because of some indiscretion on the part of the serpents, Garuda took a vow to devour them all, and eliminate them from the Earth. However, the serpents were saved from total destruction by an edict of the Supreme Being—and were given a special domain where they would be safe from Garuda as long as they remained within their bounds.

The image of the eagle fighting with serpents is not unique to the Vedic tradition. The founder of the Aztec nation in ancient Mexico was told in a dream that his people must wander the land until they came to their predestined place of settlement. He was told he would recognize this place when he saw an eagle fighting with a serpent. This omen was finally observed on the island of Tenochtitlan in the Valley of Mexico, which became the capital of the Aztec nation.[84] The symbol of the eagle and the serpent was later adopted as the coat of arms for the modern Mexican nation.

Figure 26—The Eagle and the Serpent

This ancient symbol depicts the relationship between the polarized and unpolarized subtle energies. The eagle symbolizes cosmic pure awareness, the type of awareness reflected by unpolarized subtle energy. This type of awareness alone can ascend and descend the scales of Creation like a divine bird. Only this type of awareness is competent to rule the trends of time during an entire epochal cycle.

The polarized currents of subtle matter-energy that come under the command of the eagle, or overarching cosmic awareness, are symbolized by fiery serpents. During the Golden Age, these polarized currents are aligned with and controlled by the cosmic pure awareness that rules the Earth. During the Dark Age, these polarized currents become rebellious and uncontrollable—causing untold misery to the population of the world. At that time they become the enemies of cosmic awareness and must ultimately be destroyed or neutralized.

At the beginning of a New Golden Age, when the divine bird or phoenix returns and the rule of cosmic pure awareness is reestablished on the planet, then the polarized subtle energies (serpents) are either brought under control (kept within certain bounds) or they are destroyed totally. Although such mythical accounts and stories may appear childlike, they contain an extraordinarily deep wisdom, and have served as vehicles for the transmission of sacred knowledge over many millennia.

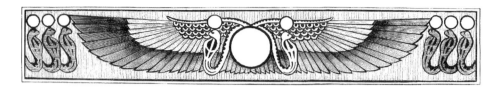

18. THE PLEIADIAN CONNECTION

The descent of pure knowledge on our planet has its origin in the pillar of celestial fire that connects the Earth with the divine abode of the Creator at the center of the Universe. It is clear that the ancient Seers knew the precise direction from which this pillar of fire descends, for this knowledge was woven into their mythological accounts of the gods.

The Pleiades in the Greek Tradition

For example, in the Greek tradition, Hermes, the Divine Messenger, was said to be the son of Zeus and Maya, one of the seven daughters of Atlas. These seven daughters were called the Pleiades and were identified with the seven stars that form the constellation of the same name. One of those stars still is called Maya, and another is called Atlas, after the father of the Pleiades.

This tells us that the ancient Seers knew that the Divine Messenger, who displays the form of the pillar of celestial fire, comes to the Earth from the direction of the Pleiades, which is the place of its birth. More specifically, it tells us that the Pillar of Divine Fire comes from the direction of the star Maya.

The star Maya thus held a special significance for the ancient Seers. To commemorate its significance, the month of May was named after this star. It is during the month of May each year that the Sun transits the Pleiades constellation and aligns itself with the star called Maya.

In honor of this event, a sacred ceremony was instituted by the Seers, which still is practiced in many cultures around the world. This ceremony now is known as the May Day celebration. In accordance with ancient tradition, during the May Day celebration, a tall pole is erected in the center of a field, and different colored strings are attached to the top of the pole. Young maidens then take the ends of the strings and circumambulate the pole in a clockwise fashion, causing the strings to become twisted around the pole as they walk. This ceremony symbolizes the coiling of the polarized energies around the pillar of celestial fire.

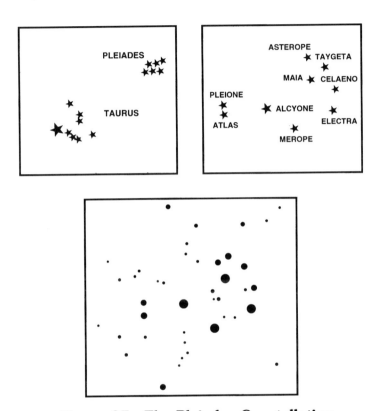

Figure 27—The Pleiades Constellation

The Pleiades constellation is a tight little cluster of stars in the sign of Taurus located about 400 light-years from our solar system. Although only six of the Pleiadian stars are easily visible with the naked eye, under a telescope one can see that there are hundreds of stars contained in this cluster. Most of these stars are hotter and brighter than our star, and are much younger. It has been estimated by modern astronomers that the average age of a Pleiadian star is only 73 million years, whereas the age of the Sun is estimated to be around four or five billion years.

It is likely that this ceremony originally was performed at noon on the exact day that the Sun transits the star Maya in the Pleiades constellation. The

May Pole then would symbolize not only the pillar of fire, but it also would point in the exact direction from which the pillar of fire descends to the Earth at the dawn of each Golden Age.

The May Day celebration thus not only commemorates the onset of spring, but it also commemorates the awakening of the human race to a new state of consciousness that is as lovely and refreshing as a beautiful spring day. Although this ceremony still is practiced in many cultures around the world, its true significance has been completely lost and forgotten.

The Pleiades in the Polynesian Tradition

The Greeks were not the only ones to assign special significance to this direction in the sky. There are many mythical traditions from around the world that associate the Pleiades with the transformation from one world Age to the next. For example, consider the following passage from an old Polynesian myth in the royal tradition of Hawaii.

> Now turns the swinging of time over on the burnt-out world;
> Back goes the great turning of things upward again;
> As yet sunless the time of shrouded light;
> Unsteady, as in dim moon-shimmer,
> From out Makalii's night-dark veil of cloud
> Thrills, shadow-like, the prefiguration of the world to be.[85]

This seemingly obscure passage refers to the end of one world ("the burnt-out world") and the beginning of a new world that is yet to come. It specifically refers to the moment of transition, "the time of shrouded light" when the sky is covered over by dark clouds, and is yet sunless. It is at this moment, when the world becomes shrouded in darkness, that there emerges from Makalii a thrilling "prefiguration of the world to be." According to this ancient myth, Makalii is the source from which the blue-print for the new world emerges at the time of transition. But who or what is Makalii? According to scholars in this field, the word Makalii is the name for the Pleiades.

Another myth from a tradition in Borneo speaks of a "whirlpool island" where there is a celestial Tree. By climbing this Tree it is said that human beings may ascend into Heaven and bring back useful seeds from the "land of the Pleiades."[86] Clearly, this is no ordinary Tree. It is the pillar of celestial fire that connects the Earth with the Highest Heaven at the center of the Universe. If one's awareness ascends along this pillar or Tree up into Heaven, one may bring back many useful seeds of pure knowledge to Earth. Where do these seeds come from? According to this myth, they come from the land of the Pleiades.

The Pleiades in the Mesoamerican Tradition

The Pleiades also played an important role in the performance of the New Fire Ceremony among both the Mayans and Aztecs.[87] This ceremony was performed every fifty-two years to mark the end of one cycle or Age and the beginning of the next. The New Fire Ceremony was performed to bind together the cycles of years. In the performance of this ceremony the Mayans and later the Aztecs would extinguish all their fires and destroy their utensils, so that everything could be reignited and made anew. One chronicler states:

> Behold what was done when the years were bound—when was reached the time when they were to draw the new fire, when now its count was accomplished. First they put out fires everywhere in the country round. And the statues, hewn in either wood or stone, kept in each man's home and regarded as gods, were all cast into the water. Also (were) these (cast away)—the pestles, and the (three) hearth stones (upon which the cooking pots rested); and everywhere there was much sweeping—there was sweeping very clear. Rubbish was thrown out; none lay in any of the houses.[88]

These actions marked the end of one cycle of fifty-two years and the beginning of a new cycle. According to scholars, the point of transition between one cycle and the next was marked by a celestial event related to the Pleiades.

The priests went to a special place to observe it, an eminence called the Hill of the Star, located on a prominent peninsula that jutted out into the lake. When the Pleiades crossed the overhead point, it was a sign to the people that the gods would not destroy the world, that people would be granted a new age.[89]

This critical transit of the Pleiades was supposed to take place on that specific day of the fifty-second year when the Pleiades constellation crossed the southern meridian at midnight. Those versed in astronomy know that the Pleiades crosses the southern meridian every day, but the transit occurs at midnight on only one day of the year, sometime in November.[90]

Why was the midnight transit of the Pleiades constellation so important? It appears that the Mayan people were deeply afraid of this transit. If we conjecture on this point, it may be that the people of Mesoamerica associated this transit with some terrible catastrophe that had occurred in the distant past. Could it be that the midnight transit of the Pleiades constellation commemorated the terrible transition from one world Age to another that occurred at the time of epochal Midnight, some 13,000 years ago? In subsequent chapters we will examine the devastating effects that this transition had upon the human population all over the globe.

The catastrophe that descended on the planet some 13,000 years ago came through the agency of the Divine Messenger. It came through the pillar of fire that lies in the direction of the Pleiades constellation. Furthermore, it came at the time of epochal Midnight. According to the epochal cycle described in chapter 2, such a cataclysmic transition can occur only once every 52,000 years. Was the fifty-two year cycle of the New Fire Ceremony designed to commemorate on a small scale the cyclic reoccurrence of this terrible global cataclysm, which then gave birth to a new Golden Age?

The Pleiades in the Vedic Tradition

In the Vedic tradition, the Pleiades constellation is named *Krittika,* which literally means a "sharp flame" or "sword of fire." Alternatively, the word "Krittika" may be derived from the Sanskrit root *krit,* which means "to twist threads" or "to wind (as a snake)." This clearly is related to the symbology of the Caduceus and the May Pole.

The root "krit" also means "to separate, cut asunder, or divide." This secondary meaning refers to the division of souls into two groups that occurs on the Day of Illumination. The subtle energy associated with the Pleiades constellation is considered a Sword of Fire because it cuts asunder or separates knowledge from ignorance. It separates Light from darkness.

In Vedic astrology, each constellation is identified with a particular *devata* or celestial being. Out of all twenty-seven Vedic *nakshatras,* or constellations, the Pleiades is the only one exclusively identified with Agni, the divine fire. In the Vedic tradition, Agni alone serves as the messenger between gods and men.

There are other deeper connections, embedded in various sacred rites. For example, consider the ancient *Ashva-Medha* (Horse Ritual). In the metaphorical tradition of the Vedic Seers, the stars that move about in the shining Heavens are called *ashvas* (horses). They are called horses because they serve as the vehicles by which the gods move about within the field of Creation. This terminology especially applies to the Central Sun of the Universe. The Central Sun is identified as the ultimate "divine horse" because it serves as the vehicle for the divine awareness of the Supreme Being within the field of time and space.

This symbology is deeply related to the ritual performance of the Ashva-Medha, a royal sacrificial performance in which a horse is given free rein to roam throughout the land for fourteen years. The fourteen years represent the fourteen stages of evolution that occur within the Cosmic Egg—i.e., the seven foundational stages of individual life, and the seven higher stages of universal life.

In the Vedic tradition, the seven foundational stages of individual life are called the *talas* (foundations). These represent the stages of evolution that lead up to the development of human life on a given planet. The mortal human soul represents the highest product of these foundational stages.

Once the human soul gains enlightenment, and realizes its immortality, it then proceeds through the seven higher stages of universal life, corresponding to the Seven Heavens, or seven layers of universal life. The whole story of evolution thus involves a total of fourteen stages of development. These fourteen stages are represented by the fourteen years of ritual performance of the Ashva-Medha.

During the ritual performance of the Ashva-Medha the horse is followed by a royal entourage. Any place that the horse roams unchallenged during the fourteen years is then claimed by the king performing the ritual as part of his kingdom. This represents the expanding territory of influence of the Central Sun, which eventually embraces the entire Creation.

In order for the ritual to be symbolically meaningful, the ancient ritual texts prescribe that the horse must have the sign of Krittika—the Pleiades—emblazoned on his forehead.[91] Why? Because the horse is symbolic of the divine horse, the Central Sun of the Universe, that lies in the direction of the Pleiades.

The Pleiades in the Mesopotamian Tradition

The same prescription is given regarding the black bull in the ancient Mesopotamian rituals. In one ritual, the cover of a ritualistic drum called the *lilissu* was made from the skin of a black bull that had the sign of the Pleiades on its forehead. This drum was used to contact Anu (or An)—the "God of Heaven." In the ancient cuneiform script of the Akkadian texts, Anu is written with a single wedge, which simultaneously stands for the number one and sixty, which are the first and last numbers in the sexagesimal number system. To the Akkadians, Anu thus represented the source and goal of all sequential stages of unfoldment in the cosmos. These stages are governed by the fundamental cycles of time that measure celestial events. Striking the drum covered by the black bull hide symbolized the enlivenment of these measures of time[92]—and the sign of the Pleiades on the forehead of the bull symbolized the place from which these measures emerged.

The knowledge that the pillar of celestial fire lies in the direction of the

Pleiades, and specifically in the direction of the star Maya, clearly was possessed by the ancient Seers. Although this knowledge has been lost for thousands of years, it is now being reawakened in our collective awareness once again.

Where is this knowledge coming from? It is coming from its ancient source. It is coming from the Pillar of Divine Fire itself, in the direction of the Pleiades. It is coming from the Divine Messenger of the gods—who variously is called Hermes, Thoth, Mercury, and Agni.

At the dawn of each new Golden Age the Divine Messenger descends along the pillar of celestial fire to awaken us and prepare us for the descent of Heaven on Earth. He comes to reestablish the Sacred Science for the enlightenment of the human soul and the glorification of the Earth. He comes to teach us the sacred alchemical science of the ancient Seers.

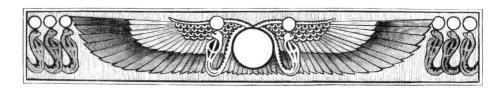

19. THE DIVINE COVENANT

Over the next few years many opportunities for rapid evolution will present themselves to us, both individually and collectively. Some of these opportunities may involve a change of perspective, a change of habits, a change of diet, a change of friends, or a change of residence. Other opportunities may involve the adoption of new spiritual practices such as meditation, breath control, chanting sacred sounds, or the performance of sacred ceremony. One of the most powerful opportunities may involve joining a coherence creating group—a collection of individuals dedicated to generating Light for the planet as a whole by performing meditation in a large group.

Such groups have sprung up at various locations all over the world during the last twenty years, and they have had a major influence on increasing the levels of spiritual Light on our planet. These groups are enormous generators of subtle matter-energy, and being a member of such a group will ensure that one's individual life is immersed in the protective, nourishing aura of the group as a whole.[93]

As we continue to progress towards the Light, such opportunities for evolution will become more frequent, and the transformations that they will bring about will become more powerful and last longer.

However, not everyone will be able to take advantage of all such opportunities. Even though one may be eager to make use of some particular opportunity, prior commitments or some disability may prohibit one from doing so. What about such individuals? Will they be left out in the cold? The answer is a resounding "No." Cosmic Intelligence is infinitely benevolent, and lovingly looks upon the human race as a mother would her children. All such contingencies have been taken into account.

If a soul sincerely seeks the Light, and is willing to devote itself to the process of spiritual evolution, then an opportunity will present itself that is appropriate for that soul's evolution, so that it too can participate in the descent of Heaven on Earth. No one who is sincerely willing to enter the Light will be left out. This is the Divine Covenant that has been given to the human race at the Dawn of this new Day.

Subtle Matter Technologies

To fulfill the terms of this Covenant, new methods of rapid evolution will be revealed to the human population over the next few years. These methods will be based upon unprecedented scientific discoveries and technological breakthroughs.

The most important of these scientific discoveries will concern the experimental discovery of an inexhaustible source of subtle matter-energy. Once this source becomes available, a whole array of subtle matter technologies will be developed, and they will be developed rapidly.

Even though electrons always have existed, development of electronic technologies began only after we developed methods for generating, measuring, and conducting the flow of electrons. Similarly, subtle matter always has been present, but subtle matter technologies can be created only after we have developed methods to generate, measure, and conduct the flow of subtle particles.

Such subtle matter technologies were known to the ancient Seers during so-called prehistoric times. However, over the course of time and the gradual decline of spiritual awareness on our planet, these technologies were lost.

Now is the time for these technologies to be rediscovered and utilized for the rapid spiritual regeneration of the human race. The new subtle matter technologies will enable us to develop methods for spiritual rejuvenation and healing that are far beyond anything imagined by modern science. Through such fundamental healing methods, otherwise incurable mental and physical diseases, as well as congenital diseases, may be completely reversed, and the body filled with spiritual Light and elevated to a state of perfect health. The subtle matter technologies thus will fulfill the Divine Covenant by enabling virtually anyone to heal themselves and prepare their subtle bodies for the coming global Illumination in a relatively short period of time.

Other technological applications of subtle matter will be made available to our planet as the human race becomes more and more spiritually responsible. These may include the generation of inexpensive and inexhaustible electric energy, the development of levitation technologies, the development of holographic information processing systems, and the development of atomic transmutation technologies.

These technologies can be given to the human race only at the appropriate time. This timing is not in the hands of any individual or organization. It is in the hands of God. Although we may have an intuitive grasp of the principles underlying these technologies, their actual manifestation on our planet cannot and will not occur until the time is ripe. Once they become manifest they will fulfill our most imaginative science fantasies.

However, this is not speculative fiction. It is our collective destiny. When the Earth becomes transformed into a World of Light, and we become spiritually responsible citizens of the Universe, the spiritual and technological keys to Creation will be handed to us. Prior to that time, in the immediate future, we will be given the technological means to heal and spiritually rejuvenate ourselves, so that as many souls as possible can receive the Light at the time of Illumination.

After the Illumination, such technologies will not seem so amazing. In truth, an enlightened human physiology is its own miracle machine, capable of healing itself and performing all kinds of miraculous feats. Enlightened souls do not need external technologies to fulfill their desires. They are complete and self-sufficient unto themselves.

But even in the Golden Age, the human population on Earth will display a spectrum of different states of evolution. The process of evolution may be much faster than before, but souls will continue to incarnate in human form and go through their own evolutionary unfoldment. The subtle matter technologies thus will serve the purpose of enabling everyone throughout society, whether they are fully enlightened or not, to experience high levels of material and spiritual fulfillment.

In such a society there will be no dichotomy between the scientific and spiritual sides of life. Matter and consciousness will coexist harmoniously in all phases of life and living. This sublime state of existence, which has been the ideal of poets, philosophers, and prophets throughout history, is destined to unfold in our generation. It is destined to unfold in accordance with the Divine Plan of human civilization, a plan that was mapped out thousands of years ago by the ancient Seers.

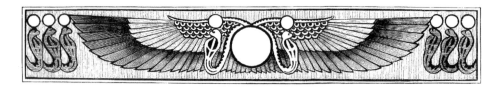

20. THE FOUR AGES OF HUMAN CIVILIZATION

According to the ancient Vedic Seers, each 13,000 year watch of the precessional cycle may be divided into four *Yugas* or Ages. These four Ages are called *Krita, Treta, Dwapara,* and *Kali.* They span a total of 12,000 years, and their periods display the relative ratios of 4:3:2:1. The period of each Age is given below.

Krita	4,800 years
Treta	3,600 years
Dwapara	2,400 years
Kali	1,200 years

Periods of the Ages or Yugas

At the junction of the Ages there is a period of transition, when one Age gives rise to another. These gaps or junctions between Ages are called *sandhis.* During the sandhi periods, the characteristics of the previous Age have not yet fully dissolved and the characteristics of the subsequent Age have not yet fully emerged. Hence the sandhi periods are counted separately.

Krita	384 years
Treta	288 years
Dwapara	192 years
Kali	96 years

Periods of the Transitions or Sandhis

The four sandhi periods together total 960 years. The sandhi periods are named after the Age that they follow and display the relative ratios of 4:3:2:1.

If the sandhi periods are included in the overall calculation, the total number of years in each full cycle of four Ages comes to 12,960 years, corresponding to one watch of the precessional cycle. The relationship between the four Ages and the four sandhis is illustrated graphically below.

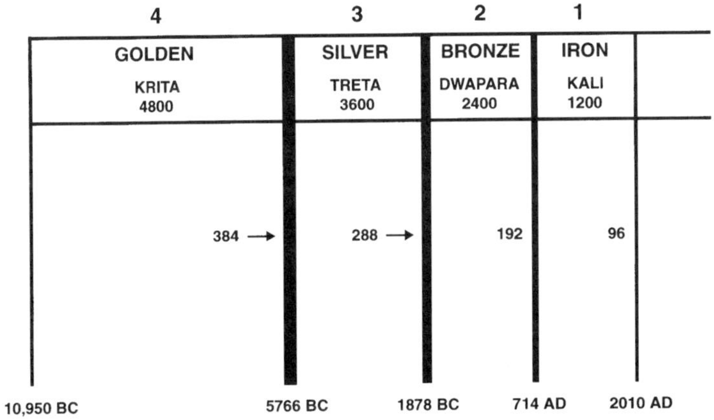

Figure 28—Timeline of the Four Ages and Four Sandhis
The four Ages and their junction periods over the last 13,000 years are graphically depicted above, along with the dates that mark their estimated starting points. The dark vertical lines represent the sandhis, the transition periods between the Ages. The ending point of each Age can be calculated by deducting the sandhi periods from the starting point of the subsequent Age.

It turns out that the period of 12,960 years, which was given by the ancients as the overall span of the four Yugas, is 72 years longer than the half-period of the precessional cycle as calculated by modern astronomers. We suspect that the number of years in the half-period is rounded off to 12,960 for esoteric purposes.

The number 12,960 is a sacred number.[94] It can be integrally divided by exactly sixty different numbers: 1, 2, 3, 4, 5, 6, 8, 9, 10, 12, 15, 16, 18, 20, 24, 27, 30, 32, 36, 40, 45, 48, 54, 60, 72, 80, 81, 90, 96, 108, 120, 135, 144, 160, 162, 180, 216, 240, 270, 288, 324, 360, 405,

432, 480, 540, 648, 720, 810, 864, 1080, 1296, 1440, 1620, 2160, 2592, 3240, 4320, 6480, and 12960.

In this sequence, the first thirty numbers (1–108) are matched in inverted order with the last thirty numbers (120–12,960). As with any set of factors that are even in number, by multiplying the matched numbers, the total (12,960) is obtained. For example:

$$1 \times 12960 = 12960$$
$$2 \times 6480 = 12960$$
$$3 \times 4320 = 12960$$
etc.

The two central numbers in this sequence of sixty are 108 and 120. As the thirtieth matched pair of numbers, they produce the equation 108 x 120 = 12,960, displaying important correspondences between the macrocosm and microcosm. There are 108 different frequency bands in the holographic spectrum of the Universe as a whole, and there are 120 years in a full astrological cycle of human life.[95] The number 12,960 thus appears to encode a host of numerological correspondences reflecting the relationship between the sequential unfoldment of human life on Earth and the sequential unfoldment of the Cosmos.

The Celestial Yugas or Ages

The four Ages described above pertain to the evolution of human civilization on Earth. There are much longer cycles that pertain to the evolution of the galaxy as a whole. In accordance with the principle "as above, so below," these longer cycles have the same names: Krita, Treta, Dwapara, and Kali, and display the same relative ratios of 4:3:2:1. However, each "year" in the larger cycle is a "celestial year" that is composed of 360 human years. The four celestial Yugas (not including their sandhi periods) thus span a total of 12,000 x 360 = 4,320,000 years.

The celestial Yugas primarily affect the evolution of the Galactic Civilization, which has its largest population density in the bulge at the center of the galaxy. According to the Vedic Seers, there was a recent important change in the galactic cycle of celestial Yugas. About 5,200 years ago the celestial Dwapara Age ended and the celestial Kali Yuga began.

In India this change was marked by the Mahabharata war, which tradition-ally is believed to have occurred around 5,200 years ago. In the West, this change was marked by the unification of Egypt and the ascendancy of the first Dynasty of Pharaohs. It was around this same time that the first alpha-betical scripts began to appear. In addition, there is a growing body of paleoclimatic data which suggests that there were major abrupt variations in both water levels and temperature around the planet at this time.[96] Thus, the celestial Yugas also have a profound impact upon our own planet.

Compared to the long, slow celestial cycle, the terrestrial cycle of Ages appears to be a fast roller-coaster ride—and it is the relatively rapid changes within this minor cycle that are of immediate concern to us now. Each of the four minor Ages has its own unique qualities and characteristics, which profoundly affect the rise and fall of human civilizations on Earth. Cycles of similar duration and characteristics are found on all evolving worlds inhab-ited by human beings throughout our galaxy.

The characteristics and qualities of the four Ages should be understood as universal archetypes. The actual manifestations of those archetypes will vary depending upon the particular planet in which those manifestations occur, and upon the location of the planetary cycle within the longer celestial cycle affecting the galaxy as a whole. In addition, the manifestations of the Ages may vary according to the climate, geography, and culture of the planetary region in which they occur. A brief description of the archetypical charac-teristics of the four Ages is given below.

Krita or Sat Yuga:
The Golden Age

Krita or Sat Yuga, which also is called the Golden Age, is characterized by mass enlightenment, world peace, and the descent of Heaven on Earth. It lasts for approximately 4,800 years.

During the Golden Age, the human population on the planet generally is small, due to the worldwide devastation that precedes and accompanies its advent. However, many of those who survive these calamities are initiated into the Light and are rapidly elevated to a high state of consciousness.

Because of their elevated consciousness, the people of the Golden Age enjoy nonlocal intuitive access to the Divine Mind, as well as telepathic powers. Hence, written language is completely unnecessary and unused. If one wants to know something, one intuitively accesses the Divine Mind, and that knowledge spontaneously manifests itself in one's own mind. On the more highly evolved planets, a single sacred language is spoken by all the people during the Golden Ages.

During this period, individuals also possess other divine powers, such as levitation and the ability to fulfill their desires by mere intention. Hence, elaborate technological aides to support human life on the planet generally are unnecessary. If technologies are used at all, they are used for purposes of spiritual rejuvenation and glorification, rather than for mere creature comforts.

———◆———

Treta Yuga:
The Silver Age

Treta Yuga, which also is called the Silver Age, lasts for a period of 3,600 years. During Treta Yuga, the level of consciousness of the general population begins to decline, the number of enlightened souls begins to decrease, and collective stress begins to accumulate in the world population. Access to the Divine Mind becomes limited to the remaining enlightened Seers, who become organized into secret esoteric societies, and serve as the spiritual leaders of the general population.

These enlightened spiritual leaders administer society by assuming the roles of both kings and priests. During this period, the priest-kings organize large scale sacred ceremonies and rituals to invoke the gods and uphold the spiritual and cultural integrity of the people. These collective performances become the main purpose and focus of society.

During the Treta Age, the Sacred Science is passed on as an oral tradition among the high initiates in an attempt to preserve the knowledge for future generations. However, the knowledge is cloaked in elaborate metaphors and esoteric symbols to prevent its misuse by the uninitiated. Towards the end of Treta Yuga, when it becomes clear that the real knowledge, which exists only on the level of pure consciousness, is about to be lost, various systems of writing are invented to record the knowledge.

Dwapara Yuga: The Bronze Age

Dwapara Yuga, which also is called the Bronze Age, lasts for about 2,400 years. During this Age the consciousness of the general population declines even further, and the number of truly enlightened souls becomes very small.

At this time, the knowledge of the Sacred Science and its associated technologies generally is lost. The ancient teachings and technological prescriptions that have been passed from generation to generation over thousands of years may still persist within the secret academies, but they tend to be accepted on faith, rather than true scientific understanding. Even those who are initiated into the sacred lore have a difficult time comprehending it, due both to their low levels of consciousness, and the thick cloak of metaphors and esoteric symbols under which the knowledge has been hidden.

Although the performance of sacred ceremony continues to play a central role in the life of society, the effectiveness and power of the ceremonies is greatly reduced. As the ceremonies lose their spiritual power, the cultural integrity of people begins to fall apart, and the population becomes prey to invasion and disease.

This social degeneration also is reflected by the kings of the Dwapara Age, who become increasingly motivated by ego. Because of their arrogance, they begin to seek conquest of other kingdoms. Passionate rivalries among kingdoms thus become rampant. This gives rise to bloody wars, and the ascendancy of feudal warrior societies, where physical strength is more important than spiritual knowledge.

During the Dwapara Age, the ancient civilizations are replaced by new civilizations based upon new languages, new ways, new religions, and new blood. By the end of Dwapara Yuga the last vestiges of the great civilizations of the Golden and Silver Ages are finally destroyed, and all that remains are memories of a glorious past era when the gods once walked the Earth.

Kali Yuga:
The Iron Age

Kali Yuga, which also is called the Iron Age, lasts for 1,200 years. During this Age the consciousness of the general population is very low. It is difficult and rare to find even a single enlightened soul. The Sacred Science is completely lost, and replaced by various false doctrines.

Violent wars, wretched living conditions, disease, plagues, and mass destruction become commonplace. As a result, the duration of life is shortened greatly and life becomes miserable. Faith in the authority of the intuitively revealed precepts is lost, and is replaced by faith in empirical sensory experience. This gives rise to objective science, or materialism, which is devoid of wholeness, and devoted to the gross material realm of existence. Due to the corruption of kings, the monarchies are overthrown, and democratic societies emerge, ruled by the masses.

According to our best estimates, the most recent Dark Age began around 714 A.D. and ended around 1914 A.D. For thousands of years prior to this time, the ancient Seers knew that a Dark Age was going to descend upon the Earth. They predicted it and tried to prepare their followers for it. In the Hermetic texts (circa 200 A.D.), the predicted effects of the Dark Age were described as follows:

> Darkness will be preferred to light, and death will be thought more profitable than life; no one will raise his eyes to Heaven; the pious will be deemed insane, and the impious wise; the madman will be thought a brave man, and the wicked will be esteemed as good. As to the soul, and the belief that it is immortal by nature, or may hope to attain immortality, . . . all this they will mock at, and will even persuade themselves that it is false. No word of reverence or piety, no utterance worthy of Heaven and of the gods of Heaven, will be heard or believed.[97]

During the Dark Age, the celestial beings themselves depart from the Earth, and the people of the Earth are left totally bereft of true spiritual guidance.

> And so the gods will depart from mankind,—a grievous thing!—
> and only the evil angels will remain, who will mingle with men, and
> drive the poor wretches by main force into all manner of reckless
> crime, into wars, and robberies, and frauds, and all things hostile
> to the nature of the soul. Then the Earth will no longer stand
> unshaken, and the sea will be unable to bear ships; Heaven will not
> support the stars in their orbits, nor will the stars pursue their
> constant course in the Heaven.[98]

At the very end of the Dark Age there are global devastations that greatly reduce the population of the Earth. These devastations generally involve a shifting of the geographic poles, a phenomenon that we will discuss in chapter 24. This shifting of the poles is referred to in the passage above: "Heaven will not support the stars in their orbits, nor will the stars pursue their constant course in the Heaven." The devastations accompanying this pole shift have a purifying effect, and herald the dawn of a new Golden Age, when the Holy Spirit descends upon the Earth and initiates a new group of human souls into the Light.

> then the Master and Father, (the infinite) God, . . . will look on that
> which has come to pass, and will stay the disorder by the counter
> working of his will, which is the Good. He will call back to the right
> path those who have gone astray; he will cleanse the world from
> evil, now washing it away with waterfloods, now burning it out with
> the fiercest fire, or again expelling it by war and pestilence. And
> thus he will bring back the world to its former aspect, so that the
> Kosmos will once more be deemed worthy of worship and
> wondering reverence, and God, the maker and restorer of the
> mighty fabric, will be adored by the men of that day with unceasing
> hymns of praise and blessing. Such is the new birth of the Kosmos.
> It is a making again of all things good, a holy and awe-striking
> restoration of all nature; and it is wrought in the process of time by
> the eternal will of God.[99]

The resultant Illumination of the world is accompanied by mass enlightenment, world peace, and the descent of Heaven on Earth. The cycle of four

Ages then repeats itself. The ancient Seers thus understood the cycle of Ages as the birth and rebirth of the world, brought about by divine will.

The Present Time Although Kali Yuga represents the darkest hour in
of Transition each 13,000 year cycle, it is the shortest of the
four Ages and comes just before the dawn of a new Golden Age. At the present time in history, we stand in the gap (sandhi) between the last dying breath of Kali Yuga and the first awakening breath of a new Golden Age.

Using various historical and astrological events to "rectify" the timetable of events over the last 13,000 years, we estimate that the current sandhi period of ninety-six years began in 1914—the year that marked the beginning of the first World War—and will end around the spring equinox of 2010 A.D. During this period, profound adjustments in the social, climatic, and geological structures of our planet are likely to occur, as the collective consciousness of the planet shifts in preparation for the onset of the new Golden Age.

The sandhi period also is the time for profound innovation, as fresh new ideas filter into our collective awareness. These new ideas are planted in the collective consciousness by the Holy Spirit, who comes at the beginning of each new Golden Age of humanity to inspire new inventions and scientific discoveries in the minds of individuals around the world.

The growth of scientific knowledge over the last two hundred years has been overseen and fostered by this Cosmic Intelligence. However, the advent of modern mundane science is only a preparation for the ultimate revelation of the Sacred Science of the Seers, which holds the keys to all the treasures of Heaven and Earth.

Although the subtle matter density on our planet has been increasing steadily since around 1914, we believe that the majority of the increase in subtle matter density will occur during the final forty year period that comes just before the onset of Krita Yuga. According to our calculations, this period began around 1970 and will end around 2010, give or take a few years.

During the final forty years of the sandhi period, the Divine Messenger begins to whisper the knowledge of the Sacred Science into the hearts of those who are ready and willing to receive it. On the Day of Illumination itself, when the rate of increase in subtle energy turns vertical, the collective awareness of the Earth as a whole will transcend and experience a state of pure consciousness. Those who receive the Light most fully then will be able to communicate with the gods on a collective as well as on an individual level. This will mark the beginning of the new Golden Age, and the descent of Heaven on Earth.

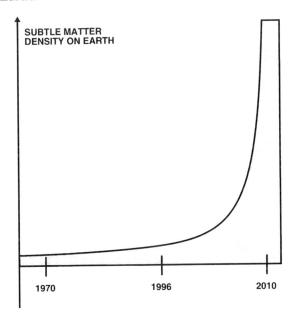

Figure 29—Forty Year Period

The graph above shows that we are still in a period of relatively slow transformation. However, around the year 2000 the subtle matter levels are predicted to increase dramatically, and they are expected to go completely vertical on the day of Illumination, which is estimated to occur around 2010.

However, the exact date of this event its unknown. The discrepancy between the exact astronomical period of the precessional cycle (12,888 years) and the given esoteric period (12,960 years) causes a blurring in our knowledge of the exact time at which the Ages begin and end.

According to recent interpretations of the Mayan calendar,[100] the Mayans predicted that the transition will occur on the winter solstice in the year 2012. This is less than two years from our estimate of the spring equinox of 2010.

However, these numbers are nothing more than estimates. In our opinion, the exact time of the Illumination will remain a deep mystery until the divine energy actually descends upon us. We know that this time is coming, and that it is coming soon, but exactly when it will occur may very well lie beyond the comprehension of human intelligence. The timing of the descent is totally in the hands of God.

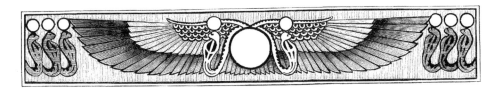

21. THE SOLAR AND LUNAR RACES

The relatively brief period of recorded history on our planet has plumbed unfathomable depths of tragedy and soared to celestial heights of joy. The surface of the Earth may be compared to a stage filled with millions of players. Upon this stage each human soul must play out his or her own unique drama during the course of a lifetime, and then disappear, like a dream in the night, behind the curtain of death.

How many souls have come and gone in this manner since the play first began? How many great and glorious civilizations have risen in hope and fallen into dust since the dawn of the first Day of human life on Earth? How many vast untold dramas are yet to unfold?

As we now stand at the threshold of a brand new Day of human civilization on Earth, it is time to reflect upon the grand mythical patterns of human existence that have been revealed in our brief sojourn on this planet. These patterns have much to teach us about our ancient roots, and they have much to tell us about our future journey.

In spite of the immense diversity of individual dramas that have been played out upon the stage of time, there are two great streams or classes of human souls that have manifested themselves upon the face of the Earth since the very beginning.

These two great streams of humanity embody the polarized energies of Mother Earth, which long to unite in perfect wholeness. Their ultimate union will complete our evolution as a collective planetary awareness, and will mark the full maturity of human civilization on Earth.

The souls belonging to these two streams display different qualities and tendencies. These qualities may be summarized as either solar (yang) or lunar (yin) in their nature. The solar qualities are hard, harsh, masculine, rebellious, innovative, and aggressive, while the lunar qualities are soft, gentle, feminine, obedient, traditional, and passive. The solar energies are fiery in nature, while the lunar energies are watery in nature.

Those who possess an abundance of solar energy tend to rely upon their own self-initiative. They prefer to look at the world through the eye of reason rather than the eye of faith. They conceive of Nature as something to be conquered and they apply themselves industriously towards this end through work and action. They are not satisfied with the slow process of natural evolution, and always look for ways to hasten the evolutionary process through the development of new technologies and processes.

Those who possess an abundance of lunar energy, on the other hand, tend to trust in the benevolence of their Lord, rather than their own self-initiative. They prefer to look at the world through the eye of faith, rather than the eye of reason. To them Nature is not something to be conquered. It is some-thing to be accepted as a gift from God. Rather than trying to change or shape Nature through action, they seek to find their place within the natural order of things through revelation. They are willing to wait patiently for the natural unfoldment of the Divine Plan, and place little trust in technological shortcuts or improvements.

Those souls who possess the solar qualities tend to evolve elaborate mathe-matical or scientific expressions of Truth, while those who possess lunar qualities tend to evolve elaborate linguistic or spiritual expressions of Truth.

In general, women possess a predominance of watery lunar energy, while men possess a predominance of fiery solar energy. Similarly, it can be said that solar qualities dominate in the western hemisphere, and in its civiliza-tions and people, and lunar qualities dominate in the eastern hemisphere, and in its civilizations and people. However, these generalities should not be taken too far. The multitude of nations within the eastern hemisphere are not strictly lunar in their nature, and the nations in the western hemisphere are not strictly solar. There are subdivisions of solar and lunar qualities within each hemisphere and nation, each community and organization, and each family and individual.

Those souls, whether male or female, in which lunar energy predominates may be said to belong to the lunar race, while those souls in which solar energy predominates may be said to belong to the solar race. The usefulness of this classification is that it enables us to understand the age-old differences between the two main contrasting forces that have shaped human destiny on Earth.

Integrating Earth's   When the Earth experiences a Golden Age,
Planetary Awareness   the two types of souls become nonlocally
unified to form a single planetary awareness. This integrates the lunar and solar qualities of the two hemispheres of the Earth. This integrated planetary awareness is reflected, at least to some degree, in the integrated individual awareness of every human being on Earth. This allows the divine quality of human awareness to shine forth more brightly at that time than at any other.

Up until the present era, we have been unable to sustain this unified, integrated state of planetary awareness for more than a few thousand years at a time, and even then, it was sustained by a relatively small number of individuals in both the eastern and western hemispheres.

One of the highest purposes of human life on Earth is to have a large population of human beings sustain this unified holistic planetary awareness at all times, during all four Ages, and during the entire epochal cycle of Day and Night. The attainment of this goal requires that a high level of consciousness be maintained by a large number of human souls at all times on the planet. This achievement would result in our planet being elevated to the status of a permanent World of Light. Given our current level of awareness, it is difficult to conceive of the immeasurable consequences that would follow from such an attainment. To say that the Earth would be transformed into a Heavenly Paradise does not do justice to the magnitude of the possibility.

Such an intensely enlightened state of planetary awareness is the goal towards which all of our human civilizations have been striving. We may see history as a sequence of failed civilizations, but the rise and fall of each civilization on Earth is a stepping stone on the path towards planetary enlightenment. Each of these steps is carefully planned and orchestrated by the gods who are the celestial overseers and protectors of the human race.

All of these steps lead towards an even higher divine purpose and goal—the complete enlightenment of every atom, molecule, cell, and individual being on our planet. In the Vedic tradition, this state of collective enlightenment was called *samitti samani*—a collection of beings established in wholeness, evenness of life. This type of collective enlightenment is celebrated in the last hymn of the last *mandala* (cycle) of the Rig Veda. It represents the culmination of individual evolution in collective wholeness.

> Go together, speak together, know your minds to be functioning together from a common source, in the same manner as the impulses of Creative Intelligence [celestial beings], in the beginning, remain together united near the source.
>
> Integrated is the expression of knowledge, an assembly is significant in unity, united are their minds while full of desires. For you I make use of the integrated expression of knowledge. By virtue of unitedness and by means of that which remains to be united, I perform action to generate wholeness of life.
>
> United be your purpose, harmonious be your feelings, collected be your mind, in the same way as all the various aspects of the universe exist in togetherness, wholeness.[101]

This is an inconceivably high goal. Although there are many permanent Worlds of Light within our galaxy, especially in the region of the galactic center, none of them yet has achieved such complete spiritual perfection. To achieve this ultimate goal, the human race as a whole will have to attain spiritual perfection, and then, in addition, it will have to assist the gods in the complete spiritualization of all the animals, plants, and so-called unconscious matter of the planet.

This type of evolutionary development does not unfold over the course of a single epochal Day and Night. It may take many thousands of epochal Days and Nights, corresponding to billions of human years. The Planetary Being may have to reincarnate over and over again in different cycles of Creation before this goal of planetary perfection is finally achieved.

During the course of this development, many trillions of human souls will come and go on the stage of life, and many great and glorious civilizations will tell their tales of joy and woe. But the human race as a whole will go on and endure throughout the Ages. Human beings may live and die and be reborn until they individually attain enlightenment, or ascend to higher worlds. But the human race as a whole, which forms the collective heart and soul of our planet, will remain here on Earth building new civilizations and continuing to evolve and grow more enlightened Day by Day, until the ultimate goal of the Creator finally is achieved.

When that goal is finally achieved, the group soul of our planet will be elevated to the status of an immortal god, and ascend to serve the Creator in divine realms that are beyond our mortal comprehension.

This story, which is the story of the human race as a whole, is not new. It is as old as time itself. Yet it is forever being told, over and over again, on planets like our own throughout the Universe. Who but the Creator alone can comprehend the endless marvels of God's Creation?

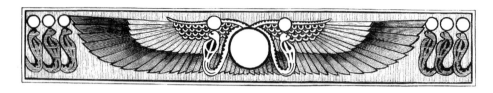

22. THE SPIRITUAL FOUNDATIONS OF HUMAN CIVILIZATION

Given the ultimate goal for which human civilization is conceived, and the grand scale of time in which this goal is to be achieved, it is incredible to realize that we scarcely have begun our adventure on this planet. The human race on Earth still is like a newborn babe.

From a cosmic point of view, it was only recently that the first human souls on our planet were initiated into the light of pure consciousness, and stepped from a world of prehistoric darkness, where their souls generally were bound by animalistic tendencies, into a fresh new world of celestial light, where their souls were liberated to soar in the realms of the gods.

Having been initiated into the Light, and having realized their own divine natures, the first enlightened human beings roamed the surface of the Earth like so many celestial beings. At the time of their Illumination, the first enlightened humans were given god-like powers, and were free to move through Nature unimpeded. Along with various nonlocal powers of intuition, they also possessed powers of physical levitation, invisibility, and mastery of the elements.

Because it was the first time that the sons and daughters of immortality walked the Earth in significant numbers with full memory of their own divine source, they were given special treatment. Like newborn infants, these first enlightened human beings were nursed with infinite care and attention. It was as if they were carried constantly in the arms of their adoring Mother, and doted over by their loving Father.

During the first Golden Age, the enlightened ones wandered through the forests, plains, and mountains in a state of perfect innocence, completely absorbed in divine Love and contemplating their oneness with the entire Creation. There was no need or desire for clothing, artificial shelters, or outer technological devices, for they were absolutely pure of heart, and everything that they desired manifested itself spontaneously through their mere intention. The weather was perfect, the fruits and vegetables grew abundantly without cultivation, the animals were docile, and the Earth truly resembled a Heavenly Paradise. This was the proverbial Garden of Eden.

Of course, these conditions were not present everywhere on Earth. It generally was true only in those regions naturally blessed with a favorable climate, suitable vegetation, and a hospitable terrain capable of supporting the early evolutionary development of human life. These were the regions where the majority of the first initiations took place. The first Seers were born in such regions primarily because of the gentle conditions of life existing there at that time—conditions that favored the development of a refined nervous system capable of supporting the experience of pure consciousness.

The first enlightened Seers allowed Mother Nature to take care of all their material needs, and thus were free to spend their time in deep meditation cognizing, through the faculty of nonlocal intuition, the divine blueprint of God's Creation, and impressing that knowledge deep into their hearts and souls.

Although they wandered naked over the face of the Earth, they were clothed in spiritual glory. Although they slept beneath the trees, they were sheltered by the vast umbrella of the starry Heavens. In a state of total innocence, they ate the fruits and roots of the plants and trees, and tasted the herbs and flowers of the meadows, and this food was like ambrosia—it gave them perfect health. These first god-like humans were relatively immortal. They lived for thousands and thousands of years and their illustrious descendants carried on in the same manner.

For many thousands of years there was a high level of civilization on our planet. This civilization left no clear traces in the archeological records, because it was in complete harmony with Nature. The illumined souls that lived at that time did not concern themselves with fabricating man-made artifacts. They did not need to. They were completely content with God's Creation. All of Nature was delivered to them for their nourishment and delight.

The modern obsession with man-made creation is only a recent development.

This characteristic has emerged only since the time of the great flood, some 13,000 years ago, which marked the beginning of our current watch. Prior to that time, during the long antediluvian period, human civilization primarily was characterized by its spiritual rather than its material development.

One might argue that such a natural lifestyle, in which the Seers walked naked through the forests and slept beneath the trees, was uncivilized. But it is difficult for us to conceive of the spiritual awareness that these beings enjoyed. For them, all of Nature was a reflection of God's divine glory, and was impressed with the divine blueprint of immortality. Nature itself was a miraculous technology that served their every need. Although their feet walked the Earth and their eyes beheld the beauty of its mountains, streams, forests, and plains, their souls soared nonlocally through the Heavens, and explored the galaxies and cosmic regions that cannot be seen by earthly eyes.

Those who equate the emergence of human civilization merely with the construction of physical buildings and monuments are sorely missing the point. The true mark of a civilized people resides in the strength of their spiritual vision and the depth of their love for all Creation, not in their engineering ability. The true foundation of human civilization inheres in the spiritual, not the material heritage of the people.

Regardless of the grandeur of the architecture, culture, or political organization of a given civilization, and regardless of its specific form of organized religion, if the people do not individually possess cosmic awareness, universal love, and deep spiritual knowledge, they cannot be said to be truly civilized—and may act like thieves in the night when given the opportunity.

Thus, the most substantial edifice that can be built by a civilized people lies not in its monumental remains built upon the Earth, but in the structure of divine truth built within their souls. Such spiritual achievements ultimately can endure much longer than any stone monument because they are passed on as a living flame from heart to heart over the ages. And even though this flame may die down at the end of each Dark Age, and the structure of pure knowledge in the human heart may be reduced to ashes, the ashes of pure knowledge do not die. They remain embedded in the human heart, and may be fanned into a new blaze by subsequent generations in each new Golden Age.

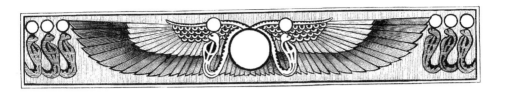

23. THE ANTEDILUVIAN WORLD

Around 13,000 years ago, there was a terrible catastrophe that struck the Earth like a thunderbolt from Heaven. This catastrophe was accompanied by earthquakes, tornado force winds, and a great flood that inundated vast regions. This catastrophe occurred at the hour of epochal Midnight, when the spiritual Light on our planet was at an all time low. Immediately after the flood, a new Golden Age dawned, and a new cycle of Ages began to unfold. The world that existed before the flood may be called the antediluvian world.

The antediluvian world was vastly different from the world that we now know. At that time people did not live in large cities. They lived in small family groups, clans, or tribes. For the people of the antediluvian world, the Earth was like a vast garden, filled with an abundance of animal and plant life. There were no national borders, no cities, no roads. Their home was the vast wilderness that covered the entire Earth.

During the long antediluvian period, the outer character of life changed little. However, there were profound changes that occurred on the spiritual levels of human existence. The real history of the antediluvian world is thus a spiritual history, rather than a mundane history. The dramatic events of this period did not involve the rise and fall of political empires. They involved the rise and fall of the spiritual awareness of the entire human race. At that time the world was not divided into different political nations—but it was spiritually divided.

All over the world the human population was divided into two distinct camps—those who walked in darkness and those who walked in Light. Although the individual players have changed, the conflict between these two classes of souls has continued throughout the ages—even to this very day.

As discussed earlier, our solar system is located in that region of the galaxy

177

known as kurukshetra—the field of action. This is the region where souls incarnate to perform action. Based upon the choices that they make and the actions that they perform, they then either ascend towards the Light or descend towards darkness.[102]

The Earth thus may be understood as the proving ground for the soul. It also is a spiritual battleground where the forces of light and the forces of darkness contend with each other to dominate the collective awareness of the human population. At certain times, the forces of light dominate over the forces of darkness, and at other times the forces of darkness dominate over the forces of light. In the antediluvian world this drama was played out in an extreme fashion.

The Nature Spirits and Terrestrial Gods

To properly understand the antediluvian drama, we must direct our attention away from the gross physical affairs of the planet to the realms of the subtle fields or spiritual beings that are always present among us. We are referring to the nature spirits and terrestrial gods—the morphic fields that are associated with and preside over all the unenlightened beings on our planet.

The nature spirits and terrestrial gods are not mythical fabrications of the primitive human mind. They are fully conscious fields of subtle matter-energy. These spiritual beings are not innately good or bad. As morphic fields they literally are produced and programmed by the individual and collective systems with which they are associated. Once they are created, however, they take on a life of their own, and can act back upon their creators to further influence their behavior. The morphic fields of an individual and of a community thus are intimately connected with the individual and the community in a self-referral feedback loop.

As we have discussed, when a morphic field presides over a collection of natural systems such as minerals, plants, or animals, it may be called a nature spirit. When it presides over a collection of human beings, it may be called a terrestrial god. One might think that if we ignore these spiritual beings they will just go away. But this is not true. They are not subject to our whims. These beings are deeply rooted in Nature. Indeed, they are essential to the well-being of every natural system on our planet. Without the presence of these collective subtle fields, no life forms would be able to exist on this Earth. They are the agencies of growth and production through which Mother Nature works her magic.

Regarding the power of the nature spirits there is the following passage in the ancient Hermetic texts:

> Thus marshaled in separate corps, the nature spirits serve under the several planets. They are both good and bad in their natures, that is, in their workings, for the essence of a nature spirit consists in its working. To these nature spirits is given dominion over all things upon the Earth, . . . they are also the authors of the disturbances [geologic, climatic, etc.] upon Earth, and work manifold trouble both for cities and nations collectively and for individual men.[103]

While the nature spirits have dominion over the natural forces and creatures that exist in the sky and on the Earth, the terrestrial gods have dominion over the minds and emotions of human beings. They actively participate in the evolution of the human populations with which they are associated, and can and do use their influence to guide whole populations towards the performance of either good or evil actions. This is an unalterable spiritual fact. It happens whether we like it or not. It happens whether we believe it or not. In effect, the terrestrial gods may be understood as embodiments of our own collective karma.

According to the ancient Seers, the only way to escape and override the influence of our past karma is to attain the state of enlightenment. Neither the nature spirits nor the terrestrial gods can have any control or influence over the enlightened soul, or Divine Ka, which reflects pure consciousness.

> But the rational part of the soul [the Divine Ka] remains free from the dominion of the nature spirits, and fit to receive God into itself. If the rational part of a man's soul is illumined by a ray of light from God, (then) for that man the working of the nature spirits is

brought to naught; for no nature spirit and no [terrestrial] god has power against a single ray of the light of God.[104]

This background information will help us to understand more clearly the spiritual drama that took place a little over 13,000 years ago as the antediluvian world was finally coming to an end. The antediluvian world had existed for many thousands of years, at least since the dawning of the previous Golden Age. Yet just before epochal Midnight, it was to enter into a Dark Age that would prove devastating beyond comprehension.

The Innocent Reflection of the Age   Generally speaking, the nature spirits and terrestrial gods tend to reflect the character of the Age and epoch in which they are found. During the Golden Age, the terrestrial gods are filled with celestial light, and are the benevolent benefactors of the human race. At such times, they appear as perfect reflections of the celestial gods in Heaven, and there is total harmony between Heaven and Earth. The seasons come on time, the harvests are abundant, and people generally live for hundreds or even thousands of years.

During such periods, the Seers may innocently invoke the terrestrial gods to attain their physical needs. When properly invoked, the gods or subtle fields instantly respond and organize the troops of nature spirits to fulfill the desire or intention of the invoker.

During the Golden Age such invocations typically require nothing more than a silent whisper of the god's name on the level of pure consciousness. During the Treta, or Silver Age, the invocations may also involve the performance of external rituals, involving simple offerings of flowers, fruit, and grains. At this time, the terrestrial gods are still filled with celestial light and are eager to assist human beings in the fulfillment of their desires.

As the Treta Age declines into the Bronze, or Dwapara Age however, there is a change of attitude on the part of the gods. This change of attitude is caused by the changed nature of human awareness during the Dwapara

Age. As discussed earlier, this is the time when warrior societies come to prominence all over the Earth—and killing and destruction become commonplace. The increased violence in human thought and action profoundly influences the fields of subtle energy that constitute the nature spirits and terrestrial gods. As a result, the terrestrial gods begin to reflect these growing violent tendencies within themselves.

By the time the Dark Age arrives, the nature spirits and terrestrial gods are so filled with violent impressions, that they no longer reflect the Light of Heaven. They no longer appear as beings of light, who are opposed to darkness. Instead, they appear as beings of darkness, who are generally opposed to the Light.

Because these beings of darkness reflect the misery and mean mindedness of the collective population of human beings during the Dark Age, the gigantic subtle bodies of the nature spirits and terrestrial gods may assume forms that are not very attractive in appearance. These frightful forms are not intrinsically evil. They merely reflect the mental impressions stored in the collective consciousness of the human population.

In effect, the frightful forms of the terrestrial gods are the instruments of Nature, created to deliver to the people the fruit of their actions and intentions. To do so, these huge spiritual beings induce the various troops of nature spirits to create collective calamities, which manifest as floods, fires, typhoons, earthquakes, etc.

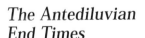

The Antediluvian End Times

The end of the antediluvian period (circa 11,000 B.C.) coincided with the darkest points of both the 52,000 year epochal cycle of Day and Night and the 13,000 year cycle of Ages. As a result, certain terrestrial gods assumed the form of powerful beings of darkness completely antithetical to the forces of light. Just before the hour of epochal Midnight, these powerful beings of darkness consciously worked to destroy all those who were promoting the Light on our planet. These beings of darkness desired to take control of the planet, and transform our world into a world of darkness, where they would have complete sway.

Under the spiritual onslaught of these powerful beings of darkness, the last remnants of the spiritual traditions that had been initiated on Earth during the previous Golden Age were about to be eradicated. The handful of remaining Seers on Earth were under intense spiritual attack, and generally hid themselves away in caves or underground chambers, where they were protected by the inner presence of Mother Earth. There they could devote themselves undistractedly to the contemplation of God. They practiced severe austerities and offered their hearts to the Supreme Being to draw more Light onto the planet, and to attract the assistance of the celestial beings.

Just when the dark forces seemed to reach their greatest strength, God directly intervened, and destroyed the forces of darkness in a terrible cataclysm. A wave of celestial fire descended on the planet like a bolt of lightning from the Heavens, causing sudden worldwide devastation.

The cosmic wave of celestial fire that descended onto the Earth at the stroke of epochal Midnight was immensely destructive. Its destructive impact was due to the contrast between the levels of subtle energy within the body of the Earth and within the descending wave.[105]

The result was a sudden worldwide cataclysm unimaginable in its effects. This cataclysm marked the end of the last Ice Age. It was characterized by violent earthquakes, huge tidal waves, intense volcanic activity, tornado force winds, and heavy rainfall. These events were followed by a worldwide flood that caused the Earth's oceans to rise several hundred feet above previous levels. This flood permanently submerged vast coastal and inland regions on all the continents, and its memory has been recorded in the numerous flood myths passed down by different traditions all around the world.

Many ancient myths describe this catastrophe, and blame it on the gigantic and rebellious beings of darkness that stalked the Earth at that time. The Hebrews called them the *Nephilim*, the Greeks called them the *Titans*, and in the Vedic tradition, they were called the *Asuras*.

For example, in the Book of Genesis when the stage is being set for the story of the flood, it is said:

> In those days . . . the Nephilim ["Giants" or literally "those who had come down"] were on Earth. They were the heroes of old, men of renown. [106]

Immediately following this enigmatic statement, the text goes on to state:

> When the Lord saw that man had done much evil on Earth and that his thoughts and inclinations were always evil, he was sorry that he had made man on Earth, and he was grieved at heart. He said, 'This race of men whom I have created, I will wipe them off the face of the Earth—man and beast, reptiles and birds. I am sorry that I ever made them.' . . .[107]

The Nephilim mentioned in the Bible were not an ordinary race of men. Nor were they aliens from outer space. They were the gigantic terrestrial gods that had been invoked by human beings for the accomplishment of many great and glorious tasks during the previous Golden Age. They were thus described as the "heroes of old." But when these gigantic subtle beings turned evil due to the dark thoughts and inclinations of men during the subsequent Dark Age, the Lord decided to wipe the Earth clean and start all over again. He then decided

> to bring the waters of the flood over the Earth to destroy every human being under heaven that has spirit of life; everything on Earth shall perish.[108]

It is clear from this passage that the responsibility for the catastrophe cannot be pinned on the Nephilim. They were simply the mirrors of human thought and action. It was human misdeeds that brought down the wrath of the celestial gods.

The Greeks, using their own language and metaphors, elaborated on this story more fully. In the Greek myth, the gigantic subtle beings were called Titans—the demigods—who in the beginning were aligned with the celestial or Olympian gods, and then later rebelled against them. It is explicitly stated that these gigantic subtle beings were instrumental in bringing about the flood. The flood was sent to the Earth by Zeus, the king of the celestial gods, as a punishment for the misdeeds of the Titan, Prometheus, who had given humanity the knowledge of the sacred fire.

The sacred fire delivered to humanity by Prometheus was not ordinary fire—it was the celestial fire of the gods.[109] It is our understanding that the knowledge of how to manipulate the celestial fire, and ritualistically invoke its presence, was given to humanity by the Titans, or terrestrial gods, during the epoch that began at the time of epochal Dusk, that is, 26,000 years ago at the beginning of the last Age of Aquarius. It was introduced at that time because it was known that the Earth was entering into the epochal Night, and human beings would be more on their own. They no longer would be waited on hand and foot by the gods, as they were during the long period of the epochal Day. They were thus given the science of sacred ritual so that they could generate additional celestial fire and invoke the gods.

These ritual practices at first were put to good use, and human beings were able to invoke the gigantic subtle beings for accomplishing many marvelous things. But later, as the cycle of Ages proceeded, the thoughts of humans turned dark and evil. The subtle beings created and invoked through the rituals reflected these evil tendencies, and had to be wiped out. According to the Greek legend, the mechanism used to cleanse the Earth of this evil influence was an overwhelming flood.

Similar stories are told around the world. For example, in the great Indian epic called the Mahabharata, it is said that in the beginning, the Asuras, or terrestrial gods, were virtuous, good, just, and charitable. They knew and obeyed the divine law (dharma), and made their offerings to the Devas (or celestial gods). But afterwards, as they multiplied in number, they became proud, vain, and quarrelsome. They made confusion of everything, and in the due course of time they were doomed.[110]

These stories are not just an old-world phenomenon. The same kind of story is told by the natives of South America. In one Peruvian myth it is said that in the beginning:

> The great Creator God, Viracocha, decided to make a world for men to live in. First he made the Earth and sky. Then he began to

make people to live in it, carving great stone figures of giants which he brought to life. At first all went well but after a time the giants began to fight among themselves and refused to work. Viracocha decided that he must destroy them. Some he turned back into stone. . . the rest he overwhelmed with a great flood.[111]

The stones referred to here were not the actual bodies of the terrestrial gods. They were the stones used in the worship or invocation of the terrestrial gods. The stones themselves were not the giants—they simply were the natural materials through which the gigantic subtle beings were invoked.

Although the flood brought untold destruction to the human race, its purpose was to purify the Earth from the darkness that oppressed it. Just as a thunderstorm brings a sweet peace and healing calm in its wake, the worldwide cataclysm was followed immediately by a new Golden Age for those that survived. The Divine Messenger then descended onto the Earth and many of the survivors were newly initiated into the Light. The civilizations that were spawned at that time, 13,000 years ago, contained numerous enlightened souls who were filled with spiritual knowledge and divine power, and it was a time of great rejoicing and thanksgiving in Nature.

Over the last 13,000 years, the civilizations that emerged after the flood have gradually matured, decayed, and died. During their early days they were filled with a spiritual glory that cannot be compared to anything that we know. However, nothing now remains of their ancient spiritual glory but a few chunks of monolithic stone, and a few surviving myths and legends. All of the great enlightened souls that once walked the Earth like celestial gods seem to have vanished into the mists of the past, like so many dreams in the cosmic night.

At the present time, the hour hand of the Cosmic Clock is approaching the junction between the signs of Pisces and Aquarius. This marks the end of the last watch of humanity's Night on Earth. It marks the time for the entire human race to awaken from its collective dream, and behold the Light of a new Day. It marks the time for all of us to arise and prepare once again for the arrival of the Divine Messenger, and for our initiation into the Light.

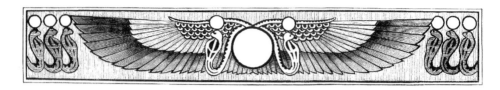

24. THE SHIFT OF THE GEOGRAPHIC POLES

The worldwide cataclysm that struck the Earth at the stroke of epochal Midnight was not merely a geological adjustment. It was not the result of purely physical forces interacting among themselves in the body of the Earth. It was a deliberate hammer stroke of the celestial gods, designed to pulverize the dark cancer that had begun to grow in the human heart and stalk the Earth.

At that time, a thunderbolt of celestial fire flashed forth from the brow of the Creator and descended onto the Earth with the force of a mighty hammer. The body of the Earth shuddered and shook under the impact of this blow, and the entire human race was as if knocked unconscious. When it awoke, the geographic poles of the Earth had shifted, and the entire antediluvian world had been destroyed.

Such global transformations are not the result of unconscious physical forces. They are not left to chance. They are orchestrated and organized by the gods to further the purpose of spiritual evolution on our planet.

The shifting of the geographic poles 13,000 years ago was not unprecedented. The poles of our planet have shifted before—and they will shift again. It is important for us to understand this phenomenon, for another shifting of the geographic poles may occur soon. Another tidal wave of celestial fire already has been ordained and unleashed by the Creator and is now propagating through the Heavens on its way to our planet.

One might wonder how a wave of almost weightless, invisible substance (subtle matter) could wreak such immense havoc on a planet as massive as the Earth. To understand this phenomenon, we must realize that the impact of this wave is not due to its mass. Rather, its impact is due to its influence on the magnetic and gravitational fields surrounding the Earth.

The Magnetic Interaction of the Stream of Celestial Fire

The stream of subtle matter-energy that descends upon the Earth from the Heavens is not a spiritual metaphor, but is very real. It consists of subtle electromagnetic particles. These particles display helical trajectories along the axis of the stream, and thus are organized into a vortex filament or fiery tornado of subtle particles, carrying powerful magnetic fields.

When the magnetic fields associated with this fiery tornado interact with the magnetic fields of the Earth, the Earth's magnetic poles may become reoriented, shifted, or even reversed in their direction. Just as the intrinsic spin of an atom will reorient itself in the presence of an external magnetic field, so also the intrinsic spin of the Earth may reorient itself in the presence of celestial magnetic fields.

Under a complete reversal, magnetic North becomes magnetic South, and vice versa. There is strong physical evidence that such reversals have occurred many times in the past, although their cause is unknown to the scientific community. Apparently the last reversal occurred during the eleventh millennium B.C.[112]

In our opinion, the exact nature of such a shift would depend upon the orientation of the Earth's magnetic field with respect to the magnetic field of the celestial tornado at the time of impact. It also would depend upon the magnetic polarity of the tornado itself. Because the angle of the Earth's magnetic axis varies with respect to the fixed stars over the course of the Earth's annual rotation around the Sun, both the exact timing of the impact and the polarity of the pillar of fire would need to be known in advance in order to venture any prediction about the exact nature of the shift. The gods alone are aware of this information. However, those who possess intuitive vision may glean the general outcome of the transformation by reading the signs within the subtle body of the Earth itself.

One should note that the Earth's magnetic poles do not coincide exactly with the rotational axis of the planet. They are about eleven degrees off center. This is because the *intrinsic spin* of the Earth, responsible for the Earth's magnetic field, is not the same as the bulk rotation of the Earth upon its axis.

The intrinsic spin of the planet is tied to the rotational kinetics of the Earth's core. It is the rotating core of the planet that generates the Earth's magnetic field. The rotating core is separated from the revolving surface of the Earth by a deep layer of hot magma, which is filled with various circulating currents. When the Earth enters into a strong celestial magnetic field, the rotational kinetics of the Earth's core are directly affected, causing the currents of magma to become reoriented.

This internal shift of magma flow may involve the rearrangement of vast quantities of fluid mass beneath the surface of the Earth. This rearrangement alone could cause serious Earth changes in the form of major earthquakes. Under certain conditions, it also could contribute to an actual shift of the geographical poles on the surface of the planet.

———— • ——◆•◆•◆—— • ————

The Gravitational Interaction of the Stream of Celestial Fire

However, this magnetic effect is exacerbated and supported by another effect, namely the influence of the subtle particles upon the gravitational field of the Earth. A detailed model of this gravitational mechanism will be presented in another volume. For now, suffice it to say that when the Earth becomes charged with a high density field of subtle matter-energy, these particles partially shield the Earth from the inertial forces that connect it to the rest of the Universe. As a result, the Earth as a whole appears to lose some of its mass.

The ancient Seers used this same shielding effect to nullify the gravitational force of the Earth, and thereby levitate heavy stones and other objects in the construction of temples after the flood. The enlightened Seers also used this effect to levitate their own bodies and fly through the air. This is not a new force. This mechanism has been used by enlightened civilizations throughout the galaxy to propel interstellar levitation vehicles for millions of years. The knowledge of this force is thus very old.

When this shielding effect is applied to the Earth as a whole, it is as if the Earth suddenly loses a small portion of its mass. This sudden loss of mass causes the Earth to slip into a slightly larger orbit around the Sun. It also may cause the streams of magma within the Earth's core to shift and rearrange themselves into a new stable flow pattern. In addition, these gravitational effects may cause the moon to shift into a larger orbit around the Earth, producing changes in tidal effects on the Earth.

Thus, at the same time as the Earth's magnetic field is being reoriented, the Earth's gravitational field also is being adjusted. These combined influences could well result in a major shift of the Earth's rotational axis.

Earth-Crust Displacement

However, yet another critical factor may also play a role in this scenario. This relates to the build-up of the polar icecaps and the theory of earth-crust displacement. This theory presents the possibility that under certain conditions, the entire crust of the Earth might slide around and be displaced in a single piece. This is not such a far-fetched idea. The Earth's crust is a rigid structure often less than thirty miles thick. It rests on a lubricating layer of molten rock and gas known as the asthenosphere. Under certain conditions, the outer crust might slide around on this lubricating layer and be displaced as a whole, while remaining intact. In fact, this theory was championed at one time by Albert Einstein.

Albert Einstein investigated the possibility that the weight of the ice-caps, which are not symmetrically distributed about the pole, might cause such a displacement. Einstein wrote: "The Earth's rotation acts on these unsymmetrically deposited masses, and produces centrifugal momentum that is transmitted to the rigid crust of the Earth. The constantly increasing centrifugal momentum produced this way will, when it reaches a certain point, produce a movement of the Earth's crust over the Earth's body, and this will displace the polar regions towards the equator."

When Einstein wrote these words [1953] the astronomical causes of the ice ages were not fully appreciated. When the shape of the

> Earth's orbit deviates from a perfect circle by more than one percent, the gravitational influence of the sun increases, exercising more pull on the planet and its massive ice sheets. Their ponderous weight pushes against the crust and this immense pressure, combined with the greater incline in the Earth's tilt [another changing factor of the orbital geometry] forces the crust to shift. . . [113]

The interactions of the Earth's magnetic and gravitational fields with the stream of celestial fire, along with the theory of earth-crust displacement, illumine some of the mechanics that may underlie a pole shift.

According to the theory of Earth-crust displacement, such a shift would not involve a displacement of the actual axis of rotation. Rather, it would represent a sliding of the Earth's entire crust upon the lubricating bed of gas and molten rock upon which it rests. This would have essentially no effect on the dynamic equilibrium of the rotating mass of the Earth as a whole.

In such a shift, the Earth's axis would retain its position with respect to the plane of the ecliptic and the fixed stars, but the position of the stars and the ecliptic as viewed from any given point on Earth would change dramatically. After such a shift, the Sun no longer would appear to rise from the same direction as it did before. The directions "East," "West," "North," and "South" would spin around and need to be relocated, and the movements of the stars in the night sky would shift accordingly. This kind of cosmic reorientation inevitably would have a profound impact upon the human psyche.

Many ancient myths record this kind of sudden changing of the celestial order. For example, Marduk, the ancient Babylonian god considered responsible for initiating the flood, is recorded as saying:

> When I stood up from my seat and let the flood break in, then the judgment of Earth and Heaven went out of joint. . . the stars of heaven—their position changed, and I did not bring them back.[114]

Evidence of Pole Shifts

There also is geological evidence of previous pole shifts. It has been documented that towards the end of the last Ice Age certain regions in what are now Alaska and northern Siberia enjoyed a temperate, even warm climate. There also is evidence that parts of Antarctica were free of ice during that same epoch.[115] To explain these anomalies, which occurred when much of western Europe and northeastern North America were buried under hundreds of feet of ice, it has been suggested that the North and South Poles were positioned at different parts of the globe than they are today.[116]

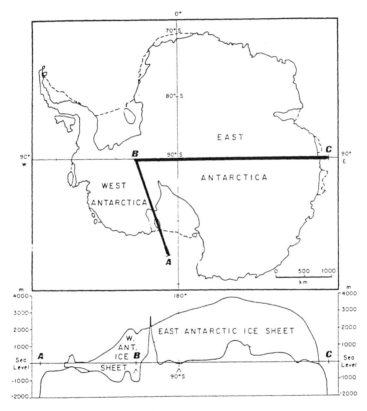

Figure 30—Ice Sheets of Antarctica

Two different views of Antarctica and its ice sheets are shown in this illustration. The bottom graph shows a topical cross section taken along the line A–B–C drawn in the top map. Notice the dramatic difference between the thickness of the ice sheets on west and east Antarctica. [Source: J. T. Hollin and R. G. Barry, "Empirical and Theoretical Evidence Concerning the Response of the Earth's Ice and Snow Cover to a Global Temperature Increase," *Environment International* 2 (1980): 437–444.]

In particular, it has been suggested that the geographic North Pole then was located at Hudson's Bay, while the geographic South Pole was situated just off the east Antarctic coast. This would imply that west Antarctica previously was at much warmer latitudes than it is today, a supposition supported to some degree by the great discrepancy between the thickness of the ice sheets deposited on east and west Antarctica.

To give some idea of this discrepancy, it has been estimated that if the east Antarctic ice dome were to melt it would raise the sea level some 164 feet, while if the west Antarctic ice sheet were to melt, it would raise the sea level only 16 to 32 feet. Furthermore, it is believed that the west Antarctic ice sheet is much younger than the east Antarctic sheet.[117]

A pole shift also would have a devastating effect on plant and animal species around the globe. There is substantial paleobotanical evidence that a pole shift or something equally catastrophic occurred around the eleventh millennium B.C. Around that time, the regions of the Yukon, Alaska, and northern Siberia, that previously had enjoyed a temperate climate, suddenly were exposed to frigid Arctic temperatures. As a result, vast herds of mammoths, antelopes, horses, and other temperate mammal species that lived in those regions at the time were flash frozen and buried beneath the permafrost that has existed there ever since. These animals were not just frozen to death. It appears that many of them were ripped apart by unknown forces and piled up in tangled heaps along with torn and twisted trees and plants. In the words of one professor at the University of New Mexico, within the frozen muck of Alaska

> lie the twisted parts of animals and trees intermingled with lenses of ice and layers of peat and mosses. . . . Bison, horses, wolves, bears, lions. . . . Whole herds of animals were apparently killed together, overcome by some common power. . . . Such piles of bodies of animals or men simply do not occur by any ordinary natural means. [118]

Although these remains were discovered some time ago and have been documented,[119] they have yet to be adequately explained by modern scientific theories.

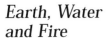Earth, Water and Fire

Other regions of the world may have faced different forms of destruction. Huge tidal waves may have been pulled out of the depths of the oceans, rising up in massive walls of water towering thousands of feet high. We believe that these watery walls of death overwhelmed the continental shelves and coastal plains, and rolled up river valleys on all continents for hundreds of miles. These tidal waves did not occur once and then go away. A whole series of such waves probably came at intervals over several days, as the Earth's crust shifted and rolled into its new position.

The cause of these tidal waves was the huge Earth tremors that rolled around the globe. These were not ordinary earthquakes, centered along fault lines. Rather, they were "Earth waves" that involved the entire crust of the Earth. At the time of the shift, the entire crust of the Earth must have developed broad swells or wave-like formations that propagated around the planet with enormous power and speed.

Unlike localized quakes associated with fault lines, which generally involve abrupt, jolting movements of one tectonic plate against another, we believe that the Earth tremors accompanying the pole shift were huge rolling swells that caused the entire crust of the Earth to rise and fall in a wave-like fashion. These swells may have had wavelengths that stretched for a thousand miles or more. The magnitude of these Earth displacements could have been millions of times stronger than what we would consider a severe earthquake today.

In our vision, these deep rolling Earth swells caused the world's oceans to rise up out of their trenches and spill over the continents in massive tidal waves that wiped out virtually all land-based life within the coastal regions of the planet. These watery walls of death would have rolled up river valleys, where the human population was most dense, obliterating whole communities along their way. We estimate that within a few hours of the first rolling tremors, the resulting tidal waves had wiped millions of human beings off the face of the Earth, along with countless animals.

Others have had similar visions. For example, a Midrashic legend of the deluge asserts that: "The waters were piled up to a height of sixteen hundred miles, and they could be seen by all the nations of the Earth."[120] A Lappish tradition paints an even more graphic picture. According to this tradition the god Jubmel promised to suddenly destroy the world in a great flood.

> I shall reverse the world. I shall bid the rivers flow upward; I shall cause the sea to gather together itself up into a huge towering wall which I shall hurl upon your wicked Earth-children, and thus destroy them and all life.[121]

The Navajo tribe of Arizona have preserved similar legends, in which huge towering walls of water once advanced across the deserts like a "chain of high mountains."[122]

Those who lived far enough inland, or at an elevation high enough to survive the watery walls of death that advanced across the Earth would not have been totally spared. They would have had to endure tornado-force winds, violent earthquakes, and volcanic eruptions. These additional forms of natural violence would have wreaked untold havoc on much of the remaining population.

During the next few thousand years, when the ice sheets over North America and Western Europe were melting rapidly, and before the new polar ice caps had built up to their present levels, the world was much more humid than it is today, and it rained almost continuously in many places. This caused a worldwide flood, which permanently inundated the coastlines of the continents. In some areas, such as off the Patagonian coast of South America, the shoreline receded by as much as three hundred miles.

The coastal regions that existed during the Antediluvian period now lie buried beneath layers of sand and silt at the bottom of the ocean. They form the continental shelves that extend far out into the sea. Who knows what archeological treasures exist there?

In addition to these violent cataclysms, the pillar of celestial fire that descended upon the Earth at that time initiated a process of intense tapas in the surviving population, and many perished due to this purification.

The Survivors   However, not everyone perished. Many of those aligned with the forces of light had been forewarned of the coming devastations. A few spiritual communities and some of the more illumined families had made preparations well in advance to survive the cataclysms. To escape the flood they moved to higher ground up in the mountains or they built boats or arks.

The mountains not only protected them from the flood, but the mountain ranges as a whole also acted as "Earth walls" (similar to "sea walls"), lessening the effect of the rolling Earth tremors in their vicinity. In addition, those who were aligned with the Light were more physically and spiritually prepared to receive the infusion of subtle energy that descended at that time. Hence, immediately after the cataclysm, many of the individuals in these groups were elevated to the status of enlightened Seers.

The powerful beings of darkness that had roamed the Earth for the previous few thousand years also were profoundly affected by the Illumination. They were not destroyed by the floods or earthquakes. These beings were subtle and could not be touched by gross physical events. Rather, they were destroyed directly by the spiritual Light that descended upon the planet like a flood of celestial fire, or a bolt of lightning from Heaven.

The beings of darkness that stalked the Earth during that period were composed of dark *(tamasic)* subtle matter. This is the same type of subtle matter out of which the dark worlds that lie in the outer regions of the galaxy are composed. The subtle matter that descends along the pillar of fire, on the other hand, is composed of luminous *(sattvic)* subtle matter. These two types of subtle matter are directly opposed and tend to annihilate one another.[123]

Thus, when the flood of celestial fire descended upon the planet, the beings of darkness were totally consumed by the Light of Heaven. Like dry pieces of cotton tossed into a blazing fire, the beings of darkness were consumed by celestial fire. The polarized currents that composed their subtle bodies were neutralized, and the various nature spirits and terrestrial gods became subdued. Once the cosmic battle was over, the terrestrial gods became subservient to the celestial gods in Heaven once again.

The Divine Messenger or Holy Spirit then initiated a new Golden Age, and the forces of light were given sovereignty over the entire planet, as in days of old. This is how the forces of darkness were overcome and the forces of light became reestablished around the world some 13,000 years ago. Since that time, the cycle of four Ages (Yugas) has unfolded, and many civilizations have risen, flourished, and perished.

A New Illumination

Now we face a new time of Illumination—a new beginning of the cycle of Ages. Another wave of celestial fire is on its way to our planet, and it will arrive here soon, within the next ten to twenty years. However, we do not foresee the same global devastation that occurred 13,000 years ago. The subtle matter density of the Earth is higher now, just before epochal Dawn, than it was then, just before epochal Midnight.

Over the last thirty years, new teachers have brought knowledge of meditation and other spiritual practices to the mass population of the world. These teachers have played a crucial role in helping to increase the Light on our planet. By instructing millions of individuals in these ancient practices, and inspiring large numbers of people to come together and perform these practices in groups, they have helped to generate enormous quantities of cosmic life force. The luminous subtle matter generated by these groups has been infused into the Earth, thereby gradually raising the consciousness of all beings. Without the infusions of cosmic life force provided by these groups, the last thirty years would have been very different, and the visions of doom and gloom associated with the end of this Age would have been more accurately prophetic.[124]

Because of the efforts of millions of people to improve and increase the levels of spiritual Light on our planet over the last thirty years, the great danger that once loomed over our heads has been largely averted. However, much still remains to be done. The Light must be increased at an even faster pace over the next few years if we are to truly avoid all danger.

To accomplish this feat, new sacred technologies must be delivered to the human race over the next decade or so that will enable us to raise the subtle matter density of the planet ever more rapidly, providing a larger and larger cushion to soften the impact of the coming wave. These technologies will be used to enhance and accelerate the spiritual evolution of millions of people around the world, and they also will be used to directly nourish the subtle body of Earth itself. All of this is part of the Divine Covenant that has been given to the human race. The gods are prepared to do their part. Now it is up to us to do ours. The transformation is inevitable. But whether it will be gentle or violent is totally in our hands.

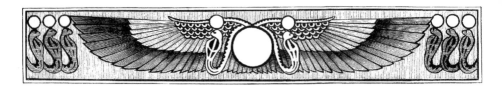

25. ANCIENT LEGENDS OF THE FLOOD

We believe that the destruction of the antediluvian world marked the darkest moment in the history of human civilization on Earth. It occurred when the Light coming from the Central Sun was minimal, and the forces of light were all but overwhelmed by the forces of darkness. It was at that point that the hammer stroke of the gods descended on the forces of darkness and untold destruction was unleashed upon the human race.

These dramatic events have been deeply ingrained in our collective psyche. Legends and myths concerning these global events have been passed on from generation to generation by various cultures and traditions throughout the world.

Modern scholarship has revealed that there are over 500 ancient legends and myths around the world concerning a great deluge or flood that overwhelmed mankind.[125] This suggests that the deluge truly was a global cataclysm and not just an isolated local event.

The Legend of Utnapishtim One of the most poignant and detailed of the flood stories is the Mesopotamian legend of Utnapishtim, a king who is reputed to have ruled the land of ancient Sumer (southern Iraq), during the days of the flood. His legend was recorded on cuneiform tablets dating back to the beginning of the third millennium B.C. The clay tablets recording his legend were excavated along with thousands of other similar tablets from the sands of southern Iraq during the last century and a half, and offer a unique glimpse into the stories of the ancient past.

According to this version of the flood myth, Utnapishtim played the familiar role of Noah. Being forewarned of the impending disaster, he built an ark, loaded it with kith and kin, as well as various animals, and rode out the flood, eventually landing on a mountain top. For preserving the seeds of humanity and of all living things, he was rewarded by the gods with the gift of immortality. The story is set in the days immediately preceding the flood, when it is said that the gods dwelt on Earth.

> In those days the world teemed, the people multiplied, the world bellowed like a wild bull, and the great god was aroused by the clamor. Enlil [the enforcer of divine decisions] heard the clamor and he said to the gods in council, "The uproar of mankind is intolerable and sleep is no longer possible by reason of the babel." So the gods agreed to exterminate mankind.[126]

But the merciful gods took pity on Utnapishtim and warned him of the impending disaster. It is said that the gods spoke to him through the "reed wall" of his house.

This "reed wall" is a metaphor for the field of celestial rays through which the gods whisper their secrets to the Seers on Earth. The Egyptians employed a similar metaphor when they spoke of the "Field of Reeds." The idea that the gods spoke to mortals through hollow tubes or reeds also is inherent in the symbology of Thoth, the scribe of the gods, who uses a pen fashioned out of reeds to inscribe the sacred words of the Gods.

In any event, a warning was whispered to Utnapishtim through the celestial reeds—along with instructions to build an ark. After building the ark and loading it with the seeds of all living things, he climbed into the ark and realized the time had come.

> The time was fulfilled. When the first light of dawn appeared a black cloud came up from the base of the sky; it thundered within where Adad, lord of the storm was riding. . . a stupor of despair went up to heaven when the god of storm turned daylight to darkness, when he smashed the land like a cup.

> On the first day the tempest blew swiftly and brought the flood. . . . No man could see his fellow. Nor could the people be distinguished from the sky. Even the gods were afraid of the flood. They

withdrew; they went up to the heaven of Anu and crouched in the outskirts.

For six days and nights the wind blew, torrent and tempest and flood overwhelmed the world, tempest and flood raged together like warring hosts. When the seventh day dawned the storm from the south subsided, the sea grew calm, the flood was stilled. I looked at the face of the world and there was silence. The surface of the sea stretched as flat as a roof-top. All mankind had returned to clay . . . . I opened a hatch and light fell on my face. Then I bowed low, I sat down and wept, the tears streamed down my face, for on every side was the waste of water. . . . Fourteen leagues distant there appeared a mountain, and there the boat grounded; on the mountain of Nisir the boat held fast, she held fast and did not budge.[127]

Having landed on top of the mountain, he eventually disembarked and offered burnt offerings to the gods in thanksgiving. This scenario, which very closely parallels the legend of Noah presented in the Book of Genesis, has been told in various ways in many independent legends and myths all around the globe.

Mesoamerican Legends of the Flood

For example, the native traditions of both North and South America are filled with flood legends. In one Peruvian legend, an Indian and his llama took refuge on a high mountain and thereby survived the flood, while the rest of humanity was destroyed.

When they reached the top of the mountain they saw that all kinds of birds and animals had already taken refuge there. The sea began to rise, and covered all the plains and mountains except the top of Vilca-Coto; and even there the waves dashed up so high that the animals were forced to crowd into a narrow area. . . . Five days later the water ebbed, and the sea returned to its bed. But all human beings except one were drowned, and from him are descended all the nations on Earth.[128]

Similar traditions exist among the North American natives. For example, the

Inuit Indians believed that at one time there was a devastating flood and earthquake "which swept so rapidly over the face of the Earth that only a few people managed to escape in their canoes or take refuge on the tops of the highest mountains, petrified with terror."[129]

Chinese and Vedic Legends of the Flood   On the other side of the globe in China, similar traditions exist. Early Jesuit scholars there uncovered legends which told of a time long ago when "mankind rebelled against the high gods and the system of the Universe fell into disorder."[130] The consequences were devastating:

> The planets altered their courses. The sky sank lower towards the north. The sun, moon, and stars changed their motions. The Earth fell to pieces and the waters in its bosom rushed upwards with violence and overflowed the Earth.[131]

Here the celestial signs of a pole shift are clearly indicated. During such a shift the movements of the heavenly bodies are irrevocably altered. As viewed from any given point on Earth, the planets will appear to follow a different course across the night sky after the shift than they did before. In addition, the place where the Sun rises in the "East" and where it sets in the "West" will be different. The night sky, which is set against the fixed stars, also will appear to be different.

According to the Chinese legend cited above, the "sky sank lower towards the north." This is consistent with the direction of the pole shift proposed by certain authors discussed earlier.[132] According to this scenario, the Earth's crust may have pivoted in a swiveling movement that would have carried much of the western hemisphere towards more southerly latitudes, while much of the eastern hemisphere, including China, would have been shifted towards more northern latitudes. This would have caused the northern horizon to appear to sink down lower in the night sky, revealing new stars that previously were hidden below the horizon.

In the Vedic tradition the flood myth is centered around Manu, the proto-typical or representative man, who discovered a small fish swimming in the palm of his hand one day while making ablutions in a river. According to the story, the divine fish begged Manu to allow it to live, so he put it in a jar. As the fish grew, he had to replace the small jar with larger ones. Eventually the fish grew so large that it had to be taken to a lake. When it outgrew the lake Manu took the fish to the sea, where it grew into a huge one-horned whale with golden scales. When the divine fish had become fully grown, it told Manu of an impending deluge and instructed him to build a ship and load it with every living species of animal and the seeds of all plants. Fastening his boat to the horn of the divine fish, Manu rode out the flood. Eventually the ark landed on top of Mount Meru. As the waters receded, Manu descended from the mountain back to the Earth below. This marked the beginning of a new Age of the world. After the flood Manu and his wife produced children and became the ancestors of the present human race.[133]

Such myths and legends clearly point towards a global cataclysm and flood that was experienced in a similar manner by people all around the world. It is no coincidence that these stories have begun to be collected within the last couple of hundred years. The voices of the ancient past are crying out to be heard all around the world. They speak not only about where we have been, but also about where we are going.

The Legend of Atlantis

One of the most popular legends concerning the antediluvian drama is that of Atlantis. Our only direct source for the legend of Atlantis is a fragmentary description provided by Plato (c. 427–347 B.C.) in two of his Dialogues—*Timaeus* and *Critias*. In these texts, Plato paints a picture of an island paradise that was originally filled with virtuous men and women, who enjoyed every kind of luxury and convenience. But eventually the civilization went awry, and engaged on a course of world conquest. Ultimately it was destroyed in a devastating cataclysm that occurred over a single day and night—and the Atlantean civilization sank beneath the waves and was lost.

It is a popular belief that the Atlantean civilization was a highly advanced technological culture that existed somewhere in the Atlantic Ocean. Others have speculated that it was located in the Aegean Sea, while still others have suggested that it existed on the continent of Antarctica.

While we will leave the discussion of the location of Atlantis to others, we do believe that the Seers who existed prior to the flood did possess various subtle spiritual technologies. However, we do not believe that these technologies took the form of devices such as electric motors, combustion engines, or computers. Rather, these technologies were comparatively simple, primarily involving certain ritualistic and alchemical techniques. Although these technologies may have been simple, they were not trivial. In many ways, their capabilities went far beyond the capabilities of modern-day technologies. Equipped with the subtle matter technologies, the ancient Seers were able to accomplish things that are only dreamed of by modern scientists.

However, the ordinary people did not possess these subtle technologies. Nor did these technologies provide the basis for a large industrial society. We believe that prior to the flood, the sacred technologies were the exclusive domain of a small handful of ancient Seers—who were the last remnants of a much more glorious time.

During the Golden Age that came after the flood, the number of Seers increased dramatically and the Sacred Science once again was taught on a larger scale. Later, during the Treta Age, some of the ancient technologies were incorporated into the fabric of society—but were available only to the kings and priests, who had been initiated into their secrets.

Since the end of the Treta Age, some 4,000 years ago, the true knowledge concerning these subtle spiritual technologies generally has been lost. Instead, over the last few hundred years we have developed a wealth of gross material technologies.

It is now time for these two types of technology—spiritual and material—to meet and shake hands. It is time to revise the technological foundations of modern civilization so as to pave the way for the descent of Heaven on Earth. We believe these changes are destined to occur—not just because we wish them to, but because they are built into the Divine Plan—a plan envisioned by the ancient Seers long ago, before our modern world was even born.

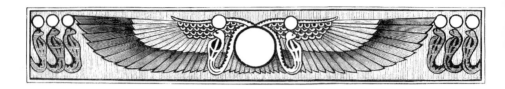

26. THE TRADITION OF ENLIGHTENED SEERS

Since the first group of human souls were initiated into the Light on our planet ever so long ago, there has been a secret, holy tradition of enlightened Seers on our planet at all times. Even during the long periods of spiritual darkness, there always have been a few enlightened Seers upholding the Light. These enlightened Seers were given the responsibility to oversee the spiritual well-being of the human race as a whole, and the authority to initiate new individual souls into the light of pure consciousness at any time.[134]

Although such enlightened Seers have been present on Earth since the beginning of human history, they generally have remained hidden away, uninvolved in the drama of public life. In general, their influence has been manifest not so much through linear transmission of knowledge from person to person, as through the nonlocal power of their spiritual presence, and their ability to intercede on behalf of humanity to the celestial beings or gods, and to the Creator himself.

On occasion, the enlightened ones have stepped into the light of public knowledge to set the ship of humanity back on course. But in general, they have remained behind the scenes, and allowed the mass of humankind to develop and mature according to its own desires and tendencies. However, they have continuously watched over us, always remaining conscious of the bigger picture—the Divine Plan and its overall time scale.

The enlightened Seers are truly universal beings. Their awareness literally is universal in its breadth, comprehending the entire seven-layered structure of universal life, and understanding the profound significance and scope of the Divine Plan for human evolution on Earth. Such Seers do not seek recognition or fame. Their innocent desire is to carry out the will of the Creator, and to assist in the accomplishment of the Divine Plan. That is their only motive for action.

Thirteen thousand years ago, just before the hour of epochal Midnight when the spiritual darkness was most impenetrable, the number of enlightened Seers on our planet reached an all time low. Only a handful of Seers were present on the Earth at that time. When the hammer stroke of the gods finally descended, and the watery walls of death washed over the land, a large portion of the population was destroyed. Those that survived became infused with the Holy Spirit, and rapidly were elevated to new levels of spiritual awareness. After the flood the number of enlightened Seers increased dramatically, and a new Golden Age dawned for all mankind.

The Seers that emerged after the flood generally chose to follow one of two paths. Depending upon their innate tendencies, whether solar or lunar, the Seers naturally were inclined to follow either (i) the path of action, or (ii) the path of knowledge.

Those who followed the path of action were charged with overseeing the temporal development of the human race. They were responsible for educating the people of the world in the various arts and sciences that would enable them to thrive and flourish on the Earth. All the mundane arts and sciences, including mathematics, astrology, agriculture, navigation, statecraft, the building sciences, sacred rituals, alchemical technologies, alphabets, writing, music, art, etc. fell under their jurisdiction, and were imparted to the general population at the appropriate times through their benedictions.

To develop this knowledge, the more active Seers organized themselves under the umbrella of a sacred academy, which was active throughout the western hemisphere during the long Golden Age. As the Golden Age came to an end, the members of the sacred academy dispersed all over the globe to disseminate the knowledge that they had developed to people in different regions. This dissemination of knowledge initiated many of the historical civilizations that emerged at the end of the Neolithic Age, during the fourth millennium B.C.

The Seers who followed the path of knowledge, on the other hand, were not directly involved in the worldly development of human civilization. They were devoted to purely spiritual pursuits. To pursue their spiritual goals in an undistracted manner, they preferred to remain hidden away in deep forests or mountain caves. Some of the contemplative Seers lived in solitude while others lived in peaceful hermitages among a small group of spiritual aspirants who were their followers.

Given the general solar nature of the western hemisphere, the Seers that emerged in the West generally displayed a more active temperament. Those that emerged in the East displayed a more contemplative temperament, and they pursued the paths appropriate to their temperaments.

Although these two groups of Seers generally displayed different temperaments, during the Golden Age all the Seers around the world belonged to the same worldwide tradition of sacred knowledge. They were all initiates of the Divine Messenger. They were all fully identified with their own higher Selves, had memory of their divine origins, and possessed the wisdom of the Seven Sages, or the seven universal spirits of God. Nevertheless, due to their different tendencies, the two groups of Seers were concerned with different issues, and evolved different types of cultures.

In the East, the Seers were primarily concerned with the cognition, preservation, and utilization of the universal language of Nature—the software of the Sacred Science. Their culture was designed around the aspiration to enliven the sacred knowledge on the level of human speech.

In the West, the Seers were primarily concerned with the cognition, preservation, and utilization of the subtle matter technologies—the hardware of the Sacred Science. Their culture was designed around the aspiration to embody the sacred knowledge on the level of physical form.

These two approaches to the Sacred Science were manifest most prominently in the Vedic tradition in the East and the Egyptian tradition in the West. We will now examine these ancient traditions and their legacies in more detail.

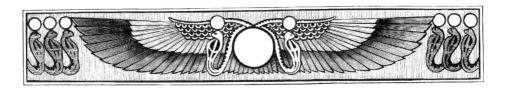

27. THE ANCIENT VEDIC TRADITION

The Vedic Rishis   During the last Golden Age (circa 11,000 to 6000 B.C.) the responsibility for the cognition and development of the software of the Sacred Science fell primarily to the Vedic Rishis (Seers).

Fundamentally, the Vedic Rishis are immortal modes of unbounded pure consciousness. During the Golden Ages, individual human beings on Earth attune themselves to these immortal modes of pure consciousness and gain access to the structure of pure knowledge inherent within those modes. In so doing, they become identified with the immortal Seers and become earthly embodiments of those Seers. However, the cognitions of the Seers do not depend upon the one-time historical appearance of a particular individual on Earth. They depend only upon the cosmic awareness of the Seer or Rishi who is an immortal mode of unbounded pure consciousness.

The cognitions of the Seers may be revealed to humans on Earth during certain times, and they may be hidden at other times, but their existence does not depend upon whether or not humans on Earth are aware of them. They are part of the underlying blueprint of pure knowledge that serves as the permanent basis of Creation on cosmological scales of reality.

In each Golden Age, new individual Seers are initiated into the Light and evolve to the point where they become identified with the cosmic Seers. They gain access to the cognitions of pure knowledge available from those cosmic perspectives, and make them available for the benefit of all humanity. These cognitions, which occur on the level of unbounded pure consciousness, are then expressed on the level of human speech and passed on from generation to generation as an oral tradition until the advent of a new Golden Age, when the cognitions are re-cognized and the tradition refreshed by a new group of Seers.

This nonlocal transmission of pure knowledge has been taking place in every cycle of Creation and on every Earth-like world throughout the Universe since the beginning of time. The availability of the Vedic cognitions is part of the Divine Plan for human evolution throughout the Universe.

According to the ancient tradition, there are seven main Rishis or Seers. These correspond to the seven universal spirits of God discussed earlier. The principal offshoots of the seven universal Seers number several hundred. Each of these offshoots is identified with a particular Vedic Rishi, who ultimately has trillions of descendants in the branching spiritual hierarchy of God's kingdom.

The Sacred Mantras   The sum total of all the cognitions of pure knowledge available through the principal Rishis is called the Veda, which literally means "pure knowledge." According to the ancient tradition, the Veda is eternal, uncreated, and indestructible. It consists of the transcendental impulses of pure consciousness that constitute the unmanifest blueprint of Creation.

Although the Vedic Rishis are called Seers, they fundamentally cognized these impulses of pure consciousness as impulses of primordial sound. These primordial sounds are organized into quantized packets or units of spiritual sound called *aksharas* (syllables). A collection of such syllables is called a *mantra* or sonic formula.

A mantra may be understood as a sacred formula that sonically encodes the divine correspondences between Heaven and Earth. The mantras encode the nonlocal connections that mediate the relationships between the macrocosm and the microcosm. In a sense, they may be viewed as the esoteric keys of Creation. Their purpose is to unlock the vast storehouses of pure knowledge that are nonlocally embedded in the very structure of pure consciousness.

The divine correspondences between Heaven and Earth embody the universal archetypes or divine laws that permanently underlie all things in Creation. They are the vibrant nonlocal impulses of organizing power that inspire evolution in Nature. They are the ultimate threads of divine intelligence that weave the fabric of the world.

The meaning of a mantra is inherent in the sequence of letters and syllables out of which it is composed. The meaning is not derived from a grammatical analysis of the mantra. Grammar by definition deals with words and their combinations into sentences. It does not deal with the sequences of letters and syllables that ultimately compose the words and sentences. As a result, the true meaning of the mantras is completely hidden to the uninitiated. According to tradition, the mantras reveal their secret meanings only when they are properly invoked on the level of pure consciousness.

To use a modern analogy, the mantras may be compared to secret codes that unlock vast memory banks within the cosmic computer. For the codes to work, the cosmic computer must be turned on—and it is turned on only by the light of pure consciousness. Without pure consciousness, there is no access to the power of the cosmic computer. In this manner, the sacred knowledge remains protected for all times, and cannot be misused by the unenlightened.

From a more technical point of view, a mantra may be understood as a spiritual resonance that exists deep within the soul of an object and constitutes its spiritual name. These resonances encode all of the nonlocal relationships among the various parts and aspects of the object. It is these relationships that enable the object to exist as a single whole, a single system, on the level of pure consciousness. These relationships are not mediated by any physical forces. They are mediated by pure consciousness alone.

The soul of an object can tell no lies. It always reveals the object's true identity. This identity is revealed as a resonant interference pattern of primordial sound within the soul of the object. This resonating pattern of consciousness contains the complete knowledge of the object, including the complete knowledge of its subtle and gross forms. It represents the true spiritual name of the object.

The spiritual name of an object is (usually) not the same as the conventional name assigned to the object by human beings. The spiritual name is the resonant vibrating soul of the object itself. While spiritual names may be cognized on the level of pure consciousness by humans who have risen to the status of Seers, such names are never the product of human creation, invention, or custom.

The Universal Language of Nature

There are thousands of conventional languages that have been passed on through human custom, and adapted according to changing circumstances in the ebb and flow of history. The same object may have a different name in each of these languages. Such languages are neither universal nor eternal. They are localized, both in the geography in which they are found and in the times in which they are spoken.

The universal language of Nature, on the other hand, is eternal. It already exists in Nature. Human awareness simply has to discover it there. The ancient Vedic Seers, who were endowed with passive lunar dispositions, did not view themselves as the conquerors of Nature. They did not impose arbitrarily invented names upon the forms and phenomena of the world. Rather they passively listened and "heard" the spiritual names that were already inherent within the objects themselves.

They were able to do this because their minds were deeply established in the silent stillness of pure consciousness. While immersed in deep transcendental meditation they were able to experience their thoughts in a state of perfect innocence. This perfect innocence enabled the first Seers to cognize the true spiritual name of whatever image or object was projected into their minds. These cognitions were stored in their soul as frequency blueprints or condensed sonic formulas. Such formulas were deemed to have magical powers, and were sought after by the Seers of every culture. In the Vedic tradition, such formulas were called mantras.

By cognizing the mantras that exist on different scales of time and space, that is, on different levels of universal life, the Seers were able to clearly see the divine correspondences that exist between the things in Heaven and things on Earth.

The rule of divine correspondence is simple: objects correspond to one another to the degree that they possess similar spiritual names. Thus, the proper naming of objects was considered an extremely important aspect of the Sacred Science.

The knowledge of the sacred mantras gave the ancient Seers complete mastery over Nature. By means of these mantras, the Vedic Seers could invoke the celestial gods, awaken the soul of any object, and program the fields of subtle matter to perform any task. In effect, the sacred mantras represented the software of Nature itself. Through this software they could program or engineer Nature according to their will.

The Secret of Divine Invocation

Although the Vedic mantras contain the sonic keys that can unlock all the secret correspondences in Nature, and invoke the presence of the gods on Earth, the mantras are powerless unless they are invoked on the level of pure consciousness. The mere passage of air through the vocal chords is incompetent to awaken the nonlocal correspondences between Heaven and Earth—correspondences that must span trillions of light-years. Such correspondences can be awakened only on the level of pure consciousness. Nothing less than pure consciousness can extend nonlocally into the vast unfathomable bosom of Heaven and call down the blessings of the gods on Earth.

However, under certain conditions the sacred mantras also can be uttered externally with powerful results. For the mantras to be effective when spoken externally, they must be properly pronounced when a high density field of subtle matter, which reflects a high level of pure consciousness, is present in the ambient environment. Such external conditions generally are available only in the Golden and Silver Ages of humanity, when the density of ambient subtle matter is much higher, and the people generally are more enlightened than in other Ages.

To increase the effectiveness and power of the mantras, the Vedic Seers developed various of ritual performances, called *yagyas* (offerings). These performances typically involved offering mineral, vegetable, and animal substances into the consecrated fire (agni). Because the consecrated fire was used to carry the offerings to the gods, it was deemed to be the messenger between human beings and the gods.

The purpose of the burnt offerings was to produce a high density cloud of subtle matter-energy which then could be programmed by the sacred mantras. The materials offered into the fire were chosen specifically because they possessed an abundance of subtle matter-energy. The subtle matter-energy inherent in the material was liberated when the material was consumed by the heat of the fire. The liberated subtle matter-energy then formed a cloud of "mind-stuff" that hovered around the fire. The mantras were then employed to invoke certain divine correspondences within the cloud of subtle matter-energy, infusing it with intelligence and organizing power, and programming it for specific purposes.

During the Golden and Silver Ages, such sacred rituals were employed by the ancient Seers in virtually every culture around the world to invoke the presence of Heaven upon the Earth. The burnt offerings served to generate high density fields of subtle matter-energy, into which sacred incantations were made to call down the blessings of the celestials for the nourishment of all beings on Earth.

To our ancient ancestors, such rituals were the key to maintaining peace and harmony in Nature. They caused the seasons to come on time and the plants and animals to thrive and grow abundantly. Sacred rituals also were performed to bring success in all types of human endeavor, and to protect the human population from calamity, disease, crime, and war.

When the Silver Age ended, around 2150 B.C., the increasing darkness and violence in human awareness carried over into the performance of the sacred rituals, and various types of animal and human sacrifices began to grow in popularity among people in different parts of the world. This dark turn of events caused the celestial beings, who are the overseers of the human race, to steer the children of the Earth away from the performance of such rituals.

Thus, new religions were introduced prior to the onset of the Dark Age, which rejected and prohibited the performance of ritual sacrifices and burnt offerings. This was accomplished by the introduction of Buddhism in the East, and Christianity and Islam in the West.

These new religions were part of the overall Divine Plan for human evolution on our planet. Among other things, their purpose was to steer the human population away from the dangers associated with the misuse of the Sacred Science. To prevent another collective disaster like that which occurred at the hour of epochal Midnight, the widespread performance of dark, violent rituals involving the destruction of animal and human life had to be avoided.

With the advent of these new religions, the practice of making burnt offerings was greatly diminished all around the world. Over the last 2,500 years, the basic knowledge concerning these ancient performances generally has been lost.

For the last two or three thousand years, human awareness has been restricted to the gross field of action so that it would not create a mess for itself. The subtle fields of existence are much more powerful than the gross fields of existence. If the sacred rituals designed to manipulate the subtle fields of life are used for violent, destructive purposes, rather than for nourishing purposes, the results can be catastrophic.

On the other hand, if the sacred rituals are performed properly, for nourishing, life-enhancing purposes, they have the potential to completely transform life on Earth for the good. The Vedic yagyas, when performed properly, have the ability to invoke the presence of Heaven into the very soul of our planet, and transform the Earth into a Heavenly Paradise. This knowledge is an important part of the Sacred Science of the Seers. It currently is being revitalized for the nourishment of human life on our planet. One of the keys to this revitalization is the existence of the Vedic mantras, which have been preserved since time immemorial by rigorous family traditions of oral recitation.

The Tradition of Oral Recitation

In the Vedic tradition, the mantras belonging to each family of Seers were considered the real wealth and treasure possessed by the family. Only those in the direct lineage of the original Vedic Rishi who cognized the formulas were allowed to memorize and recite them. This kept the vibrations of the original Rishi lively in the blood (or DNA) of his or her earthly descendants.

The people that belonged to the Vedic tradition primarily lived in the large region that lies between the Indus and Ganges rivers in north-central India and Pakistan. However, they were not the only people to inhabit this region. They coexisted along with various primitive tribes of hunter-gatherers, referred to in the ancient texts as the Khols, the Bhils, etc., but did not mix with them.

Up until the advent of the historical era, the Vedic people remained sequestered away, living in small spiritual hermitages nestled in the forests near freshwater streams and lakes. Virtually no archeological traces of these spiritual communities remain. This is because they were primarily vegetarians, and did not leave behind piles of cutting and scraping tools. They also cremated their dead and scattered their ashes in streams and lakes. There are thus no buried bodies or charred animal bones to mark their presence. Furthermore, they kept no written records, and did not build any megalithic stone structures. Their dwellings generally had a wooden frame, and were made of thatched grass, woven leaves, or tree bark. So from an archeological point of view, the Vedic people were completely invisible.

Although the Vedic Seers left behind few archeological traces, they did leave behind an enormous legacy of sacred texts, passed on through oral recitation. According to the tradition, many of the sacred texts cognized by the original Vedic Rishis during the Golden Age have been preserved in their purity up until this very day.

Most of us have played the game of passing a rumor around a circle of people, only to find it substantially changed by the time it arrives back at its source. Based upon this experience it might seem that an oral tradition would leave too much room for distortion and change over time.

But this was not the view of the Vedic Seers. The Vedic Rishis believed that in order to survive the ravages of time, the sacred knowledge had to be passed from heart to heart as a living flame, filled with the breath of life.

One of the beauties of the process of oral transmission is that it does not depend upon an intellectual understanding of the text that is being transmitted. It depends only upon the correct pronunciation of the sacred sounds. Even in modern times there have been examples of illiterate Brahman priests appearing and dictating very long sacred texts in Sanskrit verse, till then unknown and unrecorded, and apparently very ancient.[135]

One cannot imagine the discipline and rigor involved in a traditional Vedic education. During the first six months of a Vedic education, the young students are drilled for many hours every day until they perfect the pronunciation of the Vedic letters. This is done before they are taught the first rule of grammar, and before they recite the first word of actual text! Correct pronunciation of the sacred texts is a cornerstone of the Vedic tradition. It is the essential key to the utilization and preservation of the sacred formulas. And in a traditional Vedic education this is hammered home with exhaustive thoroughness.

Once the students have mastered the alphabet, they are then taught the sacred texts. They learn the texts not by looking at symbols printed in a book, but by hearing and repeating the sacred sounds, over and over again, for months and years, until the texts are imprinted indelibly within their souls. This education traditionally takes at least twelve years. By the time they have graduated from this education, the Vedic texts are an integral part of their very breath. They could recite them perfectly in their sleep. They then gain the title of a Vedic pundit. But this is not the end. The pundits are bound by duty to continue their rigorous daily recitations of the sacred texts throughout their entire lives, passing the knowledge on to their students and descendants as it was taught to them.

Of course, this tradition barely exists in India today. Over the last century, more and more Brahman families have given up their Vedic recitations in order to pursue modern careers as engineers, doctors, physicists, accountants, etc. This is a sign that we have reached the very end of Kali Yuga.

When the Vedic tradition, which is perhaps the oldest surviving ancient tradition on our planet, begins to disappear from the Earth, one can be sure that a new revival is on its way.

The Status of the Vedic Literature

It is a sad fact that western scholarship has greatly undervalued the Vedic culture from the beginning. This may have had its origin in the arrogant attitude of the British colonial rulers, who generally had no clue about the ancient Vedic texts or their importance. The Vedic knowledge and culture were completely foreign to early western scholars. Some of them believed that the Vedic texts were nothing more than a bunch of gibberish invented by the Brahman priests to subjugate the masses of the people.

The strangeness of the Vedic texts to western scholars may also have had something to do with the late date at which they were introduced to the western world. Until the eighteenth century, the Vedic texts were completely unknown to the West. The ancient Greek, Arabic, Hebrew, and Latin texts had been known and studied by western scholars for many centuries, but the Vedic texts were discovered much later.

When the Vedic texts initially began to be translated into French, German, and English by western scholars, they generally were deemed incomprehensible. The cosmic mind-set of the Vedic Seers seemed so naive that the Vedic literature was considered to be little more than elaborate nonsense. This attitude led to numerous misinterpretations and poor translations.

It is only within the last 150 years that Vedic scholarship has begun to be taken more seriously in the West. Unfortunately, there are vast portions of the Vedic literature that have been lost, and of the surviving portions, many texts remain uncatalogued and untranslated. As a result, the Vedic literature barely has been tapped by western scholarship, and the general population knows basically nothing of the vast treasures of knowledge contained therein.

These problems have been compounded by the fact that those who attempt to investigate the Vedic knowledge are confronted by a formidable language barrier. It is well known that Vedic Sanskrit is one of the most complex and sophisticated languages on our planet. Although it is deeply related to classical Greek and Latin (as well as most other European languages), it is far superior to these languages in its construction and elegance. Commenting on this, Sir William Jones, a British judge and linguist, announced to the Asiatic Society in Calcutta in 1786:

> The Sanskrit language, whatever may be its antiquity, is of wonderful structure; more perfect than the Greek, more copious than the Latin, and more exquisitely refined than either; yet bearing to both of them a stronger affinity, both in the roots of verbs and in the forms of grammar, than could have been produced by accident; so strong that no philologer could examine all the three without believing them to have sprung from some common source, which, perhaps, no longer exists. There is a similar reason, though not quite as forcible, for supposing that both the Gothic and Celtic, though blended with a different idiom, had the same origin with the Sanskrit, and the old Persian might be added to the same family.[136]

Because of the complex structure of the language, fluency in writing and reading Vedic Sanskrit generally requires ten years of hard, dedicated study. And even if one develops the grammatical skills necessary to translate the Vedic texts, the true knowledge of the texts still remains hidden away, buried behind the sequences of letters and syllables that constitute the mantras or esoteric formulas.

Over the last forty years, Maharishi Mahesh Yogi, who is a "Great Seer" (Maharishi) in his own right, and who has deep insight into the Vedic texts, has made a heroic effort to correct many of the misinterpretations that have grown up surrounding the Vedic texts.[137] This is a problem even in India, where the real tradition is barely surviving in just a few families.

Maharishi has brought to light the original organic unity of the twenty-seven different aspects of Vedic knowledge, which were recorded as separate sets of Vedic texts and preserved by different family traditions. He also has interpreted the Vedic knowledge in a modern scientific framework that is extremely illuminating.

It is significant that the ancient Vedic mantras are being introduced to the western hemisphere at this time. This indicates that the time is now ripe for a new Golden Age, when the sacred language of eastern Seers and the sacred technologies of the western Seers will meet and shake hands for the first time in thousands of years.

The profound integration of these two great streams of knowledge is destined to be the hallmark of the new Day of human civilization about to dawn on Earth. This is not happening by accident. It is all part of the Divine Plan for the full enlightenment of our planet.

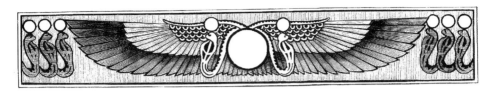

28. THE ANCIENT EGYPTIAN CIVILIZATION

Egyptian Prehistory   The western branch of Seers, unlike their Vedic counterparts, possessed an active solar nature, and were devoted to the development and utilization of the hardware, or technological applications of the Sacred Science. As a result they developed their own culture suited to their natures.

The history of the western esoteric tradition is extremely ancient. We suspect that it extends all the way back to the time of epochal High Noon (circa 37,000 B.C.), when the emanations of the Central Sun were most intense, and the levels of spiritual Light on our planet were at their peak.

According to the cycles of time mapped out earlier, the hour of epochal High Noon was marked by the onset of the Age of Leo some 39,000 years ago. We believe that this was the time when the great solar dynasty of western Seers first became established on Earth.

Although this conclusion is based upon esoteric and intuitive considerations, it seems to be consistent with the concept of Egyptian history presented by Manetho (literally "Truth of Thoth") who lived in the third century B.C.

Manetho was one of the high priests at Heliopolis, which was considered the greatest seat of wisdom in ancient Egypt. He is said to have written a text called the *History of Egypt*. Although the original text has been lost, a number of secondary sources report that Manetho estimated that the entire history of Egyptian civilization spanned a total of 36,525 years.[138] This period ranged from the "First Time," when the gods first ruled Egypt, to his own time, when Egypt was ruled by the last dynasty of mortal kings.

It has been 2,300 years since Manetho wrote his *History of Egypt*. If we add these years to the figure given above, we can see that the first god-like ruler of Egypt would have ascended the throne about 38,825 years ago.

This is remarkably close to the period of epochal High Noon (about 39,000 years ago). It is our opinion that from then until the ascendancy of Menes, the first mortal king of Egypt (circa 3100 B.C.), the western world was governed and dominated by a relatively small group of enlightened Seers. We believe these Seers belonged to an unseen spiritual academy whose purpose was to cognize and preserve for future generations of mankind the knowledge pertaining to spiritual enlightenment and physical immortality.

However, there is no reason to suppose that the sacred academy originally was an "Egyptian" institution. During the antediluvian period and during the long Golden Age that followed the flood, the nation of Egypt did not exist as such.

Egyptologists estimate that Egypt emerged as a political entity only after 3200 B.C. The ancient Vedic Seers marked this same time as the point when our galaxy entered into the celestial Kali Yuga. It was around this same time (3114 B.C.) that the Mayan Long Count began. According to the Mayan Calendar, this marked the beginning of the fourth Age of the Sun, an Age that is scheduled to end around 2012 A.D.[139]

The period around 3200 B.C. thus was considered extremely important by the Egyptian, Vedic, and Mayan cultures. In essence, it marked the beginning of the modern historical world. Prior to that time, there were no large-scale political nations anywhere on Earth. The archeological record shows that there were plenty of small communities and city-states, but no large-scale nations.

It is our understanding that before the advent of the celestial Kali Yuga, the world was ruled by spiritual power rather than by political, economic, or military power. Those who held the reins of spiritual power were the enlightened Seers. To the ordinary people of that period, the enlightened Seers appeared as immortal gods. They were revered as the spiritual leaders and protectors of the people.

The secular leaders of the small clans, tribes, and communities that existed at that time must have had their own sphere of influence, but it is highly unlikely that they challenged the authority of the Seers. They would have been in awe of the enormous spiritual power and wisdom possessed by the Seers, and it would have been inconceivable to compete with such power.

We think it likely that the enlightened members of the secret academy belonged to no particular nation or people. We speculate that they came from all over the Mediterranean region, that is, from Anatolia, Mesopotamia, Canaan, Egypt, Ethiopia, as well as the rest of North Africa.[140] However, the particular region in which they were born and raised was probably not important.

During the Golden Age, it is unlikely that the qualification to become a member of the sacred academy was based upon one's race, sex, religion, nationality, or family lineage. More probably, it was based upon one's level of consciousness. We must remind ourselves that the members of the sacred academy were enlightened Seers who considered themselves to be part of a timeless, universal tradition. They were nothing less than citizens of the Universe. They were thus immune to the petty distinctions and differences that have caused so much havoc in the world over the last few thousand years. The Seers did not really care about the color of one's body, or the particular dialect that one spoke. They were able to see into one's very soul. Thus, the only real qualification to become a member of this elite secret society was an enlightened universal consciousness. That was the key that opened the door.

The Ancient Esoteric Tradition

In accordance with their solar natures, the western Seers naturally received a wealth of knowledge concerning the technologies of the Sacred Science. These technologies are not unique to our planet. They are present on all Worlds of Light throughout the Universe.

When the population of a given planet displays the appropriate level of spiritual development and social responsibility, these technologies are bestowed upon the general population by the gods. Prior to that time, they are shared only with an elite few—the enlightened Seers—for their own spiritual development and use.

During the previous Golden Age, the Seers who received this knowledge were not allowed to share it publicly. This policy was in the best interest of humanity as a whole. At that time, the human population on Earth was not ready to receive this knowledge. It would have been misused, and this misuse could have destroyed our planet.

The sacred technologies are not trivial. They are the most powerful technologies available to human beings anywhere in the Universe. Furthermore, they have the power both to create and to destroy with equal facility.

Unlike mantras, which are ineffective unless one is established in pure consciousness, the effectiveness of the sacred technologies does not depend upon one's level of consciousness. Anyone who understands the principles of these technologies and knows how to construct them can utilize these technologies—for good or for evil. They can be used by anyone, regardless of their spiritual development or moral fiber, to create either Heaven or Hell on Earth.

That is why the ancient Seers were so concerned about the promulgation of these technologies to the general population. Even among initiates in the sacred academy, there were many different levels of knowledge. Only the most enlightened Seers who had demonstrated a sincere devotion to the well-being of humanity as a whole were given access to the highest secrets of the tradition. Others were given bits and pieces of the sacred knowledge in accordance with their spiritual status and function.

A Secret Radiation Technology

As one might expect, the sacred technologies did not involve technologies such as we are familiar with in modern times. They did not use any modern materials, such as stainless steel or plastics. Theirs was not a gross matter technology. It was a completely different type of technology that utilized natural materials, such as herbs, metallic ores, and crystals, and operated on the basis of a deep esoteric understanding of luminous subtle matter.

To the members of the sacred academy, the luminous currents of subtle matter generated by these technologies often were conceived of as fiery serpents. Some of the devices that they built were designed to radiate these currents into the environment. This is not just speculation. Such radiation devices are depicted on the walls of a small underground crypt lying directly beneath the main altar in the Ptolemaic Temple of Hathor, located at Denderah in Upper Egypt.[141]

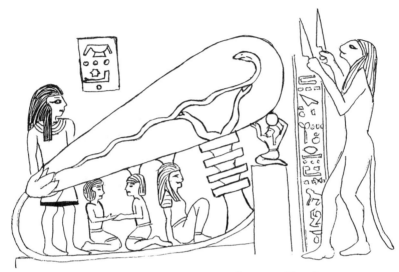

Figure 31—Egyptian Radiation Device

These engravings are unique. Nothing like them has been found in any of the other pyramids, temples, tombs, or catacombs scattered throughout Egypt. As a result, Egyptologists cannot explain them in the context of the traditional religious or mythic traditions with which they are familiar.

The Temple of Hathor at Denderah was constructed by the Ptolemies in the first century B.C. Although the Temple was built at a time when most of the practical wisdom of the ancient Seers already had been lost, we know that there still were many ancient records, in the form of temple engravings and papyrus scrolls, that were cherished by the Ptolemies as representing the lost wisdom of ancient Egypt. We suspect that the ancient technologies and wisdom preserved in these records were incorporated into the Temple so that they would be preserved for future generations.

From archeological studies we know that the Temple of Denderah was constructed upon the site of an earlier temple. Thus, the engravings depicted in the new temple may have been reproductions of engravings that were in the older temple. In addition, the inspiration for and design of the Temple appears to predate the time of its construction. Hieroglyphs engraved on the Temple declare that it was constructed "according to the plan laid down in the time of the Followers of Horus."142

Figure 32—The Temple of Denderah

The illustration above presents the Temple of Denderah in its heyday as romantically imagined by Napoleon's artists during the nineteenth century.

According to Manetho, the Followers of Horus (or Shemsu Hor) ruled Egypt prior to the first mortal king. In other words, the hieroglyphs declare that the plan for the Temple of Denderah was conceived at least 3,000 years earlier, before the First Dynasty of pharaohs. The persistence of knowledge and intent over this incredibly long period points to the silent, unseen influence of the members of the sacred academy, an influence that must have been present, at least to some extent, even as late as the first century B.C.

It should be noted that the engravings of the radiation devices were found in a small crypt located directly beneath the main altar of the Temple. The size of the crypt (1.12 x 4.6 meters)[143] is such that it is not possible to step back and view the engravings from a distance. Clearly, they were not meant to be seen by the ordinary public. Do these engravings depict a secret sacred technology known to the high priests alone? If so, then what kind of technology was it?

In our opinion, the engravings depict various subtle matter technologies designed to radiate intense currents of subtle matter-energy into the environment. The currents of subtle matter-energy generated by these devices are depicted as serpents or snakes contained within large oblong bulbs, possibly made of glass.

The currents of subtle matter appear to be discharged from a nozzle that is shaped like a lotus flower. The nozzle, in turn, is connected by a cable or tube to a small vessel located at the right-hand side of the drawing. We believe that this vessel represents a "subtle matter generator," from which the currents of celestial fire originate. This assumption is supported by the fact that the Egyptian sun-god Atum-Re is sitting on top of the vessel.[144] To the Egyptians this would indicate that the vessel is a source of celestial fire, just like the Central Sun of the Universe.

We suspect that once the celestial fire was generated within the subtle matter generator, it was conducted through the cable in the form of a current, resembling a current of electricity, until it ultimately was discharged in the bulb.

What was the purpose of this strange device? A hint may be taken from the fact that it was depicted beneath the Holy of Holies in the Temple of Hathor. Hathor was a sacred goddess who had been revered since the earliest periods of Egyptian history. She was often depicted as a cow, or as having the horns of a cow, to indicate her nourishing power. It was her role to daily nurse the king or his priestly representative with the milk flowing from her breasts. The milk of Hathor was credited with rejuvenative and supernatural power. Through the divine nourishment provided by this milk, the king received the grace of office and the supernatural spiritual power that he needed to rule and protect Egypt.[145] In addition to her role as a divine nurse-maid, the goddess Hathor also was known as the protectress of the necropolis regions of the Nile, a region where the rites of resurrection, rebirth, and immortality played an important role.

Figure 33—Hathor

We suggest that the large bulb depicted in figure 31 symbolically represents the "breast" from which the divine "milk" of Hathor was effused. In this interpretation, the streams of divine milk effused from the breasts of Hathor would correspond to currents of celestial fire effused from the radiation devices. Is it possible that these devices were used on a daily basis by the Egyptian kings and priests to elevate their consciousness and spiritualize their bodies? By absorbing the currents of celestial fire emanating from these devices, were they symbolically "drinking the milk that issued from the breasts of Hathor"?

The association of milk with celestial fire is not so far-fetched. In the Vedic tradition, the Soma, or Nectar of Immortality, was often called the "Milk of Heaven."[146] By consuming this immortal nectar the celestial gods and ancient Vedic Seers were said to attain great spiritual power, sovereignty, and physical immortality.

However, it appears that "nursing" from the breast of Hathor may have involved something different than actually drinking a liquid. The individuals kneeling below the discharge tube appear to be receiving the influence of the currents as though they were bathing in the fluorescent glow of a discharge tube in a tanning booth. More specifically, the discharges appear to be absorbed into the body through the crown of the head.

Apparently, the placement of individuals below the discharge tube played an important role in the use of these devices. In each engraving that depicts the use of such a device (and there are several such engravings located within the crypt), there is at least one individual located below each discharge tube. In most cases, these individuals are kneeling with their palms outstretched and turned upwards. This traditional gesture indicates that the individual is in a receptive mode.[147] Was this meant to signify that the individual was in the process of receiving the blessing of the goddess? Were these individuals drinking milk from the breast of Hathor?

The Breath of the Serpent

Although the process of receiving the nourishing rays of celestial fire may have elevated the minds and bodies of the kings and priests to high levels of spiritual enlightenment, this process was not without its dangers. The element of danger is indicated by the baboon-like creature standing to the right holding two knives. The baboon was one of the symbolic forms used to signify the Egyptian wisdom-god Thoth. The presence of this creature indicates that the whole process was taking place under the scrutiny of Thoth, the Divine Messenger.

The two knives held in the hands of the Thoth figure may have indicated the potential danger of the process. In order to use a device involving high-intensity discharges of celestial fire, very strict rules and conditions must have been observed by the participants. To qualify for this treatment, one probably had to be either a priest or a king. More importantly, one had to undergo the proper preparatory rituals.

These rituals were designed to gradually purify and charge one's mind and body with cosmic life force. Only the highest initiates were prepared to drink from the breast of Hathor in this manner. The physiology of the individual would have to be highly evolved to receive such powerful rays of celestial fire without being injured by the subtle fusion reactions.

If one is not sufficiently prepared to receive the nourishing milk of the goddess, then one may experience it as the fiery breath of the serpent. The nature of this breath is such that it can literally burn one up. If one's mind and body is filled with impurity, and one has not undergone the proper preparatory rituals, then upon receiving the radiations of celestial fire, the impurities in one's body may be consumed so quickly that the physiology itself may be damaged or destroyed.

Such considerations are not mere conjecture. In the Bible, it is recorded that grievous injuries sometimes were sustained by those who tended the Ark of the Covenant. According to Biblical reports, this strange device was sometimes surrounded by a mysterious cloud filled with the Divine Presence. But the influence of the Ark was not always benevolent. In at least one instance, two innocent individuals were burned up and destroyed by lightning-like radiations or sparks emanating from the Ark.148

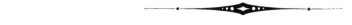

The Djed Pillar

In order to build up a high-intensity discharge of subtle matter-energy in such radiation devices, a certain amount of electrical insulation would be required. This is because particles of subtle matter or celestial fire possess electric charge.

To discharge high intensity currents of celestial fire, the device would have to be electrically insulated from the ground of the Earth. Otherwise, the subtle matter charge building up within the device would continuously drain into the ground, and an intense discharge would not be achieved.

One technology that may have played an important role in this regard is the Djed pillar. The Djed pillar is a strange-looking column or pillar that appears to be divided into sections. It is a sacred ancient Egyptian symbol that represents perfect "stability."149 It also is symbolic of Osiris, who represents the principle of spiritual rebirth, resurrection, and immortality.

In the Hathor engravings, a Djed pillar is depicted as supporting the oblong bulb that contains the discharge. It is illustrated as though it were endowed with two arms. These arms extend into the oblong bulb and appear to directly support the discharge that is taking place therein. We believe that this provides an esoteric clue as to the true function of the pillar. In our opinion, the Djed pillar was a technological device that was used to give both structural and electrical stability to the discharge.

More specifically, the Djed pillar may be interpreted as a type of high-voltage insulator used by the ancient Egyptians to isolate and stabilize the high density currents of subtle matter-energy generated during their sacred rituals. Its resemblance to many types of modern high-voltage insulators is uncanny.

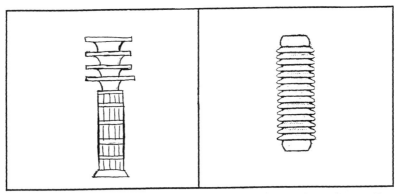

Figure 34—The Djed Pillar and a Modern High-Voltage Insulator

Unlike modern insulators, the purpose of the Djed pillar was sacred and holy. According to Egyptologists, it played an essential part in the spiritualization of the human physiology. For example, in the *Dictionary of Ancient Egypt* the Djed pillar is stated to have been

> a powerful weapon of magic for all deceased Egyptians, considered
> necessary to aid in the transformation of the human flesh into the
> spiritual form assumed by the dead in eternity.[150]

It is well known that the ancient Egyptians performed various sacred rituals designed to transform the mortal human body into a divine celestial body. These rituals are generally called the "mortuary rites."

The Mortuary Rites   According to modern Egyptologists, the mortuary rites were performed while the dead body of the priest or pharaoh was being embalmed, wrapped in linen garments, and then marched to its burial place. Having been immortalized in this manner, the mummified body was placed inside a sealed sarcophagus where it would remain more or less free from decay for a long period.

Although this may be an accurate assessment of the mortuary rites as they were practiced after the time of the First Intermediate Period (2134–2040

B.C.), it is our opinion that these rituals were a morbid perversion of the original "rites of immortality" that were practiced by the members of the sacred academy prior to that time. Although the practice of preserving the body through mummification dates all the way back to the Old Kingdom, we believe that the real rites of immortality were performed prior to the death of the physical body in an attempt to transform the living body of the priest or pharaoh into a fully spiritualized celestial form.

In accordance with this view, the Mastabas of the Early Dynastic Period and the Pyramids of the Old Kingdom originally may not have been tombs at all. We believe they were places of transfiguration where the priests and pharaohs would undergo the sacred rites of immortality in an attempt to spiritualize their physical bodies.

> By the time Egypt was unified after 3000 B.C., the people viewed the tomb as the instrument by which death could be overcome, not as a mere shelter for cast-off mortal remains. The tomb became a place of transfiguration. The *akh,* the transfigured spiritual being, emerged from the corpse as a result of religious ceremonies. The *akhu,* the deceased, soared into the heavens.

> The dead were "those who have gone to their kas." Through the intercession and guidance of these astral beings, the dead changed from weak mortals into unique immortal spiritual beings, exchanging life on earth for the perfect existence of eternity.[151]

The performance of the mortuary rites generally was accompanied by various incantations or spells. The most prominent of the surviving texts associated with these rites are the *Pyramid Texts of Unas* (circa 2600 B.C.) and the *Papyrus of Ani* (circa 1500 B.C.). In both texts, the focus is upon the ascension of the soul into the celestial regions, and not upon the dead body of the individual. In fact, the denial of death is a constant theme. Over and over again in the Pyramid Texts it is specifically stated that the individual undergoing the ritual is not dead. According to the texts, the purpose of the ritual is to prepare the person to attain immortality and ascend into the celestial regions.

Although there is no doubt that such texts eventually were associated with the mummification process, this may have been a later adaptation. Variations of these texts probably had been passed down in an oral tradition for thousands of years before they finally were written down. Once the true knowledge of immortality was lost, it seems reasonable to assume that the inheritors of the lost tradition perverted the original intention of the rites and applied them towards preserving the physical body of the deceased through mummification.

In spite of the fact that modern Egyptologists believe that the mortuary texts were intended to govern what happens to a person after his or her death, there is no direct mention of the person's death at all. Modern scholars have interpreted such phrases as "to moor" or "to unite with the land" as signifying death. Other phrases such as "the day of mooring," the "good day," or "that day of come hither" are interpreted as indicating the time of death. However, these phrases may also be interpreted as referring to the day of spiritual ascension, when the individual establishes a nonlocal connection with the celestial regions and ascends to commune with "those who are yonder."[152]

In the ancient esoteric tradition there are two types of death. The first is a living death. This type of death corresponds to ordinary life as experienced by unenlightened individuals. From the point of view of the enlightened Seers the ordinary life of most individuals is no life at all; it is a form of living death. One overcomes this first type of death when one gains spiritual enlightenment.

The second type of death corresponds to the actual death of the physical body. Once an individual has gained enlightenment, there is no death of the subtle spiritual body, but the gross body can die. We believe that the ancient Egyptians performed the rites of immortality to avoid and overcome both types of death, and thus attain true immortality. They performed the rites of immortality to charge their bodies with cosmic life force, gain spiritual enlightenment, and attain a celestial form even while they were alive in the physical body.

The Process of Spiritual Ascension

The 3,500 year old *Papyrus of Ani,* also called the *Egyptian Book of the Dead,* provides a highly symbolic, illustrated version of the Egyptian rites of immortality as they were practiced around

1500 B.C. Although this text was written some 650 years after the end of the Old Kingdom, when much of the ancient wisdom already had been lost, it appears that much of the ancient symbology had survived.

The introductory illustration in this ancient text is very significant. It provides an esoteric key that symbolically encodes the entire process of spiritual transformation governed by the text. This illustration has been reproduced below.

Figure 35—
The Djed Pillar and the Process of Spiritual Ascension

In the above illustration, the *ankh* symbol, which represents the *akh* or spiritualized form of the Self, is rising out of the Djed pillar and ascending towards the solar disk, symbolic of the Central Sun of the Universe.

The various elements in the scene all have hieroglyphic significance and carry esoteric meaning. The arch at the top of the illustration is an elongated version of the hieroglyphic sign "pet" which means "sky" or "heavenly region." Directly under this sign is the solar disk, which signifies the Central

Sun of the Universe. As we have seen, the Central Sun is the most glorious seat of the Divine Presence in the Universe. It represents the throne of God, and may be viewed as the goal of all forms of spiritual ascension.

On either side of the Central Sun are six baboons. They are facing upwards towards the heavenly regions with hands uplifted in praise of the Central Sun. These baboons are personifications of the six spheres of universal life that lie above our own earthly region, and that surround the Central Sun on all sides. They are personified as baboons because in the Egyptian tradition the baboon was one of the symbols of Thoth, the Divine Messenger. In our interpretation, the six baboons and the ankh taken together represent the seven universal spirits that surround the throne of God.

The *ankh* symbol, also called the Egyptian Cross, represents the spiritualized form of the human soul after it has been transfigured or transformed into an immortal celestial being. At that time, it becomes the very embodiment of the Divine Messenger.[153]

Of the seven universal spirits, the ankh is given primary importance because it represents the resurrected human soul, the higher Self, which bears the greatest resemblance to the Creator himself.

Technically speaking, the resurrected form of the soul consists of unpolarized celestial fire—the neutral type of subtle matter-energy that reflects pure consciousness. In the symbology of the Egyptian cross, this neutral form of subtle matter-energy is represented by the inverted tear drop that sits on top of the cross. This tear drop is symbolic of the head, which acts as an inverted cup, designed to capture and hold within itself the glorious essence of life, the celestial fire. The two arms of the cross upon which the tear drop rests represent the two polarized currents of celestial fire inherent within the neutral current. The symbolic motif of the ankh thus appears to be deeply related to that of the Caduceus, and on a cosmic scale may be interpreted as an Egyptian version of the pillar of celestial fire that connects Heaven and Earth.

The ankh symbol in this particular vignette is endowed with two human-like arms that are reaching up to embrace the solar disk. These arms are painted red, the same color as the solar disk itself. The two arms play a role similar to the two wings of the Caduceus. They represent the power to nonlocally embrace or comprehend the celestial regions as well as the highest abode of God within the expanding awareness of the Seer.

The fact that the ankh symbol is seated upon the Djed pillar is highly significant. The Djed pillar represents the spinal column in the body, divided into sections. The spinal column may be understood as the pillar that supports the neutral current of celestial fire that flows along the spine. However, as discussed earlier, we believe that there also is a technological interpretation of the Djed pillar. In our view it corresponds to an insulating device that provides the structural and electrical stability required to sustain the generation of a high density field or current of celestial fire. This is also the function of the spine in the human body. It supports the current of celestial fire that rises up into the head.

The Myth of Osiris

In Egyptian mythology, the Djed pillar not only symbolizes stability, it also symbolizes the god Osiris, the most revered of the divine kings of ancient Egypt. Because Osiris was the first earthly king to ascend into the celestial regions, his story became transformed into a great and enduring myth that illumines the whole principle of spiritual resurrection and ascension.

According to this myth, Osiris originally ruled Egypt along with Isis, his sister and queen, for a long and fruitful period. At a certain point Osiris embarked upon a world civilizing tour, and was gone for a long time. When he returned, he was slain by his brother Set, who then usurped the throne. The lifeless body of Osiris was placed by Set and his co-conspirators in a sealed wooden coffin and set afloat on the Nile. The wooden coffin floated down the Nile into the Mediterranean until it finally came to shore at Byblos—an ancient port located on the coast of Lebanon. The details of the Osirian episode at Byblos are intriguing.

> The myth tells us how Osiris, still sealed inside his coffer, is carried out into the sea and washed up at Byblos. The waves lay him to rest among the branches of a tamarisk tree, which rapidly grows to

234

a magnificent size, enclosing the coffer within its trunk. The king of the country, who much admires the tamarisk tree, cuts it down and fashions the part which contains Osiris into a roof pillar for his palace. Later Isis, the wife of Osiris, removes her husband's body from the pillar and takes it back to Egypt to undergo rebirth.[154]

After Isis removes the dead body of Osiris from the pillar, she and her sister Nephthys magically bring him back to life. After conceiving a son with Isis— named Horus, the hawk-headed god—Osiris ascended into the celestial regions, the Duat, where he attained immortality. Horus then became the prototype for the kings while they lived on Earth and ruled the political nation of Egypt, while Osiris became the prototype for the kings after they had renounced their earthly rule and prepared themselves to ascend into the celestial regions and attain immortality.

The myth of Osiris thus played a central role in the ancient immortality rites. The Egyptian pharaohs who were preparing to ascend into the celestial regions were invariably identified with Osiris, who had ascended before them.

Given the importance of the Osirian myth, it becomes clear that the vignette displayed in figure 35 represents a symbolically condensed version of this myth. In this interpretation, the Djed pillar may be interpreted as the pillar containing the dead body of Osiris. The placement of Isis and Nephthys on either side of the pillar signifies the process by which the spiritualized form of Osiris is extracted and magically resurrected from the pillar. The resurrected form of Osiris is symbolized by the ankh rising out of the Djed pillar.[155]

In effect, Isis and Nephthys sitting on either side of the pillar play the role of Osiris's divine nursemaids, a role deeply connected with the cult of Hathor. Indeed, Hathor and Isis possess similar divine attributes, and were often identified with one another by the ancient Egyptians. Through their magic, the divine nursemaids were able to resurrect the body of Osiris, so that he might ascend into the celestial regions.

Because Osiris was magically resurrected by his two sisters, Isis and Nephthys, they may be interpreted as symbols of the process of spiritual resurrection—a process that may have involved the use of sacred radiation devices similar to those depicted in the Temple of Hathor. In fact, the two goddesses kneeling on either side of the Djed pillar may be interpreted as divine personifications of such devices.

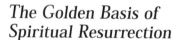

The Golden Basis of Spiritual Resurrection

This interpretation leads to another important insight. In the illustration, the two goddesses are kneeling on what appear to be raised stools or seats. These raised seats actually are depictions of the hieroglyphic sign "neb" which means "gold."

Figure 36—"Neb" the Sign for Gold

Symbolically, this indicates that the magical rejuvenative power of the two goddesses, which is the key to the entire process of spiritual resurrection, has its underlying basis in metallic gold. This has a deep alchemical meaning. As we will see later, all of the precious metals, but especially platinum, gold, and mercury, may be alchemically prepared so that they become blazing sources of celestial fire.

Regarding the alchemical nature of gold, the following discourse was presented in the *Alchemical Catechism*, a medieval work in the hermetic tradition.

> Q. How many species of gold are distinguished by the Philosophers?
> A. Three sorts:—Astral Gold, Elementary Gold, and Vulgar Gold.
>
> Q. What is astral gold?
> A. Astral Gold has its centre in the sun, which communicates it by its rays to all inferior beings. It is an igneous substance, which receives a continual emanation of solar corpuscles that penetrate

all things sentient, vegetable, and mineral.

Q. What do you refer to under the term Elementary Gold ?
A. This is the most pure and fixed portion of the elements, and of all that is composed of them. All sublunary beings included in the three kingdoms contain in their inmost centre a precious grain of this elementary gold.

Q. Give me some description of Vulgar Gold ?
A. It is the most beautiful metal of our acquaintance, the best that Nature can produce, as perfect as it is unalterable in itself.

Q. Of what species of gold is the Stone of the Philosophers ?
A. It is of the second species, as being the most pure portion of all the metallic elements after its purification, when it is termed living philosophical gold. A perfect equilibrium and equality of the four elements enter into the Physical Stone, and four things are indispensable for the accomplishment of the work, namely, composition, allocation, mixture, and union, which, once performed according to the rules of art, will beget the lawful Son of the Sun, and the Phoenix which eternally rises out of its own ashes.[156]

The esoteric connection between the Sun, the phoenix, and gold was not a medieval invention. It goes all the way back to Old Kingdom Egypt. In the ancient Heliopolitan tradition, the phoenix was known as the bennu bird, and was worshipped in the form of the benben stone, which was considered to be the concretized essence of the sun-god Atum-Re. In effect, the benben was a stone that embodied the blazing glory of the Sun. It was the original Philosopher's Stone.

The relationship between the benben stone and gold is hidden in the symbolic nature of the Egyptian language. Regarding this hidden symbolism, it has been said:

Modern language proliferates daily into new jargons, making it increasingly difficult to see the connections between fields and to express them. The language of Egypt was designed to an exactly opposite aim, with the names of things often containing clues to their inner relatedness. So, ais is the word for the physical mass of brain tissue. And the word sia (ais spelled backwards) is the word for consciousness; thus language embodies both the connection and the distinction. It obeys that cosmic principle of inversion that lies at the root of creation, which is the calling forth of matter out of spirit.[157]

In the case of the sacred stone, a similar case of inversion has been employed to convey the esoteric connection between the word *ben* "sacred stone" and the word *neb* "gold" (*ben* spelled backwards).[158] Just as consciousness *(sia)* is located within the physical mass of the brain *(ais)*, so also, gold *(neb)* is located within the physical mass of the sacred stone *(ben)*. In our opinion, the benben stone was identified with the sun-god Atum-Re because it consisted of the *living philosophical gold*—the alchemically prepared form of gold that was considered to be the "Son of the Sun."

The implication is that the two goddesses are seated on the sign for gold to indicate that the entire process of spiritual resurrection has its underlying basis in the living philosophical gold. We believe that this alchemically prepared form of gold was used not only to fabricate the sacred benben stones, but also as the source of celestial fire in the Egyptian radiation technologies.

The Giver of Eternal Life

Although no benben stones dating back to the Old Kingdom have ever been found, it is now generally believed that these sacred objects were pyramidal or conical in shape. Even though later replicas may have been made out of ordinary granite, marble, or limestone, we believe that the original benben stones were fashioned out of an alchemically prepared form of gold.

The hieroglyph that most closely represents such a conical or pyramidal object is typically used as a verb, meaning "to give" or "to bestow." Very often this verb is followed by the ankh symbol, which means "eternal life." This combination of signs is generally translated "to give eternal life."

This suggests that the conical object, whatever it was, which served as the original esoteric model for the hieroglyph "to give," was viewed by the ancient Egyptians as the "Giver of Eternal Life." Because this also was the role of the benben stone, and because the benben stone was conical in shape, it seems reasonable to assume that the "Giver of Eternal Life" was none other than the benben stone.

**Figure 37—Hieroglyph:
"To Give Eternal Life"**

**Figure 38—
The Pillar of Light**

The Pillar of Light

There is another very interesting hieroglyph that incorporates a conical object. This hieroglyph is generally translated as "pillar" or "pillar of light."

This sign may be related to the ancient Heliopolitan tradition, where the benben stone was placed upon a sacred pillar and worshipped as the embodiment of the sun-god. Did the conical object on top of the pillar represent the sacred benben stone, which was a source of celestial fire and spiritual Light? Did the original pillar of light located at Heliopolis symbolize the pillar of celestial fire that connects the Earth to the Highest Heaven at the center of the Universe?

The Chamber of Light

We suspect that the esoteric meaning of the hieroglyph illustrated above may be closer to a "chamber of light" rather than a "pillar of light." This interpretation is based upon a remarkably similar symbolic illustration found in the tomb of Huy, the viceroy to Nubia and the Sinai during the reign of King Tut—or Tut-Ankh-Amun (circa 1333–1323 B.C.).[159]

Figure 39—An Egyptian Chamber of Light

To make sense of this figure, imagine that the tall conical object at the top of the drawing is a sacred benben stone, composed of a large mound of alchemically prepared gold, capable of generating large quantities of celestial fire. This conical mound appears to be sitting in a hemispherical bowl, at the bottom of which is attached a vertical tube or shaft. The shaft descends into an indistinct region that appears to be associated with several circular symbols. It then descends further into a pair of underground chambers where two individuals are located.

Each of these underground chambers is equipped with two discharge tubes, one of which hangs down from above and another of which rises up from below. These tubes are shaped like lotus stalks, with a lotus flower on the end. This symbology is consistent with the lotus-shaped discharge heads used on the radiation devices in the Denderah engravings. Were the lotus stalks within the underground chambers symbolic of radiation discharge devices? Were they used to discharge the celestial fire generated by the benben stone above into the chambers below?

The depiction of leopard skins on either side of the chamber is clearly meant to indicate that the chambers were encased in leather or animal skins. Why would animal skins be used to encase the chambers? Is it because animal skins act as insulators of subtle matter-energy?

Metaphorically speaking, our bodies may be compared to golden cups designed to hold and retain the subtle matter-energy or celestial fire generated within them. This is true not only of the human physiology, but also of all animals and plants. The skin on the surface of the body is specifically designed to keep the subtle matter-energy from leaking out. It acts as an insulator of celestial fire. This is especially true of the skins of the big cats, which excel in their insulating properties.

That is why powerful yogis, such as Lord Shiva, like to sit on the skins of leopards and tigers. It is not for aesthetic purposes. It is for pragmatic purposes. During meditation a great deal of subtle matter-energy is built up within the system. If this subtle matter-energy remains within the body, it will engender subtle fusion reactions (tapas) within the body, and the body will become rapidly spiritualized. On the other hand, if the subtle matter-energy is allowed to leak out of the body into the ground, then the body will not evolve very quickly. The animal skins were used to provide an extra layer of insulation between the body and the ground, keeping the subtle energy from leaking out.

Apparently the same principle was employed by the ancient Egyptians in their chambers of light. In addition to the animal skins, it appears that some other kind of insulation may have been used, indicated by the stacked layers of mysterious cylindrical objects on the outer side of the leopard skins.

The remarkable thing about this depiction is its similarity with the hieroglyph that denotes a pillar of light.[160] They appear to present condensed and elaborated versions of the same object.

Figure 40—Two Versions of the Chamber of Light

The striking similarity between these two depictions is unlikely to be coincidental. Is the conical object atop the chamber the sacred benben? Was the sacred pillar at Heliopolis actually a chamber of light used by the members of the sacred academy for the purpose of spiritual regeneration?

As we have seen, the benben stone was symbolic of the bennu bird, or phoenix. According to Herodotus, the phoenix (or bennu) is said to embalm the holy ashes of its former self in an egg of myrrh, which then is carried to the Temple of the Sun-God in Heliopolis. Is the legendary egg of myrrh the sacred benben itself? Was it the Giver of Eternal Life?

The Bread of Life From other depictions of Egyptian art, it appears that the benben stone was not just incorporated into architectural sites, or used to power the chambers of light. White conical objects were also presented as an offering to the gods. In the paintings illustrating these objects, they are depicted as having subtle radiations emanating from them into the air. One such illustration is given in the drawing that immediately follows the opening vignette in the Papyrus of Ani.[161]

Figure 41—The Offerings of Ani

This illustration depicts the Scribe Ani and his wife Tutu standing before an altar table laden with various types of offerings. On top of the heap of offerings is a hemispherical bowl in which are placed three white conical objects having the same general shape as the hieroglyph "to give." We have already determined that this sign represents the benben stone, which is composed of the living philosophical gold. Do the white conical objects in the bowl represent mounds of alchemically prepared gold, which is a blazing source of celestial fire?

In the 3,500 year old painting, the white conical objects are represented as giving off subtle radiations into the air. Were these luminous radiations of celestial fire?

It turns out that the painting is embedded in a hieroglyphic text which extols and praises Osiris as the "King of Eternity, Lord of Everlasting, who passes millions of years in his lifetime."

At the end of the sacred hymn, the Scribe Ani asks for a boon. He says:

> May there be given to me bread from the House of Cool Water and
> a table of offerings from Heliopolis. . . . May the barley and emmer
> which are in it belong to the Ka of the Osiris Ani.

This reference to bread is highly symbolic. Just as ordinary bread gives physical sustenance by nourishing the gross body, the Bread of Life gives Eternal Life by nourishing the subtle body, or the Divine Ka. The ordinary bread that was prepared by the Egyptians was made from barley and emmer. These were the "seeds" that nourished the mortal physical body. The "seeds" that nourished the immortal spiritual body, on the other hand, were not ordinary food grains. They were the fully spiritualized atoms out of which the Philosopher's Stone was composed. Most likely the "seeds" consisted of alchemically prepared atoms of gold, copper, and silver. These metals were readily available to the Egyptians from their mines in the Sinai, and were probably the materials most commonly used to prepare the Stone.[162]

We believe that the sacred Stone was sometimes called "Bread" because the initiates in the sacred academy used to eat this substance to spiritually rejuvenate their subtle bodies and nourish their Divine Kas.[163] Although the consumption of the sacred Bread was kept a deep secret, the following drawing taken from ancient Egyptian temple art illustrates the point.[164]

Anubis, the divine dog, is also known as Ap-uat, the Opener of the Ways. In figure 42 he is portrayed lying on a closed chest or ark that contains an unknown treasure or mystery. As such he is given the title the "guardian of the secret." Clearly something mysterious and secret is being depicted here. What does this scene symbolize? Why is the King offering Anubis, the guardian of the secret and opener of the ways, a white conical object which is known as the white bread or white nourishment?[165]

To answer this question, let us first step back and consider the nature of animal symbolism in the Egyptian tradition. Modern scholars generally consider Egyptian animal symbolism to be a form of zoolatry in which the representation of the animal is taken as a primitive religious idol, associated with pagan nature worship. But there is a much deeper and more profound explanation.

Figure 42—Anubis, the Opener of the Ways

The divine black dog known as Anubis is depicted here lying on the chest of mysteries as guardian of the secret. The King or Pharaoh is offering him "white bread" or "white nourishment" in the form of a white conical object. Abydos, Nineteenth Dynasty.

The Egyptian seers based all of their symbolism upon the divine correspondences that they observed between certain universal principles or divine functions in the Heavens and mundane places, objects, and animals on Earth. These correspondences formed the basis of their hieroglyphic language. Having a solar nature, they used pictograms to symbolize these functions visually.

Regarding Egyptian animal symbolism in general, and the symbolism of Anubis in particular, it has been said:

Egypt's symbolism was sacred, and it was a science—an adjunct to

the sacred science of myth. It was a means of reinforcing and eluci-
dating the truths enshrined in myth in certain cases; in other cases
it was employed as the chief means for the simultaneous communication of both the essence and the detail of a given situation.

The image is concrete (bird, snake, dog, etc.), and it represents a
synthesis, a complex of qualities, functions and principles. Careful
study of the symbols usually reveals the reason why the given
symbol, and not some other, was chosen. So the bird represents
the volatile, or 'spirit'. The stork, which returns to its own nest,
hence a migratory bird par excellence, is the bird chosen for the
'soul'. The serpent symbolizes duality and dualising power. *The
dog symbolises digestion,* but given the dog's preference for
carrion over fresh meat, the choice of this symbol emphasises that
aspect of digestion which is the *transformation of dead matter
into living.* [emphasis added][166]

According to the author above, Anubis is identified with the divine function
of digestion. Thus, in tombs containing mummies, a dog's head often is
placed as a lid on the Canopic jar containing the stomach. It is all part of an
elaborate symbolism based upon divine correspondences.

Given this symbolic key, we can now make better sense of the illustration
given above. It appears that the King is offering white bread to his own
digestive system, personified as Anubis, the opener of ways. However, this
is not just ordinary bread; it is the Bread of Life. This is made clear by the
fact that the bread is shaped into a conical form. We have seen that this
form is symbolically associated with the benben stone and the hieroglyph
known as the "giver of immortal life." We suspect that the Bread of Life was
not prepared by an ordinary baker, but was prepared through an alchemical
process by the high priests. In particular, we believe that it was made out of
alchemically prepared precious metals, such as gold, silver, and copper.
These may be understood as the divine seeds, symbolized as barley and
emmer, out of which the Bread of Life was prepared.

From the depiction, it appears that the Egyptian Kings, as well as the high
priests, literally consumed the Bread of Life, offering it to their digestive
system during a sacred ritual presided over by Anubis, representing the
divine function of digestion.

Because the alchemically prepared metals were abundant sources of celestial fire, when the Bread of Life was ingested, it would fill the body with the Light of Life. The increased levels of luminous subtle matter within the body would forge new pathways throughout the physiology and increase the nourishment flowing to the Divine Ka in the heart. Once the Divine Ka was awakened, all the pathways of Heaven would become open to the soul. That is why the digestive system (Anubis) is called the Opener of the Ways. It is capable of digesting the Bread of Life, and incorporating the divine seeds into the body.

Once the ways of Heaven are open, then all the secrets of the Universe dawn in one's awareness. For this reason, Anubis also was known as the guardian of the secret. He was perched upon the chest of mysteries, the sacred ark, which contained the divine presence of God.

Anubis thus was deeply connected with the secret rites of immortality. He was considered to be the guardian or watchdog of the necropolis, where these rites were performed. He was also called the "lord of the sacred land" and "foremost of the divine chamber." This indicates the important role that the digestive system must have played in the rites of immortality.

Levitation Technology?

Based upon their ability to generate and radiate currents of celestial fire, the Egyptian Seers were able to take on gargantuan tasks that otherwise would have been impossible for ordinary mortals. Among these tasks was the construction of the enormous stone temples and Pyramids that uniquely characterize the land of Egypt.

Building the Pyramids and temples of Egypt involved the quarrying and transportation of millions and millions of huge stone blocks weighing many tons. Are we to believe that they transported these stones hundreds of miles and put them into place using ordinary manpower—without the use of wheels? Even if they floated these stones down the Nile, the idea of hauling and lifting them to the construction site, and then precisely fitting them into place using crude rollers, levers, and pulleys is almost inconceivable.

Based upon our understanding of the gravitational shielding effect of subtle matter-energy, we suspect that there may be another explanation. In particular, we believe that the Egyptians used their sacred radiation technologies to charge large blocks of stone with subtle matter-energy, or celestial fire. This conjecture is consistent with the Denderah illustrations, where the radiation devices appear to be highly portable.

Once they were charged with subtle matter-energy, the stones temporarily would be shielded, at least partially, from the gravitational field of the Earth. Depending upon the degree of the charge (i.e., the ratio of negative mass-energy to positive mass-energy), they could have been made as light as large blocks of cork.

Using this technique, stones that originally weighed tens or hundreds of tons could have been transported and placed in position by only a few men. Afterwards, as the subtle matter-energy within the stone gradually discharged into the Earth, the stone would have slowly regained its original weight. Was this how the ancient Seers constructed their megalithic monuments and temples?

The Builder Gods and the New World Order

There is mounting evidence that during the peak of the Golden Age (circa 10,500 B.C.) the members of the sacred academy mapped out various sacred sites in the Nile valley and built the Sphinx and other temples and monuments on those holy spots.[167]

These original Seers were conceived of by later generations as the "Builder Gods." According to texts inscribed upon the walls of the Temple of Edfu (circa 200 B.C.), the Builder Gods originally came from an island—the "Homeland of the Primeval Ones." After enduring a great flood, the Builder Gods resettled in the Nile valley and began to construct there a New World Order.[168]

To accomplish their mission, the Builder Gods decided to construct a huge network of light that was rooted in the Earth and yet reached towards the Heavens. This network of light was intended to serve many purposes simultaneously. It was to serve as a reflection of the celestial regions to which the Seers wanted to ascend. It was to provide a shield of luminous subtle energy that would protect and uplift the people living under its protection. And it was to serve as an architectural cryptogram, containing many esoteric secrets and hidden treasures, which would be left behind for future generations to decipher.

To construct their New World Order, the Builder Gods, or members of the sacred academy mapped out the natural patterns of subtle energy within the Earth that existed during the peak of the Golden Age (circa 10,500 B.C.). This was the time when the divine correspondences between Heaven and Earth were most fully manifest. At that time, the subtle energy patterns within the Earth were most harmoniously related to the subtle energy patterns within the Cosmos as a whole.

Mapping these subtle energy patterns did not require a geodetic survey. It was not done with surveying tools. Rather, it was accomplished by means of the subtle vision of the Seers. They simply looked for those places where the subtle energy density on the surface of the Earth was highest. Such places marked intersection points of subtle energy currents deep within the body of the Earth. These currents are known as *telluric currents*.

These high-energy spots were described as "mounds." They were conceived of as being spiritually "higher" than other places. In some cases, they were also physically higher, having a higher elevation. But this was not the main criterion for the selection of the sacred spots. The sacred spots were sacred due to the abundance of subtle matter-energy that naturally was found there.

The knowledge of the sacred spots on Earth and their divine correspondences with the sacred spots in the celestial Heavens is a deep science. It requires a fully enlightened vision, which is capable of comprehending the seven layers of universal life, and perceiving their nonlocal correspondences within the body of the Earth.

According to the Edfu texts, the one who was most qualified to carry out this spiritual survey was Thoth, the embodiment of the Divine Messenger. To identify the sacred spots, Thoth had to rely upon the wisdom of the seven

Sages—the seven universal spirits of God—who were merely aspects of his own higher Self.

According to the Edfu Texts,

> the "words of the (seven) Sages" [or seven universal spirits] were copied down by the wisdom-god Thoth into a book that codified the locations of certain "sacred mounds" along the Nile. The title of this lost book, according to the texts, was *Specifications of the Mounds of the Early Primeval Age,* and it was believed to have contained records not only of all the lesser "Mounds", or temples, but also of the Great Primeval Mound itself, the place where time had supposedly begun.[169]

The sacred mounds may be understood as the "acupuncture points" of the Earth. They were the intersection points of telluric energy in the body of the Earth, where the density of subtle matter-energy was naturally higher. It was at these sacred mounds that the members of the Sacred Academy built the various pyramids, monuments, and temples that dot the Egyptian landscape. These temples were designed to play the same role as acupuncture needles. They were designed to enliven and enhance the conduction of the telluric currents within the Earth so that the Planetary Being would become more awakened.

During the peak of the Golden Age, the temples that marked the sacred mounds probably consisted of nothing more than raised stone pillars (or chambers of light) upon which was perched a sacred benben stone.[170] The benben stones themselves may have consisted of little more than a "mound" of living philosophical gold, as illustrated in figure 39. It seems reasonable to assume that the Seers built such chambers of light (or resurrection temples) at these locations, because the density of subtle matter within the body of the Earth was highest there. This meant that the process of spiritual resurrection could be accomplished more easily and powerfully at those spots than at other locations.

Just as the Central Sun is the source of the celestial fire that illumines the Universe, so also, the benben stones served as the source of the celestial fire that illumined the land of ancient Egypt. By placing a benben on a sacred pillar at each acupuncture point, the Seers would have created a network of subtle energy, connecting all the sites, that corresponded to the subtle energy networks of both Heaven and Earth.

We suspect that the benbens were placed upon pillars (possibly Djed pillars) to electrically isolate them from the ground of the Earth. This enabled their radiations to be emitted directly into the atmosphere. The end result would have been a network of high density morphic fields, capable of reflecting the Light of Heaven, that automatically enlivened the divine correspondences between Heaven and Earth.

This network would have raised the spiritual vibration of the entire region and protected the people that lived under its umbrella from all sorts of calamities. The network of spiritual Light also would have served to attract the attention (through morphic resonance) of the most powerful and glorious denizens of Heaven. It was a sacred invocation made in stone and rooted in the body of the Earth. It laid out the cosmic blueprint for the New World Order that the pharaohs of Old Kingdom Egypt were to follow for thousands of years.

In accordance with their solar heritage, the original Egyptians chose to preserve their knowledge in symbolic, architectural, and technological forms, rather than in verbal language. Instead of sacred texts transmitted through an oral tradition, they left behind sacred objects and symbolic hieroglyphs that were imbued with the essence of their knowledge.

The Egyptian high priests are known to have constructed hidden chambers beneath their monuments. We feel certain that some of these chambers—especially those beneath the Sphinx—were used to store and preserve various sacred objects that when found will speak volumes about their sacred knowledge.

However, these chambers will not be found easily. They are watched over by powerful fields of subtle matter-energy created specifically for that purpose by the ancient Seers.

The ability to technologically create and program subtle matter fields is only one aspect of the knowledge possessed by the ancient Seers. The proverbial story of the "genie in the lamp" that is prevalent throughout the Near East is not fiction. It recalls a time when powerful subtle matter fields or nature spirits were technologically created and stored in pots, lamps, arks, or statues and programmed by the Seers and priests to perform miraculous feats.

Figure 43—The Sphinx

These subtle beings cannot be seen by the gross eyes. In fact, they may be understood as nothing other than mental phenomenon. But this does not mean that they can be dismissed as unreal. The subtle beings are "mental" in their functioning because they are formed exclusively out of chitta (subtle matter-energy)—the same stuff out of which our minds and spiritual bodies are made.

Nevertheless, they are very real, and are capable of wielding enormous influence. This influence is felt primarily on the level of mental experience. In weak minds they are easily capable of creating fear, or obsession, or confusion. Due to the influence and protection of these subtle beings, one can be certain that the ancient chambers will not be opened, despite the best efforts of modern scientists and archeologists, until the time is right. There always will be some obstacle, usually created by other people, until the appropriate time.

In spite of their technological proficiency, the Egyptian high priests could not forestall the inexorable cycles of time. They foresaw that the knowledge was going to be lost and they made their best efforts to circumvent this loss. Thus, under the scrutiny of the high priests, the Pyramid texts were compiled and inscribed upon chamber walls towards the end of the minor Treta Yuga.

The Pyramid texts constitute an elaborate array of hieroglyphic inscriptions that were inscribed on temple walls over a period of several hundred years during the Fifth and Sixth Dynasties (2465—2152 B.C.). It is believed that some parts of these texts were composed by the Heliopolitan priesthood in that era, and that other parts had been passed on since predynastic (or prehistoric) times.[171]

We suspect that these texts represent a feverish effort by the last rulers of the Old Kingdom to preserve their ancient traditions for subsequent generations. They could foresee that the knowledge was soon to be lost, and were desperate to circumvent that eventuality. In all likelihood, the Heliopolitan priesthood also broke with tradition at that time, and began to record various aspects of the sacred knowledge on papyrus scrolls.

Nevertheless, about 2150 B.C., the Old Kingdom finally fell. At this time, the knowledge of spiritual enlightenment and physical immortality was essentially lost, and true scientific understanding of the sacred technologies became obscured.

By the time the Egyptian tradition of entombment and mummification became highly popular, the true knowledge of immortality had become hidden behind a shroud of esoteric symbols, and replaced by a complicated set of superstitions. The memory of the past was preserved in the form of various esoteric texts and prescriptions, but the power and wholeness of the knowledge was lost. After the Old Kingdom dissolved, Egypt quickly devolved into a warrior society, and was subjected to long periods of foreign rule.

Between 945 B.C. and 47 B.C., Egypt was ruled successively by the Libyans, the Sudanese, the Assyrians, the Persians, and the Macedonians. By the time Egypt was conquered by Alexander the Great in 332 B.C., the ancient knowledge was little more than a legend. However, much of the ancient lore had been preserved by the Heliopolitan scribes and priests on papyrus scrolls.

These scrolls began to be collected by Ptolemy I, who became the king of Egypt after Alexander's death in 323 B.C. Even though the knowledge contained in the ancient scrolls was preserved in an esoteric style that was mostly unintelligible to the scholars of that time, the Ptolemaic kings of Egypt considered this knowledge to be one of the greatest treasures in their possession.

The Ptolemaic dynasty believed that if the esoteric knowledge contained in the scrolls could be properly interpreted and understood, the wisdom and greatness of ancient Egypt could be resurrected. As a result, the act of collecting and preserving the ancient scrolls became an obsession of the early Ptolemaic kings. The collection of scrolls continued to grow during the reign of Ptolemy II, and also during the reign of subsequent Ptolemaic rulers.

Because the Ptolemies were of Macedonian descent, they did not share the concerns of the Old Kingdom rulers and priests regarding the secrecy of the sacred knowledge. The Ptolemies had no intention to keep the sacred knowledge secret. Rather, they made an effort to dig through all the texts written by the ancient scribes in an attempt uncover the sacred knowledge. They wanted to make the sacred knowledge known to all the scholars of their day, so that the ancient glory of Egypt could be revived. That is why they built the Alexandrian library—to show off the sacred wisdom of Egypt.

During its heyday, the great library at Alexandria is said to have contained over 700,000 scrolls.[172] Unfortunately, much of this vast storehouse of ancient wisdom was lost when the library was destroyed by fire during the siege of Julius Caesar in 47 B.C., and it was utterly destroyed when the library was burned down by the Christians during the fifth century A.D.

Although the actual texts were destroyed, some vestige of the ancient Egyptian wisdom may have been preserved by the Arab and Greek scholars who studied at the great library of Alexandria prior to its destruction. It appears that these scholars brought pieces of the esoteric wisdom of ancient Egypt back to their homelands and incorporated it into their own esoteric traditions where it became known as the Hermetic art, or alchemy.

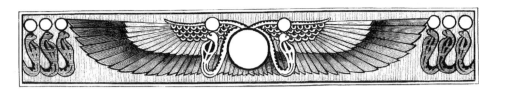

The tradition of alchemy has roots in virtually every ancient culture on the planet. The ultimate dream of the alchemist was to produce the Elixir of Life or the Philosopher's Stone. These were believed capable of transmuting the ordinary human body into a perfect, incorruptible, spiritualized body, and of transmuting ordinary metal into a perfect, incorruptible metal—gold.

The alchemists of medieval Europe considered themselves to belong to the Hermetic tradition, which purportedly was founded by the divine Seer Thoth-Hermes. According to ancient sources, Thoth-Hermes was identical to the Biblical patriarch Enoch, who in turn was identified with the Islamic prophet Idris. It appears that they are all different manifestations of the same cosmic Seer, who is none other than the Divine Messenger.

Thoth was venerated by the ancient Egyptians as the source of all wisdom. He was considered to be the inventor of the alphabet, mathematics, astronomy, astrology, geometry, and surveying. He was considered to be the namer of things yet unnamed, and the one who first taught men how to invoke the gods. In short, he was the repository of all wisdom and knowledge, and the patron of all forms of magic, invention, and science. Above all, to the followers of the Hermetic tradition, he was the father of alchemy.

The Hermetic tradition appears to have both a philosophical side and a practical, alchemical side. The philosophical side is embodied in the *Corpus Hermeticum*, a collection of treatises traditionally ascribed to Hermes Trismegistus and his immediate disciples. Although these texts are believed to have been written down sometime during the first or second century A.D., the traditional view is that they were part of a secret oral tradition that had been passed down from the earliest times. As a result, no one knows the real antiquity of these texts or who really authored them. Although these texts present a unique window into the esoteric traditions of the western Seers, very little is said in these texts about the actual practice of alchemy. They deal primarily with the spiritual and theoretical underpinnings of the Sacred Science. The practical aspects are left out.

The most distilled essence of the theory of alchemy is supposed to be contained in a short but famous text called *The Emerald Tablet*. Like the *Corpus Hermeticum,* this text was ascribed to Hermes Trismegistus. A translation is given below.

The Emerald Tablet

True it is, without falsehood, and most true,

What is below is like what is above, and what is above is like what is below,

to effect that one truly wondrous work.

And just as all things have been [derived] from the one,

by the design of the one,

so all things have been born from this one thing, by adaptation.

Its father is the sun; its mother is the moon.

The wind carried it in its belly; its nurse is the Earth.

This is the father of all works of wonder throughout the whole world.

Its power is perfect, if it shall have been turned towards the Earth.

You will separate Earth from fire, the subtle from the gross,

sweetly, with great ingenuity.

It ascends from Earth to Heaven, descends again towards Earth,

and receives the force of the things above and below.

Thus you will have the glory of the whole world.

Thereof all darkness will flee from you.

This is the strong strength of all strength,

because it will conquer everything subtle and penetrate everything solid.

Thus was the world created.

Hence will be the wondrous adaptations, of which this is the method.

And so I have been called Hermes-Trismegistus (Thrice-Great Hermes),

having three parts of the wisdom of the whole world.

What I have said about the working of the sun is complete.[173]

The earliest known version of this text was written in Syriac. The later and more complete versions were written in Latin. As before, no one knows the true antiquity and authorship of this text. Most likely it had been passed down through oral tradition for a long time before it was finally written down.

Notice that according to this text, the key to accomplishing all of the alchemical wonders depends essentially upon the divine correspondences between what is above (in Heaven) and what is below (on Earth).

The "one truly wondrous work" that is based upon these correspondences is the unification of Heaven and Earth. This is the Magnum Opus, or Great Work, that is the ultimate goal and purpose of all alchemical endeavors. On a practical level, the accomplishment of this goal involved the production of the Philosopher's Stone.

The Philosopher's Stone is a specific physical substance, which has a powdery consistency. During its preparation, the powder is said to pass through various stages associated with different colors. The colors most often mentioned are black, white and red. These powders are credited with miraculous powers.

The essential material used in the alchemical process was the chemical element mercury. Gold, silver, and sulfur also are mentioned as important sources of the sacred Stone.

In the school of Hermetic alchemy, the vessel or pot in which the alchemical process took place was required to be "hermetically sealed." This meant that the vessel was airtight, so that the vapors released during the alchemical process could not escape.

The alchemical process itself generally involved a procedure of distillation, in which the liquid was boiled, evaporated, and condensed. The Hermetic vessel or pot within which this distillation took place often was referred to as the Philosopher's Egg. This was due both to its egg-like shape, and because the Elixir or Stone was said to develop therein like an embryo in an egg. On a deeper level, the alchemical vessel represented the Cosmic Egg of the Universe as a whole. Indeed, the alchemical process was thought to mirror on a human scale the process of creation by which the Creator created the entire Universe.

Distillation may be understood as a process of evaporation and condensation. Various types of stills were developed. In one type, evaporation and condensation occurred within a single sealed vessel, in such a manner that the condensed fluids continuously were returned to the boiler. This allowed the process to take place without interruption.

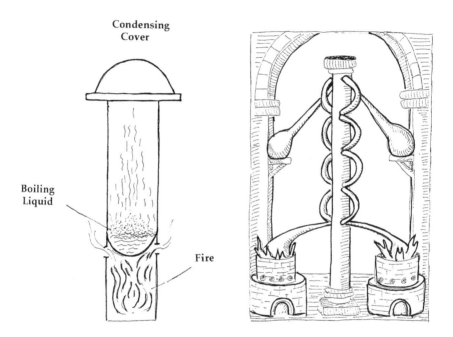

Figure 44—Alchemical Furnaces

In the illustration on the left, the alchemical furnace is built in the form of a tower with a domed roof. It has a lower chamber for holding the fire, a bowl or basin for holding the boiling liquids, and a domed top, which condenses the vapors and allows the condensed drops of liquid to drip back into the boiling pan below. In the illustration on the right, the furnaces are low brick structures into which the vessels holding the liquids are placed. The metal vapors then rise up through the collimated tubes and eventually condense into other vessels placed on the side. The condensing coils of this device were clearly designed with the shape of the Caduceus in mind.

The continuous-process type of still was an embodiment of the basic alchemical principle that the original material contains within itself all that it needs for its own nourishment, transformation, and perfection. The purpose of the alchemical procedure was to liberate the subtle life force from the gross material substance, and then feed it back to the gross substance, thereby causing the substance to grow more subtle or spiritualized. In this way, the substance could be used to nourish itself. This process was represented by the self-consuming serpent or Ouroboros.

Figure 45—Ouroboros— The Self-Consuming Serpent

The alchemical operation supposedly provided the proper conditions for this self-nourishment to take place. The material of choice for this operation was mercury, which often was symbolized as the quintessence of the serpent (subtle life force) itself.

For the material within the egg to reach perfection, it was held that it must be repeatedly subjected to the alchemical process over an extended period of time. For example, the medieval alchemists sometimes would distill the same liquid hundreds of times during the course of many months. This incubation process purportedly culminated in the production of the Elixir, Tincture, or Stone—often used as synonyms. This material then was capable of transmuting both the human body and metals, elevating them to a perfect, incorruptible, spiritualized condition.

The tradition of alchemy also has deep roots in the Vedic tradition. In the Vedic tradition, it constitutes a part of *Ayurveda*, the science of longevity. Like Thoth-Hermes, the father of this tradition is a divine personage, called Dhanvantari. Lord Dhanvantari is said to have appeared at the dawn of Creation, when the world was first churned out of the ocean of consciousness. He appeared holding a metal vessel *(kumbha)* or pot *(kalash)* filled with the Elixir of Immortality *(Amrit)*.

Figure 46—Lord Dhanvantari

Lord Dhanvantari is the bearer of the ambrosial Nectar of Immortality that is delivered to the celestial gods at the beginning of Creation. As the bearer of the divine Nectar, he may be compared to Aquarius or Ganymede, the bearer of the divine Nectar in the Roman and Greek traditions. In this light, the pot or vessel carried by Lord Dhanvantari may be viewed as nothing other than the Aquarian urn.

The Elixir of Immortality was Lord Dhanvantari's gift to the world. It represented the highest material essence generated during the process of creation, and supposedly was capable of producing perfect health, physical immortality, and spiritual enlightenment for anyone who drank it.

The practical part of Ayurveda that deals with the production of this Elixir is called *Rasayana* (The Way of Mercury). In the ancient Sanskrit texts, the word *rasa* is used synonymously for the elixir and for mercury. Other related words are Soma (the divine drink of the gods) and Amrit (Nectar of Immortality).

In Vedic alchemy, mercury was considered the ultimate key to all alchemical processes. In addition to being referred to as rasa (essence or elixir), it was variously known as *parada* (that which gives transcendence), *rasendra* (lord of the essences), and *suta* (that which engenders). It was considered to be the most powerful alchemical agent. To symbolize its creative potency, it was identified with Shiva—the field of pure consciousness that underlies the entire field of Nature. One text goes so far as to state that all the names of Shiva also are the names of mercury.[174]

Mercury is also referred to as "the semen of Shiva"—the creative energy of the Absolute. Although fully spiritualized gold may represent the highest attainment of the metals, fully spiritualized mercury transcends the category of metals altogether. It becomes a conscious living being—the very embodiment of the Light of Life itself.

According to the Vedic tradition, gold, even in its most spiritualized form, can never be as subtle as mercury. Mercury is a living embodiment of Shiva, capable of moving at will on Earth or in the air. Mercury alone was deemed to possess the supreme power of transmutation, capable of bringing about the perfection of the body *(deha siddhi)* and the perfection of metals *(loha siddhi)*.

However, ordinary mercury cannot perform this miracle. Ordinary mercury is highly toxic, and has to be purified. In order to purify mercury, it has to be repeatedly killed and resurrected. These are technical terms. According to the ancient texts, this process generally involves placing mercury in a sealed crucible along with sulfur and various other ingredients and heating it over and over again.[175] When this process is repeated many times, the mercury gradually is transformed through distinct stages to higher and higher levels of spiritual power.

Six stages of development typically are enumerated. It is said that mercury must be killed six times before it attains its highest form.[176] This is symbolic of the ascension of the soul through the six layers of universal life. As it passes from one layer to the next, the previous form of the soul is symbolically killed, only to be resurrected on a higher level. After passing through the sixth such transformation, the soul emerges triumphant in the Seventh Heaven, at the very center of the Universe, where the density of subtle matter-energy is greatest. In this way, the various stages of initiation into the Light also were ascribed to the process of purifying mercury.

Once the mercury was fully purified, it became a living embodiment of Shiva himself. It then was able to transmute hundreds, thousands, and millions of times its own weight of base metals into gold. It also was able to transmute the physical body into a state of perfect health, spiritual enlightenment, and physical immortality. In order to exercise these miraculous transmutative properties, it did not have to be consumed by either the metals or the body. It was capable of exercising its powers by its mere "smell," "smoke," "sight," or "sound."[177]

In other words, one only had to be in the presence of the fully purified mercury to experience a powerful evolutionary influence. This is not due to any chemical property of the substance. It is because the sacred material serves as a powerful generator of celestial fire. It is surrounded by a high density field of subtle matter-energy. Anything within the luminous aura of this substance thus will experience intense subtle fusion reactions, and will be elevated to higher levels of spiritual evolution.

The ancient texts thus describe the use of a stone that was made of purified mercury and placed in the mouth without being swallowed. Those who held this stone in their mouth developed extraordinary powers (siddhis) such as levitation and invisibility, powers otherwise attainable only through the arduous practice of yoga.

The relationship between mercury and the power of levitation also is indicated in other unrelated Vedic texts, which describe the construction of flying vehicles employing mercury engines as the means of propulsion. The description of this engine closely resembles the Hermetic description of the alchemical apparatus. It consisted of a sealed vessel containing mercury above, and a heating apparatus below. When the mercury was heated by controlled fire from below, the mercury developed thunder power, and with the roar of a lion, the engine lifted off the ground.

Although the process of purifying mercury has been described in a general way in both the Vedic and Hermetic texts, the secret details of this process were kept an oral secret, and this secret now has been lost. It is now time for that secret to be rediscovered and utilized for the benefit of all mankind.

Mercury also played an important role in the Chinese tradition of alchemy. In China, the alchemical tradition had its roots in Taoism. The Taoist alchemists used the theory of chi to explain alchemical transmutations. Chi is subtle matter-energy. It is the subtle electromagnetic life force that connects the physical body with the transcendental spirit. The equivalent concept in the Vedic tradition is chitta (conscious substance).

Because everything, including all material substances, are just coagulated forms of chi, the Taoists conceived a unity of substance underlying all things. By operating on the level of chi they reasoned that it should be possible to transmute one material substance into another. This is the basic idea behind Taoist transmutation theory.

Because chi is the subtle precursor of all gross material substances, and because it is the subtle matter-energy by which all mental processing occurs, it is intimately involved in the spirit-body connection, which according to the Taoist tradition is the source of all vitality, health, and longevity. Anything that increases the amount of chi within the body or increases its circulation throughout the body thus will enhance the spirit-body connection. This will increase the vitality of the system, eliminate disease, and may retard or even reverse the aging process.

The Taoist alchemists, like the Vedic alchemists, generally were focused more on the spiritual or healing aspects of the alchemical art than on transmutation. They primarily sought the Elixir of Immortality. According to the theory, the Elixir, when consumed, would generate so much chi within the body that the spirit-body connection would become perfect, giving rise to an immortal spiritualized body.

The Taoist Masters also believed that the one essential ingredient in producing the Elixir was the chemical element mercury. It turns out that the Chinese alchemists employed similar processes and substances as their Western and Vedic counterparts, and used similar equipment. They too believed that the transformation or purification of the original material involved repetitive procedures conducted over a long period of time.

There also is an ancient Hebrew tradition of alchemy. This tradition goes back to the time of Moses and the days when the Hebrews lived in Egypt. Most of us are familiar with the basic outline of the story told in the Book of Exodus. Another more elaborate version of this story is provided by Josephus, a Pharisee who lived in Jerusalem during the first century A.D. Drawing upon texts that have since been lost, Josephus wrote his *Antiquities of the Jews*, which chronicled, among other things, the life of Moses and the exodus of the Jews from Egypt. According to both Josephus and the Book of Exodus, the Jews lived in Egypt for about 400 years. It is generally believed that this took place between 1650 and 1250 B.C.[178] During that period the Hebrew people served as craftsmen, and learned many of the Egyptian metallurgical arts.

Although much of the sacred knowledge of spiritual enlightenment and physical immortality already had been lost by that time, a great deal of the practical, technical knowledge that had been developed during the Old Kingdom probably had survived, and been passed on from generation to generation by the craftsmen guilds. During their Egyptian sojourn, many of the Hebrews probably became members of these guilds and were trained in various crafts and became experts in the fields of metallurgy, gem setting, and goldsmithing.

But the true origins of Hebrew alchemy lay not with the skills of the craftsmen, but with the profound enlightenment of their spiritual leader and emancipator—Moses. According to Josephus, the birth of Moses was predicted in advance by an Egyptian "sacred scribe" who warned the

Pharaoh that this individual who was to be born among the Israelites would "surpass all men in virtue and win everlasting renown" and "abase the sovereignty of the Egyptians."[179] Accordingly, the Pharaoh commanded that all male children subsequently born to the Israelites should be cast into the river and thereby destroyed. Of course, Moses survived and was adopted by the daughter of the ruling Pharaoh, where he was instructed "in all the wisdom of the Egyptians."[180]

According to Josephus, Moses showed such wisdom and promise that he even was viewed as a potential successor to the throne. This would have entitled him to be initiated into the deepest secrets of Egyptian magic or alchemy. Although the essence of this knowledge already had been lost, Moses himself was not an ordinary student—he was destined to be a great Seer. When exposed to the ancient texts and oral traditions preserved by the Egyptian priests, he was able to penetrate into the true meanings of those texts and traditions. He discerned the truth hidden behind the esoteric symbols—and could well have single-handedly revived the lost alchemical knowledge of ancient Egypt through his own intuitive insights.

The idea that Moses possessed enormous spiritual power is clear. This was demonstrated by the various plagues that he called down upon Egypt, the parting of the Red Sea, and the subsequent destruction of the Egyptian army. Although Moses ascribed these events to the workings of God, we believe that he was the most powerful and enlightened Seer of his time. Through his own intuitive insight, and through his exposure to the ancient Egyptian secrets, we believe that he was able to revive the lost alchemical knowledge of ancient Egypt and deliver its fruits to the Hebrew people.

The first of these fruits manifested itself as the Manna, or Holy Bread, which according to the Bible miraculously appeared like hoar-frost on the ground when the Hebrew people were on the verge of starvation in the wilderness. The Biblical account of this event is quite esoteric in its description.

> That evening a flock of quails flew in and settled all over the camp, and in the morning a fall of dew lay all around it. When the dew was gone, there in the wilderness, fine flakes appeared, fine as hoar-frost on the ground. When the Israelites saw it, they said to

one another, 'What is that?', because they did not know what it was. Moses said to them, 'That is the bread which the Lord has given you to eat.'[181]

We believe that this passage presents an esoteric description of a secret alchemical process. The flock of quails may be symbolic of the process of distillation, by which the original alchemical material is first volatilized or converted into a vapor. After ascending like a flock of birds, and then cooled as by the cool desert night, the vapor particles then recondense or settle down back into a liquid or solid state. Upon heating the condensed vapor once again and drying it, as the dew would be dried by the rising Sun, a crystalline white powder "fine as hoar-frost" is left. This fine white powder was called "Bread" or "Manna" by Moses and his followers. They consumed it as a sacred food or holy substance for forty years while they were in the wilderness.

> Israel called the food manna; it was white, like coriander seed, and it tasted like a wafer made with honey.[182]

In accordance with the ancient Egyptian tradition of preserving a symbol of the sacred technology for posterity, Moses ordered that a portion of the Manna be saved for future generations.

> 'This', said Moses, 'is the command which the Lord has given:
> "Take a full omer [measure] of it [manna] to be kept for future generations, so that they may see the bread with which I fed you in the wilderness when I brought you out of Egypt."' So Moses said to Aaron, 'Take a jar and fill it with an omer of manna, and store it in the presence of the Lord to be kept for future generations.' Aaron did as the Lord commanded Moses, and stored it before the Testimony for safe keeping. The Israelites ate the manna for forty years until they came to a land where they could settle . . .[183]

The Manna was stored in a golden jar on the altar before the Ark. It became known as the "Shewbread" or the "Bread of the Presence." From the text, we know that the Bread of the Presence had to be prepared.

Who prepared the Bread of the Presence? Clearly it could not prepared by ordinary bakers because it was not made out of wheat or barley. So who was competent to prepare it? It turns out that Moses specifically asked Bezalel to prepare the Bread of the Presence. Why? Because he was an expert metallurgist and goldsmith.

> Moses said to the Israelites, 'Mark this: the Lord has specially chosen Bezalel, son of Uri, son of Hur, of the tribe of Judah. He has filled him with divine spirit, making him skilful and ingenious, expert in every craft, and a master of design, whether in gold, silver, and copper, or cutting precious stones for setting, or carving wood, in every kind of design.[184]

Bezalel was commanded by Moses to instruct the artisans and oversee their work in the construction of the following items:

> The Tabernacle, its tent and covering, fasteners, planks, bars, posts, and sockets, the Ark and its poles, the cover [of the Ark] and the Veil of the screen, the table, its poles, and all its vessels, and the *Bread of the Presence* . . . [emphasis added][185]

The Bread of the Presence was the Manna that was stored in a golden vessel in the presence of the Lord. It was ritualistically consumed by the high priests who tended to the Ark. Because the Bread of the Presence was consumed, it had to be continually replenished by Bezalel, who knew the alchemical secrets of how to prepare it. Because the white powder consisted of spiritualized precious metals, who would be better suited to this task than an expert metallurgist?

In this manner, we believe that the Hebrew tradition of alchemy goes back to the time of Moses and Bezalel, who ultimately received their training and education in the Egyptian tradition of knowledge. From that time forward, the sacred knowledge was preserved among the Levite priests within the Hebrew tradition. According to traditional sources, this knowledge was eventually lost when the first temple of Solomon was looted and destroyed by Nebuchadnezzar in 587 B.C.

Although it is clear from written records that alchemy was widely practiced with varying degrees of success in the ancient Egyptian, Greek, Islamic, Judeo-Christian,

Vedic, and Taoist cultures, what has been passed down as "alchemy" over the last 2,500 years represents little more than a vague memory of the Sacred Science and its associated technologies.

Because alchemists during the Dark Age (714–1914 A.D.) did not possess the complete knowledge, and because the time was not propitious, their efforts generally were in vain. As a result, in Europe the alchemists often were derided as failures and charlatans. With the advent of modern science, which tried to divorce itself from the subjective or spiritual aspect of life, the whole esoteric tradition of alchemy eventually was thrown out as "false science." This attitude persists today. The fulfillment of the alchemists' dream thus was destined to wait until the onset of the Aquarian Age, which is almost upon us.

Once again, this is not by chance. The Age of Aquarius is specially marked. It is destined to be the time when the knowledge of alchemy once again will become manifest in human awareness. This was clearly known to the ancient Seers.

For example, in the Greek tradition, Aquarius was considered the Water Bearer of the god Zeus. The symbol of Aquarius thus depicts a robed man holding a pot from which a stream of liquid is being poured. This is not any ordinary liquid. It is the ambrosial drink of the gods—it is the Nectar of Immortality.

In Greek mythology, Aquarius also is identified with Ganymede, the cupbearer of the gods and the very embodiment of youth and beauty. The story is that Ganymede was swept up to Heaven by Zeus, who had assumed the form of a divine eagle. In Heaven, he was raised to the status of an immortal. Thereafter he carried the golden cup from which the gods drank the Nectar of Immortality.

We have already seen that in the Vedic tradition, the Amrit—the Nectar of Immortality—was contained in the pot or urn that was delivered to the gods by Lord Dhanvantari. This pot is none other than the Aquarian urn which pours out its ambrosial fluid at the beginning of each new Golden Age.

During the Age of Aquarius the Nectar of Immortality comes to enlighten the masses. It comes in two ways. It comes as the celestial stream that is poured by the gods from the urn of Aquarius. This descends upon the Earth in the form of the universal stream of celestial fire. In addition, it is delivered to humankind through an alchemical process.

Figure 47—Aquarius—The Water Bearer of the Gods

The illustrations above are Greek and Egyptian depictions of Aquarius, respectively.

The advent of the celestial stream is out of our hands. It is in the hands of the gods. But the development and utilization of the alchemical Stone is our responsibility. The gods can inspire us with knowledge, but it is our job to take that knowledge and act upon it. It is our job to produce and utilize the sacred alchemical Stone for the benefit of the world.

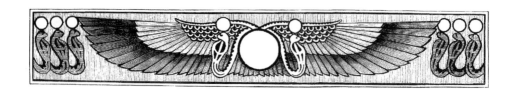

Although the alchemical process has remained one of the most closely guarded secrets of the ages, we believe that it is now time for it to be revived. The revival of this knowledge will mark a profound turning point in the history of the human race.

In essence, the alchemical process represents a process of spiritualizing atomic matter. It represents a process of increasing the amount of celestial fire generated by the atomic elements.

The complete spiritualization of matter is the ultimate goal of Creation. It is the Great Work, the Magnum Opus, that is enjoined upon all the workers of light throughout the Universe. Through this one process both the goal of material Creation and the goal of spiritual evolution simultaneously are satisfied.

In the Vedic tradition, the Great Work is called Yagya (offering). Yagya may be defined generally as any prescribed performance that serves to unite Heaven and Earth. It is considered a prescribed performance because it is based upon the divine correspondences that exist between Heaven and Earth. Because the Seers alone are capable of comprehending these correspondences, they alone are competent to prescribe the actions that are capable of uniting Heaven and Earth.

Such actions generally are considered to be ritualistic because they are performed over and over again according to prescribed rules. Regarding the performance of Yagya there are the following passages:

Having created mankind along with the Yagyas, the Creator anciently said: "By this [Yagya] may you bring forth [abundance]; may this fulfill all of your desires. By this may you nourish the celestial gods, may the celestial gods nourish you. By nourishing each other you shall attain the highest Good."[186]

Through Yagya the celestial gods [Devas] have ascended to
    Heaven.
Through Yagya they have gained victory over the terrestrial gods
    [Asuras].
Through Yagya adversaries become friends.
Yagya is the foundation of everything.
That is why it is said, that Yagya is the highest.[187]

In the rich mythological lore of the Vedic tradition, there is a prominent myth that tells the story of Creation. Although this myth applies generally to all scales in Creation, it relates specifically to the creation of the galaxy, which was conceived by the ancient Seers as a miniature Universe.

It is said that the creation of the galaxy involves the performance of a great ritual or Yagya. This particular ritual is not performed by human beings. It is performed by the subtle beings—the Devas and Asuras—corresponding to the celestial and terrestrial gods.

At the time when the great Yagya is performed, the gross structure of the galaxy does not yet exist. The galaxy then exists only in a subtle form. The subtle form of the galaxy may be understood as a hierarchically structured subtle matter field that has its own fine structure, consisting of many subfields linked together by various rays of celestial fire.

The fine structure of the galactic subtle matter field is composed of two types of subfields—unpolarized and polarized. The unpolarized fields correspond to the subtle bodies of the celestial gods (Devas). The polarized fields, on the other hand, correspond to the subtle bodies of the terrestrial gods and nature spirits (Asuras).

271

On the scale of the galaxy as a whole, the Devas and the Asuras represent huge collective fields of subtle matter-energy. These fields include within themselves all the individual souls that eventually will incarnate into physical Creation.

In particular, the Devas include within themselves the souls of all the more or less enlightened beings that eventually will inhabit the luminous stars and Worlds of Light throughout the galaxy.

The Asuras include within themselves the souls of all the more or less unenlightened beings that eventually will dwell on terrestrial, nonluminous planets like our own. They also include the souls of all those that eventually will dwell in the worlds of darkness that lie beyond the outer rim of the galaxy.

Figure 48—The Churning of the Milky Ocean

This illustration symbolizes the rotation of the galactic subtle matter field, consisting of both the Devas and the Asuras, around the center of the galaxy. The churning process is symbolic of the Great Work, designed to unify the celestial and terrestrial, or unpolarized and polarized forces of Nature.

Prior to the creation of the galaxy, the individual souls remain asleep, but their collective forms are awake. It is these collective beings that the ancient Vedic Seers referred to as the Devas (celestial beings) and the Asuras (terrestrial beings). They are responsible for performing the great Yagya that eventually gives rise to the creation of the galaxy.

The great Yagya is conceived of as the cosmic process of churning the Milky Ocean. The Milky Ocean represents the intergalactic subtle matter field in which all the Devas and Asuras are embedded. In the beginning, the density of subtle particles within this intergalactic field is extremely low. To begin to manifest the structure of the galaxy, the subtle matter density of this field must be increased and concentrated towards the center of the galaxy. To accomplish this purpose, the Devas and the Asuras begin to churn the Milky Ocean.

The purpose of the churning process is to churn out the Amrit—the Nectar of Immortality. The Amrit represents the concentrated form of subtle matter-energy that emerges at the center of the galaxy through the cosmic churning process.

In order to churn the Milky Ocean, the cosmic mountain is used as a churning rod or axis, and Vasuki, the divine serpent, is used as a rope. The Devas and the Asuras then exert themselves to make the cosmic mountain rotate or spin on its axis.

A similar motif was used in the Egyptian tradition to represent the process by which Upper and Lower Egypt were unified. In the Egyptian portrayal (see figure 49), the churning rod appears to be an upright pillar or drill, called the *sma*. It was operated by Horus (on the left), and Set (on the right). Horus may be understood as the representative of all the celestial forces, while Set may be understood as the representative of all the terrestrial forces. Although the churning process is conventionally interpreted in a political context as representing the unification of Upper and Lower Egypt, its true esoteric significance is the unification of Heaven and Earth.

Although both the Vedic and Egyptian representations of the churning process employ the analogy of a mechanical churning rod or drill, the actual churning process itself is not mechanical. Initially, the rotation of the subtle matter fields is initiated through the collective intentions of the Devas and the Asuras.

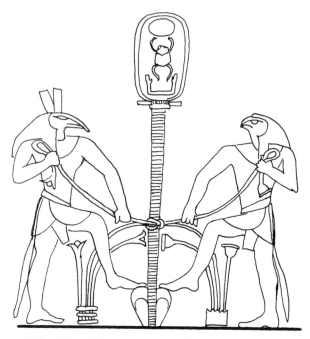

Figure 49—The Unification of Upper and Lower Egypt

As a result of the intentions of the Devas and Asuras, vast swirling currents of subtle matter-energy are set into motion around the galactic center. These swirling currents give rise to a huge whirlpool of subtle matter-energy in intergalactic space. This cosmic whirlpool spans hundreds of thousands of light-years and marks off the future domain of the evolving galaxy.

At the center of this cosmic whirlpool is a point of silence and stillness, resembling the eye of a hurricane. The silent stillness of the physical vacuum within this region represents the very heart of the Galactic Being. It is the fecund womb into which the divine seed is deposited, and from which the Light of Life emerges.

Although the swirling currents that surround the galactic heart are formed of tiny particles of subtle matter-energy, each one of which is much lighter and smaller than an electron, because of the vastness of the galactic currents, the amount of mass that is set into rotation around the heart of the galaxy is astronomically huge.

Under the influence of this rotating mass, the physical vacuum at the heart of the whirlpool spontaneously undergoes a phase transition. It begins to manifest new particles of subtle matter from within itself, and becomes a fountainhead of celestial fire. The particles of subtle matter (chitta) issuing forth from the galactic heart are extracted from the unmanifest field of primordial matter-energy *(Prakriti)* that underlies and pervades the entire Creation. These particles represent the most subtle grade of matter-energy to emerge from the field of primordial Nature.[188]

Through this spontaneous creation of subtle matter-energy, the density of celestial fire at the center of the galaxy continuously grows, until eventually it begins to reflect universal pure consciousness. This represents the first drop of Amrit to be generated by the churning actions of the Devas and Asuras. It represents the awakening of the Divine Ka for the galaxy as a whole.

This same churning process then is repeated over and over again on smaller scales to develop the Divine Kas of all the stars throughout the galaxy. Each star may be understood as having its own domain within the larger galactic field. As more and more matter and energy is churned out of the Milky Ocean through the actions of the Devas and Asuras, the density of the galactic subtle matter field continues to increase. This gives rise to intense subtle fusion reactions, which eventually culminate in the formation of the elementary particles and atoms, out of which the gross forms of the planets and stars are formed. This additional mass continues to rotate around the center of the galaxy, and thus adds more and more power to the churning process.

Ultimately, the churning process is ubiquitous. It is inherent in all forms of revolving or rotating mass everywhere throughout the Universe on all scales of time and space. The revolution of galaxies around the center of the Universe, of stars around the galactic center, of planets around stars, and of nucleons around the center of the atomic nucleus—all provide the churning action needed to generate the Amrit, the most concentrated form of celestial fire that reflects pure consciousness.

As the most concentrated form of subtle matter-energy, the Amrit represents the end result or culmination of the churning process.

In the Vedic myth, at the end of the churning process, Lord Dhanvantari appears holding an urn. This urn contains the Nectar of Immortality that is to be distributed among the celestial gods.

Lord Dhanvantari may be seen as the Vedic representation of Aquarius, the Water Bearer of the gods. The urn that he carries in his hands contains the ambrosial fluid, the Nectar of Immortality, which nourishes and gives immortality to the gods. From this perspective, we see that the Vedic myth has an alchemical significance tied to our own epoch—the Age of Aquarius. It is during the Age of Aquarius that the knowledge of how to produce the Nectar of Immortality dawns in human awareness.

Human beings can produce the Nectar of Immortality by imitating the actions of the Devas and the Asuras on our own scale of behavior. How can this be accomplished? It is clear that human beings cannot control the motions of the planets, stars, and galaxies. The celestial churning process thus must be left to the gods.

However, human beings can control the motions of elementary particles and atoms. We already have demonstrated this in our modern technologies. But in order to produce the most powerful churning action on the vacuum, human beings must master the movements of the nucleons (protons and neutrons) within the nucleus of the atom. Protons and neutrons represent the most concentrated forms of mass known to man. They are spinning around inside atomic nuclei at enormous speeds.

Unlike the rotating arms of a windmill, or the spinning wheel of a bicycle, the spinning motions of nucleons with the atomic nuclei are truly perpetual. These spinning motions are not slowed down by friction. The whirling of nucleons within the nucleus may continue for millions and even billions of years without diminishing in any way.

Although these particles are already spinning at enormous speeds, in a typical atomic nucleus the spinning motions of the nucleons largely cancel one another out, and their potential churning action on the vacuum thus is minimized.

The alchemical process is designed to maximize the churning potential inherent within the nucleus of certain atoms—the heavy, precious metals—so that these atoms become transformed into blazing sources of celestial fire. This is the key to understanding the alchemical process and the true nature of the Philosopher's Stone.

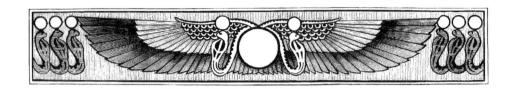

The alchemical process may be understood as a type of yagya or ritual action that mimics the process of Creation and enhances the evolution of the entire Universe. It increases the density of subtle matter-energy in Creation by maximizing the churning potential inherent in certain types of atoms.

To maximize the churning potential of an atom, it must be raised to the status of an enlightened atom. The alchemical process thus may be understood as enhancing the rate of atomic evolution, giving rise to enlightened or fully spiritualized atomic matter.

This concept of atomic evolution is radically different from that which is taught in standard physics. To understand this new (but actually ancient) concept of atomic evolution, we must revise our picture of an atom. The atomic elements are not just inert lifeless chunks of matter. They are tiny living beings. Like all living beings, the atomic beings represent evolving systems.

In order to survive and evolve, each atom must have an ample supply of "food." The food that is consumed by the atoms consists of chitta or luminous subtle matter. All atoms continuously consume and emit streams of subtle matter to sustain their very existence. They consume subtle matter, digest it, and then emit it back into the environment as a waste product.

Atoms not only consume subtle matter from the environment, but they also generate subtle matter from within themselves. We know from modern physics that the nucleus of every atom contains a certain number of nucleons within itself. The nucleons can either be positively charged particles, called protons, or neutral particles, called neutrons. As stated previously, the nucleons are whirling around inside the nucleus at enormous speeds.

For the last fifty years or so, modern physicists have tapped the energy of the nucleus through the processes of thermonuclear fusion and fission. Unfortunately, these processes are extremely violent, and may produce negative side effects for organic life. Such processes naturally occur at the heart of the Sun, where no organic life exists. That is their natural place in the scheme of things. If we try to import such processes onto the surface of the Earth, we are creating an unnatural situation that can be detrimental to the forms of life that exist on the Earth.

Although nuclear energy as it has been developed by modern physics is clearly an inappropriate technology for the planet, this does not mean that the energy of the nucleus cannot be harnessed in appropriate ways. We simply must find a way to tap this energy that is more natural and conducive to the evolutionary processes on our planet.

It turns out that the ancient Seers developed a method to tap the energy of the nucleus in all of their subtle matter technologies. The energy of the nucleus can be harnessed by taking advantage of the subtle matter-energy that naturally is generated by the whirling motions of the nucleons. This is the source from which the ancient Seers derived their currents of celestial fire. Furthermore, this source is completely inexhaustible.

The nucleus of every atom is a tiny dynamo that continuously churns out additional matter and energy from the physical vacuum in the form of subtle charged particles. These particles possess both yin (feminine) and yang (masculine) charge, and constitute the field of chitta or chi that is the basis for all mental and physical phenomena. The reason that these particles have not been detected by modern scientific equipment is because they are extremely subtle. They are far too subtle to be detected by ordinary particle detectors. Another reason why these particles have not been detected is that the majority of atoms on our planet are poor generators of subtle matter-energy.

In order to increase the amount of subtle matter-energy generated by the atoms, the churning potential of the atoms must be maximized. When the churning potential of a collection of atoms becomes maximized, the amount of subtle matter generated by the atoms may become so large that unusual and miraculous effects begin to be observed. This is what happens in the case of the sacred Stone.

The churning potential of an atom is directly related to its level of spiritual evolution. The more evolved the atom, the more powerful are its churning actions, and the more celestial fire will be emanated in its presence. Because the alchemical Stone consists of enlightened atoms, it is a blazing source of celestial fire.

In some cases, the emanations of the Stone may become so intense that the Stone displays a fluorescent-like glow. With even higher rates of discharge, the Stone may disappear from physical sight in a blinding flash of light, ascending into a higher realm of spiritual existence.[189]

The materials from which the alchemical Stone is prepared generally consist of various metals, especially the precious metals. These metals include copper, nickel, palladium, silver, platinum, gold, and mercury as well as less well-known elements such as osmium, iridium, and rhodium.[190] The precious metals are used as sources of the Stone because they possess a large number of nucleons, and because they lie at the center of the periodic table of elements.[191]

This last bit of information is rather technical. The elements at the center of the periodic table have about as many filled electron shells as empty ones. Such atoms are inherently unstable, and as a result, their nuclei may be subject to deformation and spontaneous fission.[192]

An ordinary nucleus displays a spherical shape. Deformed nuclei have been categorized into three classes: (i) deformed, (ii) superdeformed, and (iii) hyperdeformed. Although these nuclear configurations sound strange, they actually represent higher states of atomic evolution, and can easily be envisioned. Roughly speaking, a deformed nucleus has the shape of an egg; a superdeformed nucleus has the shape of a football; and a hyperdeformed nucleus has the shape of a banana.

In an ordinary spherical nucleus, the rotations of nucleons within the nucleus may occur in any and all directions with equal probability. This means that the nucleons typically do not display cooperative motions in churning the vacuum. They are all churning in different directions.

In a deformed or superdeformed nucleus, the nucleons have a higher probability of rotating around the same long axis. This increases their cooperative efforts, and enhances the churning power of the atom. Within such atoms, the nucleons not only revolve much more quickly and regularly than in ordinary atoms, but their angular momenta combine to produce a powerful churning action upon the vacuum.

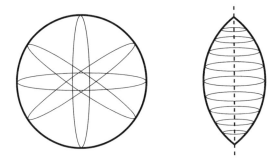

Figure 50—Ordinary and Superdeformed Nuclei

An ordinary nucleus has a spherical shape. A superdeformed nucleus is defined as a nucleus that has been elongated into a shape, resembling a football, that has a 2:1 ratio between its length and breadth. The nucleons within such nuclei spin with greater speed and regularity than nucleons in ordinary spherical nuclei. This enhances the stirring action of the nucleus on the all-pervading ocean of consciousness.

The alignment of rotations within deformed (or high-spin) nuclei maximizes the churning potential of the atom. When this occurs, the atom becomes a powerful source of celestial fire. Such atoms may be understood as enlightened atoms.

From a practical point of view, there may be many different methods of producing such enlightened atoms. The classical alchemical texts state that the Stone may be produced in bulk by mixing the precious metals with various herbs and chemicals, and repeatedly heating the mixture in a closed crucible. It is said that when the precious metals are subjected to this fairly simple process, they eventually undergo a change of state and assume the form of the alchemical Stone or Ash.

Modern alchemical researchers hold that when the process is complete, the metal no longer looks like a metal. It is transformed into a white, salt-like powder.[193]

The Vedic Seers called this powder *bhasma* (Ash), because it resembled a fine white ash, and because it was the final product left over when ordinary matter was exposed repeatedly to the fiery process of tapas or spiritual evolution. The Hebrews called the powder Manna or the Bread of the Presence. And the medieval alchemists called it the alchemical Salt or the Philosopher's Stone.

The Philosopher's Stone was revered by the ancient Seers as both the Salt of the Earth and the Foundation of Heaven. It represents the most fully spiritualized state of atomic matter. Even more, the Stone is not only charged with celestial fire, but it also is a self-sufficient generator of celestial fire. Every individual atom out of which the alchemical Stone, Salt, or Ash is composed is an intense generator of celestial fire. It is capable not only of supplying its own internal needs, but it is capable also of supplying the subtle matter needs for a large number of other atoms in its environment.

The power and value of this fully spiritualized atomic substance cannot be overestimated. As the most highly evolved form of matter in the Universe, and an intense source of celestial fire, the alchemical Salt, Stone, or Ash may serve as the ultimate source of subtle matter-energy for the new Golden Age.

Once this spiritualized white powder has been precipitated, it is capable of continuously generating large quantities of subtle matter-energy without requiring any further input of energy for long periods. It thus represents the ultimate "superfuel" of the future. This superfuel may provide an endless source of subtle energy to run all of the sacred technologies of the new Golden Age.

It also may be used to spiritually rejuvenate the human physiology. When the human body develops a certain proportion of such enlightened atoms within itself, it becomes flooded with spiritual Light and the individual human soul automatically becomes enlightened.

When the body of a planet like the Earth develops a certain proportion of such atoms within itself, the planet as a whole attains the state of planetary enlightenment—and becomes a permanent World of Light. It thus is no exaggeration to say that the alchemical Stone has the power to transform the Earth into a Heavenly Paradise. Because this transformation is the ultimate goal of all forms of human civilization, the production and utilization of the alchemical Salt, Stone, or Ash should be viewed as an essential key to the advancement of human society on our planet.

Although this knowledge has been lost for thousands of years, it is now time for it to resurface in our awareness once again. The time has come when all the sacred knowledge that has been buried beneath the sands or hidden behind closed doors must come forth and be seen in the light of day. It is time for the white Stone to be given to humanity once more. Thus, the Revelation of John states:

> To him who is victorious I will give some of the hidden manna; I
> will give him also a white Stone, and on the Stone will be written
> a new name, known to none but him that receives it.[194]

The time has come for us to receive the white Stone—the Stone that is filled with pure consciousness and imbued with the Word of God. When we have received this Stone, our souls will become filled with spiritual Light and we will begin to experience the sublime spiritual sounds of Heaven—the so-called music of the spheres—within our awareness.

Then we will know our own higher Selves, cognize our true spiritual names, and reclaim our birthright as the sons and daughters of immortality. This is the ultimate destiny of every human being on Earth. However, whether this destiny will occur sooner or later may very well depend upon the personal choices that each of us makes over the next few years.

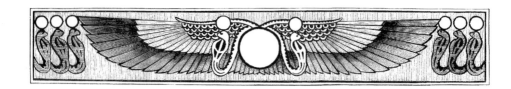

The technological process of preparing the sacred Stone was not the most important part of the sacred alchemical science. It was considered the lower knowledge. The higher knowledge concerned the process by which spiritual enlightenment and physical immortality were developed within the human soul. These two fields of knowledge also were known as the outer and the inner alchemy.

To achieve spiritual enlightenment and physical immortality, the ancient Seers of the previous Golden Age combined their knowledge of practical alchemy with their knowledge of the divine correspondences between Heaven and Earth. They used this knowledge to perform the sacred rites of immortality.

During the rites of immortality, the ancient Seers would either consume the sacred alchemical preparations (the Bread and the Nectar), or bathe in the radiations of the Stone, so that their bodies would naturally become filled with spiritual Light.

Having filled the mind and body with spiritual Light, the Seers then would invoke the Divine Archetypes present in the Highest Heaven into their minds and bodies, so that they would become perfect embodiments of Divine Life. This invocation generally was performed mentally using sacred sounds and visual symbols. These sounds and symbols corresponded to the divine names and forms that were being invoked. This is how the ancient Seers enlivened the divine correspondences between Heaven and Earth within their own souls.

Unlike the performance of external rituals, these rites were not performed for the sake of fulfilling some worldly desire. They were performed only for the sake of gaining spiritual enlightenment and physical immortality.

In general, the rites of immortality involved two steps. First, the Seers would "offer" the sacred alchemical substance—the food of the gods—into the fire of their own digestion. By doing so, the high-spin metal atoms inherent in the sacred substances would be incorporated into their physiologies. The result was that their bodies became filled with a high density field of celestial fire or spiritual Light, and they experienced a profound state of pure consciousness.

We have seen that in some cases, especially in the West, the Seers also would bathe in a high density field of subtle matter-energy, or celestial fire, generated by external radiation devices. By exposing their bodies to this high density field of celestial fire, the Seers could rapidly charge their bodies and minds with subtle matter-energy, and become filled with spiritual Light. By combining the method of internal ingestion with the method of external exposure, the Seers of the Egyptian tradition developed very powerful methods to spiritually rejuvenate the body and soul of any qualified initiate.

Once the body was filled with the light of pure consciousness, the Seer then would enliven the divine correspondences between Heaven and Earth within his or her own unbounded awareness through the performance of mental techniques, often employing sacred mantras. During such sacred rituals the awareness of the Seers would become filled with the ineffable glory of Heaven, and they themselves would become embodiments of the celestial gods.

In some instances, the physiologies of the Seers would become so spiritualized and filled with divine glory that they would physically levitate and disappear in a flash of light. They would then be free to physically ascend into the fathomless bosom of Heaven or remain on Earth. Such ascended Seers were called *Siddhas* or "perfected ones."

It appears that the food of the gods was prepared differently in different regions. In some communities the divine food was prepared as a liquid. In others, it was prepared as a powder or paste that was formed into wafers or cakes, and then consumed like bread. Regardless of how it was prepared, the sacred substance was considered the ambrosial food of the gods. It gave the people enlightenment, perfect health, and physical immortality.

In the ancient spiritual traditions of Egypt and the Middle East, the spiritualized substance was known as the Bread of Life or the Water of Life. According to the clay tablets found in ancient Sumer (circa 2900 B.C.), the Bread of Life and the Water of Life were considered miraculous substances capable of restoring life even to a dead corpse.[195]

The Egyptians referred to the food of the gods as bread and ale. But this was not ordinary bread and ale. It was divine food. This divine food was administered to the pharaohs in preparation for their ascension into the immortal realms.

In the Hebrew tradition during the time of Moses, the spiritualized substance was known as the "Bread of the Presence," the "Shewbread," or the spiritual Manna.

In the Vedic tradition, the spiritualized substance was known as Soma—the elixir of immortality. In the Taoist tradition, it was known as the Golden Elixir of Life (*Chin-tan*—literally "golden ball" or "golden pill").

Although the secret methods for preparing these sacred substances were lost long before the Christian tradition began, the Christian mass, which involves drinking the "blood" of Christ, and eating the "body" of Christ, is symbolic of these ancient long-forgotten rituals that involved eating and drinking spiritualized substances.

These substances were not hallucinogens. They were spiritualized alchemical substances. They derived their spiritual potency from the overabundance of subtle matter-energy that they possessed. Because of the subtle matter-energy inherent in these substances, the enlightened Seers who regularly partook of them were raised to the status of gods and obtained immense spiritual power. Through these substances, the ancient Seers refined their gross physical bodies into celestial bodies. In addition to developing certain supernormal abilities, and spiritual enlightenment, they attained great longevity. They lived for hundreds and even thousands of years. The ancient spiritual and religious traditions around the world are filled with examples of such long-lived individuals.

For example, in the Book of Genesis it is stated that all of the original Biblical patriarchs lived for hundreds of years: Seth lived for nine hundred and twelve years; Kenan lived for nine hundred and ten years; Mahalalel lived for eight hundred and ninety-five years, Methuselah lived for nine hundred and sixty-nine years, etc.[196] How did these individuals achieve such extended life spans? Is it possible that the Biblical patriarchs were aware of a secret science of immortality—a science that has since been lost?

In addition to attaining great longevity on Earth, some of the greatest Seers actually attained an immortal status and ascended into the celestial regions, taking their physical bodies with them. In the process of ascension, their gross bodies literally were consumed in a blazing conflagration of celestial fire, and they became fully spiritualized beings of light.

Such instances are noted in the ancient records of most of the major religions. For example, in the Old Testament, both Enoch and Elijah are said to have ascended to Heaven without physically dying.

In the Book of Genesis, it is stated that Enoch, the sixth descendant from Adam, and the great grandfather of Noah, lived for

> three hundred and sixty five years. Having walked with God, Enoch was seen no more, because God had taken him away.[197]

Enoch is a mysterious figure who was greatly revered by esoteric traditions throughout North Africa and the Middle East. Although little mention is made of him in the standard version of the Old Testament, there is an ancient apocryphal book ascribed to him in which he describes his ascension into Heaven.[198]

In the esoteric traditions, Enoch was believed to be identical with Thoth or Hermes Trismegistus—the Divine Messenger—who also was credited as being the father of alchemy. This suggests a link between Enoch and the science of alchemy. Is it possible that Enoch attained his immortal and celestial status by alchemically producing and then consuming the sacred white Stone?

Interestingly, there are additional links between Enoch and the sacred Stone. According to both the Jewish historian Josephus and the esoteric Masonic lore, Enoch was concerned that the sacred knowledge was going to be lost at the time of the flood. To prevent the sacred knowledge from being destroyed and to preserve it for future generations, Enoch excavated nine underground vaults somewhere in Canaan (modern Israel, Lebanon, and Syria), and concealed the Grand Secret, engraved on a sacred white Stone, deep in the bowels of the Earth.[199]

Although the location of this site is now unknown, we suspect that Enoch's underground chambers may be found beneath the huge stone platform at Baalbek, an ancient holy site that is located in the Bekaa valley in the mountains of Lebanon. This was the site where the Romans chose to build the largest temple complex in the entire Roman empire. The Roman temple was built upon a huge stone platform or foundation that contains some of the largest blocks of quarried stone of antiquity. A number of these stones exceed 600 tons. By comparison the largest stones used in constructing the Valley Temple and Pyramids at Giza barely exceed 200 tons. The largest stones at Stonehenge are only 54 tons.

Although modern scholars believe that this foundation was constructed by the Romans, the local legends hold that the great stones of Baalbek were put into place long before the Romans arrived. Some of these legends claim that the stones were put into place before the great flood, and that the site was originally named "Enoch."[200] Was this the place where Enoch buried the sacred white Stone? Was the "Grand Secret" engraved upon this Stone the secret of immortality?

The other individual described in the Old Testament as ascending into Heaven was Elijah. Elijah was a Biblical prophet who lived after the time of King Solomon. According to Kings II, Elijah knew in advance that he was going to ascend into Heaven. After informing his son Elisha of this fact, Elijah tried to slip away, but his son would not leave his side. Knowing that the time of ascension was near, they were walking and talking together, when suddenly there appeared chariots of fire and horses of fire, which separated them one from the other, and Elijah was carried up in the whirlwind to heaven.[201]

This whirlwind was not an ordinary whirlwind. It was a fiery tornado—a pillar of celestial fire. Although Elijah ascended to Heaven, he did not die. Even today, it is a common Jewish custom to set an extra place for the prophet Elijah at the table, for he is considered to be still alive.

Perhaps the most well-known example of one who physically ascended into Heaven is Jesus Christ. The essential mystery of Christ lies in his victory over death. According to the reports of his disciples, after Christ died on the cross his body was placed in a cave. Later the body of Christ was miraculously resurrected. When they looked for him he could not be found. His body had disappeared from the cave. When he finally appeared to the disciples, he did so by passing through locked doors.[202] The disciples were shocked and startled by this, and thought they must have been seeing a ghost. But Jesus assured them that he was no ghost. He said: "Touch me and see; no ghost has flesh and bones as you can see that I have."[203] Although the disciples could touch and feel his body, it was no longer a mere mortal body. It had been transfigured, transformed into a celestial body. It had been transformed into a vehicle of light that was capable of physically ascending into Heaven. After talking with the disciples, it is reported that Jesus "was taken up into Heaven, and he took his seat at the right hand of God."[204]

Similar examples can be found in the Vedic literature. In one instance, it is said that when Shukadeva, the son of Vyasa, physically ascended, the whole Cosmos resounded with a loud noise as though the Cosmic Egg itself had cracked open.

The Vedic literature is filled with numerous examples of individuals who have attained enlightenment and various supernormal powers, and who have developed the ability to live for many thousands of years. Many of these examples pertain to the exalted individuals who have lived on the permanent Worlds of Light throughout our galaxy. The history of the Earth included in the Vedic literature pertains to the true Earth World, of which our own planet is just a small part. To the Vedic Rishis, the true Earth World was none other than the entire galaxy.

Examples of spiritual ascension are found in all the ancient traditions because the process of ascension was experienced by ancient Seers all around the world. Fundamentally, the mechanics of ascension are related to the density of subtle matter-energy within the body. As the density of subtle matter-energy or celestial fire increases within the body, subtle fusion reactions begin to occur. This increases the sattvic nature of the body, and it generates intense heat (tapas). It also profoundly alters the nature of the physical material out of which the body is composed.

Through an internal process of atomic evolution, many of the lighter atoms are rapidly transmuted into fully spiritualized metal atoms. However, this does not mean that the body becomes heavier. Because of the intense subtle matter fields generated by the high-spin metal atoms, the body becomes increasingly shielded from the gravitational field and thus becomes lighter in weight, even though the proportion of so-called heavy metal atoms has increased.

At a certain point, when the proportion of high-spin metal atoms reaches a certain critical value and the resultant subtle matter field reaches a critical density, the entire body can levitate and even disappear from the field of ordinary physical perception. When this occurs, the Seer is said to have ascended. He or she still has a body, but the body has become spiritualized. Such an ascended body is capable of assuming either a physical or a celestial form depending upon the intention of the Seer.[205]

The important thing to understand about the process of ascension is that one does not physically "die" in ascending to Heaven. One transmutes one's physical body into a celestial body while remaining on this Earth. The advantage of this is that one can then ascend or descend the scales of Creation and assume an appropriate body on any scale of universal life at will.

It is only when one has completely spiritualized the physical body that one gains true mastery over Nature. Complete mastery means that even unconscious gross matter will shape and transform itself in accordance with one's intentions. In the Vedic tradition, those who possess complete mastery over Nature are called Siddhas (perfected ones). They have the ability to physically ascend and descend the stairway between Heaven and Earth, and to command the laws of Nature on every level of universal life.

During the Golden Age, there were many Siddhas that walked the Earth. At that time, the sacred Stone did not have to be processed from metallic ore. It naturally was available in the sap of many of the sacred plants and herbs that grew in abundance on the surface of the Earth.

These plants were said to grow on the "summit of the Earth." This has the same connotation as the Egyptian "mounds" discussed earlier. The term "summit" does not particularly describe geography. The term is used to describe the spiritual quality of a place. The Seers could see these "higher places" through their subtle vision, and would go there to gather the herbs they needed for their sacred rituals.

These regions possessed a greater abundance of subtle matter-energy because the soil possessed a higher proportion of spiritualized atoms. Because the plants growing in these regions drew their nourishment from the soil, they naturally absorbed these spiritualized or enlightened atoms into their cells. The plants growing in these regions thus contained a higher proportion of spiritualized atoms within their structure than the plants growing elsewhere.

It should be understood that within a plant, the spiritualized atoms (which are always metal atoms), are most concentrated in the sap or juice of the plant. This also is true of humans and animals, where the metal atoms are most concentrated in the blood, the sap of the body. When you bite your lip, your own blood has a strong metallic taste. This is due to the presence of metal atoms in the blood.

The plants collected from the spiritually higher regions were called "Soma plants." The ancient Vedic Seers collected the Soma plants, crushed their stalks and leaves to extract the juices, and then repeatedly cooked and filtered the juice to extract the purified essence. This essence was called Soma—the Nectar of Immortality. The Soma acquired in this manner contained a high concentration of spiritualized metal atoms, which were blazing sources of celestial fire. The purified Soma then was mixed with milk and either externally offered into the sacred fire or internally consumed by the priests, depending upon the purpose of the yagya.

If the purpose of the yagya was to generate an external subtle matter field that could be programmed to fulfill some worldly desire, then the Soma fluid was poured into the fire. Such offerings exposed the high-spin metal atoms to the intense heat of the fire. This caused the nuclei to spin even faster, increasing the amount of celestial fire generated by them. The remaining organic material in the residue was burned away, and the metal atoms, stripped of their organic sheaths, fell into the hot coals, where they would remain as sources of subtle matter-energy for the entire duration of the ritual. After the ritual was over, the sacred ashes were saved, and used for medicinal and spiritual purposes. That is why the sacred alchemical material in the Vedic tradition is referred to as bhasma (Ash).

If the purpose of the yagya was to gain physical immortality and spiritual enlightenment, the Soma fluid would be consumed internally by the person performing the ritual. The ancient Vedic Seers who consumed the Soma were invigorated with enormous spiritual energy. Their awareness expanded to embrace the entire Universe, which they conceived as their own divine body. Becoming identified with the celestial gods, they experienced the sovereign power that runs the Universe as flowing through their own being. The glorious nature of this experience is evident from the following verses from the Rig Veda:

> Like the winds violently shaking (the trees), the draughts (of Soma) have lifted me up, for I have often drunk of the Soma.
>
> Both heaven and Earth (are) not equal to one half of me, for I have often drunk of the Soma.
>
> I excel the sky in greatness, (I excel) this great Earth, for I have often drunk of the Soma.

Lo! I will place this Earth (where I will), either here or there, for I have often drunk of the Soma.

I will drive the scorching (sun) either here or there, for I have often drunk of the Soma.

One of my wings is in the sky; the other I dragged below (on the Earth), for I have often drunk of the Soma.

I am the greatest of the great, raised (all the way) to the celestial regions, for I have often drunk of the Soma.[206]

Once again, let us emphasize that these sacred substances were not intoxicants. Their influence did not rely upon chemical reactions within the body. Their influence was due entirely to the abundance of subtle matter that they generated within the physiology.

To use an analogy, the gross body may be viewed as a vessel or cup designed to hold this subtle matter. When the sacred substances are consumed, the body becomes filled with a high density field of subtle matter-energy, like a cup that is filled to its brim with ambrosial nectar. Once the subtle matter grows to certain critical levels within the physiology, the soul automatically becomes spiritually awakened and the body develops the ability to internally transmute, though subtle fusion reactions, whatever material it needs to support its further evolution and refinement. It becomes its own alchemical vessel. It also becomes an intense generator of subtle matter-energy. The vessel of the enlightened body thus may be understood as the true Holy Grail, which contains the fountain of Eternal Life within itself.

As the density of subtle matter-energy increases within the body, the soul also becomes filled with primordial sound. The awareness of the individual begins to resonate with the nonlocal impulses of pure consciousness that constitute the blueprint of Creation. These primordial sounds are the sonic keys that open the doors to all knowledge. They are the keys to the living library of Creation. They constitute the Divine Word of God.

The consumption of the spiritualized substances brought purity and enlightenment to the mind, heart, and intellect of those who consumed them. It also was said that their consumption restored sight to the blind, and made the lame whole again.[207] It rejuvenated the physical body and enabled the enlightened Seers to live for hundreds and even thousands of years in a state of perfect health and full vitality.

Although the knowledge of how to produce these sacred substances was lost long ago, it is now time for this knowledge to reemerge in our awareness. It is time for the Nectar of Immortality to flow in our bodies once again. This is not just a fond wish. It is a reality that is now upon us.

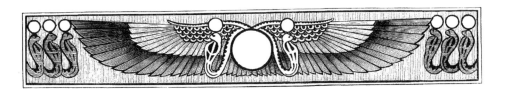

The sacred rites of immortality also played an important role in the culture of ancient Egypt. The pyramids constructed throughout the Nile valley were especially designed for this purpose. These pyramids were not randomly placed. They were located at the sacred "mounds" mapped out by Thoth during the previous Golden Age.

The pyramids may be viewed as powerful subtle matter technologies. They are esoteric machines. When the pyramids were finally completed during the Old Kingdom, they served as initiation chambers for the high priests and pharaohs. In this respect, the pyramids may be viewed as powerful chambers of light.

In order to function as chambers of light, it is necessary for the pyramids to be capped by a benben—the sacred Stone of ancient Egypt. The purpose of these capstones was to radiate subtle energy into the environment, and simultaneously charge the interior of the pyramids with a high density field of subtle matter-energy. The mere stone structure of a pyramid is dead and inert without the life-giving power of the sacred capstone. Even if a capstone is in place, if it is not a sacred Stone, which is a blazing source of celestial fire, it will have no appreciable effect.

In effect, the pyramids had a double purpose. They were used as beacons of spiritual Light to call down the blessings of Heaven upon the Earth, and they were used as chambers of light. The secret chambers within the pyramids were used as initiation rooms. These were the places where the high priests and pharaohs came to bathe in the Light of Universal Mind and commune with the celestial gods.

The striking geometric and mathematical features of the pyramids and their inner chambers are well known. Some believe that these features were built into the pyramids to convey some esoteric message across the sea of time to our current generation. While this may be true, it was not the primary purpose of the unusual construction.

The pyramids were not designed primarily for the purpose of encoding the knowledge of the ancient Seers for future generations. They were designed to structurally embody the divine correspondences between Heaven and Earth. In effect, the correspondences were "written in stone" and encoded within the very structure of the pyramids. When the pyramids became charged with celestial fire, the correspondences encoded within them served to invoke the presence of certain celestial gods.

Each pyramid was designed to embody a particular celestial being. These celestial beings generally were identified with particular stars or constellations. In a sense, the Egyptian Seers used the pyramids, and the entire network of light that covered the land of ancient Egypt, as a celestial tuning fork. The divine correspondences woven into the land and the architecture of ancient Egypt nonlocally attuned the land and each particular monument to certain specific regions of the Cosmos.

By placing themselves in the chamber of light associated with a particular monument, the ancient Egyptian Seers could ascend to the celestial region that corresponded to that monument, and nonlocally commune with the celestial beings that lived there. The most highly evolved initiates actually could ascend to those regions in their physical bodies, through a process of nonlocal reconstruction.

The process of nonlocal reconstruction is the means by which the Siddhas or perfected ones travel nonlocally around the Universe, without requiring the use of an interstellar vehicle of any kind. Basically, it requires that the body be fully spiritualized, or charged with a high density field of subtle matter-energy. When the physiology becomes fully spiritualized, it disappears in a flash of light, and automatically becomes nonlocally correlated with a vast region of space, which one experiences as one's own Self.

Once this global nonlocal correlation is established, the Divine Ka of the individual can travel anywhere within this vast nonlocal domain along the celestial rays that connect the Earth with the Cosmos.

The pyramids thus may be understood as divine portals or nonlocal gateways to the Cosmos. The beauty of the design of the pyramids and the entire landscape of ancient Egypt is that each monument or pyramid was attuned to a particular celestial target.

In their brilliant book, *The Message of the Sphinx*, Graham Hancock and Robert Bauval have presented a formidable case that the Pyramids of Giza were attuned to the three stars in the belt of Orion.

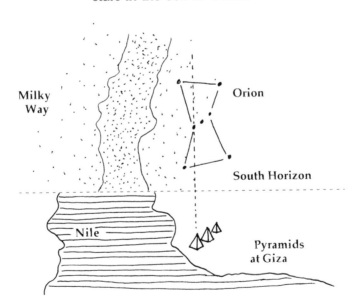

Figure 51—The Pyramids and the Orion Constellation

According to Robert Bauval and Graham Hancock, the Great Pyramids of Giza present an earthly image of the celestial constellation of Orion as it appeared around 10,500 B.C.

Equally important, the physical layout of the Giza plateau suggests that the Pyramids were perfectly attuned to these stars only around 10,500 B.C.—at the peak of the Golden Age. This was the time when the sacred "mounds" in the Nile valley were mapped out by the Divine Messenger, Thoth.

The map of the sacred "mounds" laid out the blueprint for the New World Order that emerged after the flood. This blueprint was meticulously adhered to by subsequent generations of initiates over many millennia. These initiates played the role of the high priests in Old Kingdom Egypt. They were the ones who oversaw the construction of the pyramids and other monuments, and made sure they were in accordance with the Divine Plan conceived by the Seers long ago.

But why did the ancient Seers specifically choose to map the Orion constellation on the Giza plateau, through the Great Pyramids? Why not some other constellation?

From modern astronomy, we know that the Orion constellation lies in the direction of the outer arm of the Milky Way galaxy. The stars in this region are much older and more evolved that our own Sun.

From an intuitive point of view, we believe that many of the worlds belonging to these star systems are permanent Worlds of Light, filled with enlightened Seers and Siddhas. Although these worlds lie within the luminous disk of the galaxy, and thus fall within the field of action, they have reached a point where they are self-sufficient in their ability to generate enormous quantities of celestial fire.

This means that, unlike the Earth, they no longer are dependent upon the cosmic pillar of celestial fire. Just as a baby no longer is dependent upon its umbilical cord after it is born, so also, after a Planetary Being becomes enlightened, and the planet becomes a permanent World of Light, it no longer is dependent upon the pillar of celestial fire for its evolution.

The ability of a planet to become a permanent World of Light depends upon the degree of spiritualization of matter on the planet. On a permanent World of Light, the material out of which the planet is composed has a much higher proportion of high-spin metal atoms within it than the material of the Earth.

As a result, the planet as a whole is continuously refreshed with spiritual Light. The plants, animals, humans, and other beings that live upon such planets enjoy an exalted level of spiritual evolution. Such worlds enjoy a permanent Golden Age, and generally serve as administrative outposts for the Galactic civilization.

We have seen that the true administrative center for the Galactic civilization lies at the center of the galaxy. This, in turn, is an outpost of the Divine Society, which lies at the center of the Universe.

Among other responsibilities, the enlightened Seers and Siddhas who dwell on the permanent Worlds of Light within the luminous disk of the galaxy have the responsibility to assist and oversee the evolution of human beings on nearby unenlightened planets like our own.

Based upon their geometric correspondences, it seems clear that the Egyptian Seers used the Pyramids at Giza as nonlocal communication links with the permanent Worlds of Light in the Orion constellation. Were they intended to serve as nonlocal gateways between the Earth and our local administrative center?

By bathing in the high density field of subtle matter within the Great Pyramid, and becoming filled with the illuminating power of the sacred alchemical Stone, we suspect that the Egyptian Seers were able to ascend into the Heavens. Some of them literally may have disappeared from physical sight, vanishing in a powerful subtle fusion reaction that transformed their gross physical bodies into universally correlated vehicles of celestial light.

Those who achieved this goal then would have been free to assume whatever form they desired—subtle or gross—within the realm of their ascension. Having become celestial beings of light, they were free to come and go, ascend and descend between Heaven and Earth as they pleased. Such Siddhas or perfected ones could have ascended to the permanent Worlds of Light in the Orion constellation, where they would enjoy a more or less immortal heavenly existence. These worlds in turn could serve as stepping stones to even higher worlds in the seven-layered structure of universal life.

Of course, this deep and mysterious knowledge was not available to or understood by the multitudes. It was part of the secret wisdom shared only among the highest initiates in the sacred academy. However, it seems likely that the general population had some idea of what was going on.

Those who had the most insight into the Sacred Science were the craftsmen, who actually constructed the pyramids. The craftsmen also belonged to the sacred academy, although they did not belong to the highest orders of initiates. Their domain was the lower knowledge, which pertained to the actual production of the sacred Stone and the construction of the sacred temples.

They were not privy to the deepest secrets of the higher knowledge, which related to the processes of attaining spiritual enlightenment and physical immortality. But they must have had some idea of what was involved. As a result, the craftsmen knew many of the practical secrets associated with the Sacred Science.

It is curious to note that the Great Seal of the United States—the seal printed on the back of every U. S. dollar bill—presents a depiction of the Great Pyramid, on top of which is placed the sacred benben. On the other side is illustrated the eagle, symbolic of the phoenix.

The capstone placed on top of the Pyramid is illustrated as having an "all-seeing eye" at its very center. This depicts the esoteric purpose of the capstone as a source of subtle matter-energy, capable of reflecting pure consciousness. Beneath the Pyramid is the inscription "Novus Ordo Seclorum," which literally means "New World Order."

The founding fathers apparently chose these two symbols to signify the founding of the United States, which they viewed as the founding of a New

World Order. Why they chose the pyramid and the eagle for this purpose is still a matter of debate. It seems these symbols first were presented by an artist and then chosen by the founding fathers on the basis of unknown considerations. Some have speculated that these symbols were selected because some of the founding fathers such as George Washington, Benjamin Franklin, Thomas Jefferson, and John Adams belonged to the Freemasons and Rosicrucians, who trace their knowledge to the ancient Egyptians.

Figure 52—The Great Seal of the United States

It should be noted that Charles Thompson, who was responsible for overseeing the design of the Great Seal, was a member of Franklin's American Philosophical Society, an organization that delved into many different fields of esoteric knowledge. Indeed, Benjamin Franklin is believed to have served as the Grand Master of the Rosicrucians, an esoteric secret society deeply involved in Egyptian and alchemical lore.[208]

Regardless of why or how these particular symbols were chosen, most people have no idea what the Great Seals of the United States signify—even though they encounter and use them every day. This provides an excellent example of how the most sacred knowledge may survive unnoticed through the millennia even though it is placed beneath our very noses. It survives through the use of esoteric symbols that endure long after their true meaning has been forgotten. However, at the beginning of a new Golden Age, it is inevitable that these symbols become understood and seen in their true light once again.

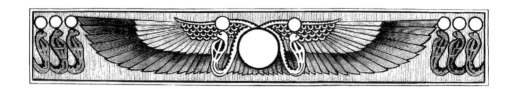

Although the sacred alchemical science largely was lost when the Old Kingdom fell around 2150 B.C., it appears to have been temporarily revived by the advent of a great new Seer in the middle of the second millennium B.C. This new Seer was called Moses.

We have already seen that Moses was raised within the royal court of Egypt, where he was given a royal education. Most certainly this included initiation into the secrets of the Heliopolitan priesthood. We believe that Moses used his own intuitive insight and his royal Egyptian education to construct one of the most unusual objects ever described in any written scriptural text—the Ark of the Covenant.

Figure 53—The Ark of the Covenant

It is said that Moses received instructions on how to build the Ark from God himself on Mount Sinai. These instructions are recorded in the Book of Exodus.

> Make an Ark, a chest of acacia-wood, two and a half cubits long, one cubit and a half wide, and one cubit and a half high. Overlay it with pure gold both inside and out, and put a band of gold all round it. Cast four gold rings for it, and fasten them to its four feet, two rings on each side. Make poles of acacia-wood and plate them with gold, and insert the poles in the rings at the sides of the Ark to lift it. The poles shall remain in the rings of the Ark and never be removed. Put into the Ark the Token of the Covenant, which I shall give you. Make a cover of pure gold, two and a half cubits long and one cubit and a half wide. Make two gold cherubim of beaten work at the ends of the cover, one at each end; make each cherub of one piece with the cover. They shall be made with wings outspread and pointing upwards, and shall screen the cover with their wings. They shall be face to face, looking inwards over the cover. Put the cover above the Ark, and put into the Ark the Tokens that I shall give you. It is there that I shall meet you, and from above the cover, between the two cherubim over the Ark of the Tokens, I shall deliver to you all my commandments for the Israelites.[209]

The Biblical accounts of the Ark clearly indicate that it was some type of sacred technology, endowed with enormous spiritual power. This sacred power was considered to be the manifest presence of God on Earth. It was not to be tampered with by the unknowing, or intentionally misused in any way, or disastrous consequences would follow.

There are a number of accounts in which innocent well-intentioned servants of the Ark were devoured and killed by the flames of celestial fire that radiated from it.[210] Furthermore, due to the enormous power of the subtle energy that it contained, whenever the Ark was moved, it was wrapped in three layers of insulating material as a precautionary measure.

> When the camp is due to move, Aaron and his sons shall come and take down the Veil of the screen and cover the Ark of the Tokens with it; over this they shall put a covering of porpoise-hide [hide of

sea-cow] and over that again a violet cloth all of one piece; they shall then put its poles in place.[211]

Figure 51—The Ark Covered with Layers of Insulation

The Veil, which was made of "finely woven linen"[212] constituted the first layer. Then came a layer of leather (taken from the hide of a sea-cow), and then another layer of cloth. Moses directed that these three layers should be put into place before the carrying poles were attached, and before anyone actually touched the Ark. The three layers all were composed of insulating materials. These layers were designed to contain the powerful currents of subtle matter-energy that otherwise would discharge onto the individuals handling the Ark, burning them with spark-like emanations. Accounts of these spark-like emanations have been reported in many ancient legends concerning the Ark.[213]

The slab of gold on top of the Ark was called the throne of mercy. It was the place where the two cherubim sat facing each other. Some accounts say that a cloud appeared upon the throne of mercy in which the presence of God was manifest.[214] This was not a cloud of steam or water vapor. It was a cloud of celestial fire or subtle matter-energy. On one occasion, Moses is said to have heard a voice coming from the region of this cloud above the throne of mercy, between the two cherubim. In other legends, it is said that this voice descended from Heaven "in the form of a tube of fire"![215]

Clearly, the Ark is more than just a holy relic—it represents something completely unique in the Biblical literature—something so strange and unusual that it has captivated the imagination of western civilization for thousands of years.

What was the Ark? How did it work? Was it pure spiritual magic, or was Sacred Science involved? As stated previously, we believe that Moses was initiated into the secret Egyptian tradition of alchemy and knew how to produce the alchemical Stone, Salt, or Ash. In our opinion, the Stone tablets or "Tokens" that were contained within the Ark were composed of the same sacred alchemical material as the benben stones and statues of the temple gods in ancient Egypt.

The statues of the temple gods are not the same statues that one sees on public display.

> The statues of the temple gods were never seen by the general population of worshippers. They resided in an inner chamber of the temple accessible only to the priests. Within this sacred space there was a perfect miniature of a Nile boat with a cabin on the deck. The statue was kept inside this cabin. It was roughly two feet in height. On festival days the boat, with the statue of the god inside, was taken out of the temple and paraded through the streets, but the god itself was never openly displayed.[216]

The temple gods of ancient Egypt thus were kept in a small box or Ark similar to that used by the Hebrews to house their god. In fact, this box literally was kept upon a boat or Ark. Neither the temple gods of ancient Egypt nor the Tokens of the Covenant ever were shown publicly. They were accessible only to the high priests. This is because they were filled with celestial fire—or the Holy Presence of God—and were capable of emanating powerful lightning-like radiations that only the high priests could handle.

It is interesting to note that the wilderness in which the Jews wandered for forty years was located on the Sinai peninsula. As pointed out earlier, this region was well known as a source of metal ore, and was dotted with ancient mines. This was the place where Moses led the people after their exodus from Egypt, and this was the place where Moses received the sacred Stone tablets that were placed inside the Ark.

Were the sacred tablets within the Ark composed of the sacred alchemical Stone? Were they composed of high-spin metal atoms? Was this why they manifested the Divine Presence so strongly?

It is conceivable that Moses used the forty days atop Mt. Sinai to prepare the alchemical substance out of which the sacred Stones were composed. It is stated that while he was on top of the sacred mountain, "Mount Sinai was all smoking because the Lord had come down upon it in fire; the smoke went up like the smoke of a kiln [or forge]."[217]

Did Moses build a forge on top of Mount Sinai to prepare the sacred white Stone? Were these Stones literally filled with the Word of God—the primordial sounds that nonlocally unite Heaven and Earth?

When Moses carried the sacred Stones down from the mountain it is said that his face shone so brightly that it made people afraid, and he had to cover his face with a veil.[218] Was this because he had been overexposed to the powerful radiations of the sacred Stone, which was filled with the presence of God? Was the radiance of his face due to the intense subtle fusion reactions occurring within his body?

Such events cannot be explained within the ordinary framework of modern science. But they can be explained by the Sacred Science of the Seers—a science that embraces all of the subtle and gross fields of matter and energy that exist in the Universe.

This is the only type of science that is capable of doing justice to the grand scheme of the Universe. It is the only type of science that is capable of upholding the nonlocal wholeness of Life, on all seven levels of universal existence. And it is the only type of science that is competent to reconstruct the lost technologies of the ancient Seers.

The knowledge of the Sacred Science was used by Moses to construct the Ark. It was used by the Egyptian high priests to ascend to the stars. And it was used by the Vedic Seers to invoke the blessings of Heaven on Earth. This same knowledge also will be used by the men and women of our generation to prepare the world for the coming Illumination. This is our destiny. It is our responsibility. And it is our greatest joy.

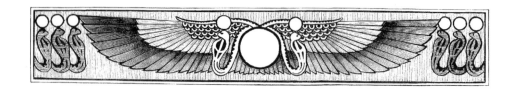

The time has now come for the complete practical knowledge of the Sacred Science to reemerge in human awareness. It is time for the human race to reawaken to its divine status. The epochal Night is over. The first light of Dawn now is shining on the eastern horizon. With this light the presence of the Divine Messenger has descended once again into our collective awareness.

The Holy Spirit has come to breathe fire and life into the human soul, so that the veils of ignorance may be lifted from our hearts and minds. He has come to revive the Sacred Science and teach us how to invoke the presence of God within our souls and within the very fabric of the Earth.

The global transformation that we have spoken of is imminent and inevitable. The Breath of God already has been released. It is now descending along the pillar of celestial fire towards the Earth from the direction of the Pleiades. When the fiery Breath of God washes over our planet, everything will be illumined and changed in a single moment. Every atom, every cell, and every being on our planet will be filled with celestial fire. An intense process of tapas or subtle fusion will begin to take place everywhere, causing the spiritual awakening of all beings.

When the wave of celestial fire descends upon our planet, the Planetary Being itself will awaken and stretch its aching bones. The very rocks of the Earth will be readjusted. Although a shift of the magnetic and geographic poles is a distinct possibility, no one knows the extent of this shift or if it will happen at all. The Earth changes that inevitably must occur still are being computed by Cosmic Intelligence. Whether the Earth's structural transformation is gradual and gentle, or sudden and violent, depends to a great extent upon the course of action that we take, individually and collectively, between now and then.

We cannot stop the advent of the Golden Age—but we can influence the amount of destruction that accompanies its birth. In order to avert radical global changes that may involve massive destruction, we must begin to nourish the subtle body of our planet, raising it to higher levels of spiritual realization and power, prior to the moment of global Illumination.

Through both inner spiritual methods and outer alchemical methods, we must increase the generation of subtle matter on our planet, so that the subtle body of the Earth may become increasingly charged with spiritual power prior to the moment of Illumination. This will soften the impact of the wave of celestial fire, and allow the Earth to evolve to its new level of internal self-organization gradually and gently, rather than suddenly and violently.

This same principle holds true for all of us as individuals. We must begin to expose ourselves to higher and higher levels of subtle matter-energy, so that the channels of subtle energy may be opened up within our bodies. These channels must be developed to the point where they can handle the influx of spiritual power that will descend at the time of Illumination. Otherwise, at the time of Illumination, the channels of subtle energy will experience such an overload that they will short-circuit.

To protect against this possibility, a new knowledge and a new technology is being given to the human race. The knowledge concerns the Sacred Science of subtle matter-energy. We have tried to introduce this subject in this book, and show its roots in the most ancient traditions of knowledge on our planet. But it is a vast subject. It cannot possibly be dealt with in a single book. Ultimately, it will require the sincere and concentrated efforts of many great souls over many years to unravel its subtle mysteries and uncover its hidden treasures.

The new technologies that we see on the horizon will be based upon this sacred alchemical science—the science of subtle matter-energy. They will be based upon the sacred white powder, composed of fully spiritualized precious metals. By providing a powerful source of celestial fire, this material may serve as the ultimate superfuel of the future.

Look at what has happened to the world since the discovery of electricity. One hundred years ago who would have been able to envision our modern world? Even in the last fifty years the world has undergone an enormous transformation. But the pace of global transformation continues to increase daily. With our modern communication and information processing capabilities, things are happening more and more quickly.

Previously, it took decades to translate new ideas into new industries. Today, new ideas can be translated into new industries almost overnight. The world appears to be caught in a spiral of technological development that is building to a great crescendo. What will this rising crescendo reveal? Will it reveal the greatest secret of the Ages? Will it reveal the Light of God shining within all things?

Who knows what technological marvels will be developed over the next ten years? With a proper understanding of the sacred alchemical science and a material source of subtle matter-energy, there are no limits to the heights that the human race might achieve.

We believe that the world is on the verge of both a spiritual and technological revolution that is completely unprecedented in history. The coming technological revolution will be based upon the discovery and application of subtle matter-energy. This subtle energy revolution will make the electric energy revolution seem pale by comparison.

This does not mean that ordinary electronic technologies will be abandoned. We envision a greatly expanded use of electric power around the world, especially in those countries that have lagged behind the more industrialized nations. Current means of generating electric power rely heavily upon fossil fuel, hydroelectric, and nuclear technologies. We anticipate that these conventional technologies ultimately will be replaced by new technologies, which utilize subtle matter-energy to generate electrons from the very vacuum of empty space.

We believe that these new subtle matter technologies will provide an unlimited, inexpensive, and extremely efficient source of electric power. Furthermore, these new technologies will not have the destructive, polluting impact on the environment that current technologies have. Because such technologies will be portable, they should provide an ideal on-board power source for electric vehicles, further substantially reducing the polluting uses of fossil fuels. With the availability of an inexpensive, nonpolluting, and portable source of electric power, the quality of life in developing nations should rise quickly, helping to create for the first time in known history a material abundance that is shared equally among the family of nations.

By using the perpetual dynamism inherent in the nucleus of the atom to tap the unlimited energy of the physical vacuum, these subtle matter technologies will appear to draw power from an all-pervading, invisible, and inexhaustible source. In a sense, they will provide a very concrete demonstration of the unlimited potential inherent within every human soul.

In addition to an energy revolution, we anticipate a revolution in the field of materials processing. Using subtle matter technologies, we believe it is possible to grow the heavier and rarer atomic elements from the lighter, more abundant atomic elements through a process of alchemical transmutation. The more exotic elements, including the precious metals, could be grown in the laboratory from silica, calcium, or carbon, using the same basic process by which they are grown deep within the Earth. This transmutation technology ultimately should give rise to complete mastery over the elements. It should virtually eliminate the need to rip open the bowels of the Earth to acquire the minerals needed for our industrial civilization. Such technologies also will help establish   balance in the world economy by freeing the mineral-poor nations from dependence on the mineral-rich nations—an inequity that has caused many wars throughout history.

We also see a profound revolution in the field of information processing. Rather than using currents of electrons to process information, we believe that information processing will be based on currents of subtle matter-energy. This should open the door to completely new, holographic methods of information processing. Although such methods already are being developed on the basis of ordinary electronic technologies, they are currently in a very crude state of development. To bring this emerging technology to maturity, a new form of electromagnetic technology must be introduced that is based on generating and conducting currents of subtle matter-energy rather than of electrons.

The new holographic method of information processing will not rely upon digital processors, but upon holographic processors. Rather than being referred to as "computers," they should be called "holographers." The new holographers will utilize certain types of refractive crystals to read and write holographic interference patterns, each of which will encode a high-resolution image of the environment. Each such image will contain gigabytes of information, and it will be possible to store thousands of these images in a single tiny crystal, smaller than the tip of a pencil. Such solid-state devices will make complex image and language recognition very simple, ultimately enabling our machines to "learn" from experience. This could pave the way for truly intelligent machines to surface on our planet.

There are many other seemingly miraculous applications of subtle matter-energy that will have equally profound implications for our modern society. We believe that the flurry of inventive activity that took place after the discovery of electricity will appear mild compared to that which will unfold over the next twenty years. We see these new possibilities emerging in a rising flood of technological innovation. There is nothing anyone can do to stem this flood, because it is not going to come from a single source. It is going to come from many sources simultaneously, like a celestial rain. It will wash over all boundaries and pour into every industry and market on our planet.

We thus believe that even on a mundane technological level our world is going to change dramatically. But these technological changes will not be taking place in a spiritual vacuum. They will be part of a worldwide spiritual and scientific revolution that will alter our most fundamental views about the world in which we live.

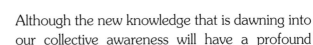

Although the new knowledge that is dawning into our collective awareness will have a profound impact upon our world both economically and technologically, our most immediate concern should be with our spiritual well-being. It is essential that we begin to spiritually regenerate ourselves—to raise the level of subtle matter-energy within our body, mind, and soul so that we will be prepared for the global transformation that is to come.

For this specific purpose, we foresee the rapid development of medicinal and rejuvenative elixirs made out of the sacred white powder. The research and development of these materials will require the participation of many different individuals. It also will require the cooperation of medical doctors, health facilities, and governmental agencies all around the world. We are not naive. We are fully aware that various vested interests may attempt to delay the availability of this material for some time. Nevertheless, we hope that the immense value of this material will soon be recognized by all. We hope that those in positions of power will honor their responsibilities to mankind and will join in the investigation and development of this precious resource for the benefit of all.

In addition to various methods of internal therapy involving the consumption of elixirs, we envision the rapid development and utilization of Chambers of Light all over the world. These Chambers of Light may be similar to the chambers of light used by the ancient Egyptian Seers. They will be designed to hold a high density field of subtle matter-energy in which individuals may bathe to receive spiritual and physical regeneration.

There is a mysterious reference to such a chamber in the *Corpus Hermeticum*. As stated previously, these texts were ascribed to Hermes Trismegistus, who was also identified with both the Biblical patriarch Enoch and the Egyptian wisdom god Thoth.

The following dialogue between Hermes Trismegistus and his son Tat describes a great vessel or chamber in which men and women were invited to bathe. This vessel did not contain water. It contained universal Mind. When one bathed in this bath of Mind, one gained the knowledge of all things on Earth as well as all things in Heaven. In addition, one gained direct intuitive knowledge of God.

> Tat: Tell me then, father, why did not God impart Mind to all men?
>
> Hermes: It was his will, my son, that Mind should be placed in the midst as a prize that human souls may win.
>
> Tat: And where did he place it?
>
> Hermes: He filled a great *kratur* [bowl, vessel, or chamber] with Mind and set it down among humans; and he appointed a Herald, and bade him make proclamation to the hearts of all humans: "Hearken, each human heart; dip yourself in this chamber, if you will, recognizing for what purpose you have been made, and believing you will ascend to Him who sent the chamber down." Now those who gave heed to the proclamation, and dipped themselves in the bath of Mind, these individuals got a share of the knowledge of God; they received Mind, and so became complete human beings. . . as many as have partaken of the gift [of Mind] which God has sent, these, my son, in comparison with the others, are as immortal gods to mortal men. They embrace in their own mind all things that are, the things on Earth and the things in Heaven, and even that which is above Heaven, if there is aught above Heaven; and raising themselves to that height, they see the Good . . . . Such, my son, is the work that Mind does; it throws open the way to knowledge of things divine, and enables us to apprehend God.[219]

This passage has a historical ring to it. The descent of the chamber of Mind may represent an actual event that happened long ago. Could this be a veiled reference to the chambers of light initially used by the members of the sacred academy, and later by the Egyptians?

Although these technologies have been hidden away and buried beneath a landslide of esoteric symbols and forgotten myths for thousands of years, it is now time for them to reappear in our midst. The time has come for a new Chamber of Light to be set down among us. The Herald or Divine Messenger is already among us. Soon all the people on Earth will be invited to come and bathe in the glorious chamber of Mind so that they might gain knowledge of all things on Earth and in Heaven, and attain true knowledge of God.

Regardless of the logistic or financial considerations involved, it is essential that these technologies be made available to everyone around the world. People of every religion and belief, every cultural and ethnic background, must have access to these technologies so that they may become filled with spiritual Light and contribute to the awakening of our planet.

By repeated exposure to the high density field of subtle matter within such chambers, we believe it will be possible for the people to gradually absorb subtle matter in controlled doses, and experience an enhanced rate of evolution. These chambers will thus embody the same fundamental principles used by the ancient Seers to achieve spiritual enlightenment and physical immortality.

To house the Chambers of Light and provide residential facilities for individuals and families who will come to receive the benefits of this extremely powerful method of spiritual regeneration, we envision the establishment of Centers of Light all around the world. These Centers will provide the proper supervision to guide people through the profound mental, physical, and spiritual transformations that they will experience from their exposure to the Light within the chambers.

We expect that the most successful of these Centers will operate on a nonprofit basis. This will ensure that the treatments given to different individuals will be given on the basis of truly altruistic humanitarian purposes. It also will provide a beautiful opportunity for philanthropic individuals and institutions to make an enormous contribution to the spiritual and physical well-being of the human race and our planet as a whole. What higher purpose can be served with our resources than to elevate the spiritual awareness and physical well-being of the human race, and pave the way for a new Golden Age?

These preparations and developments will require a collective effort. They are not and cannot be the exclusive work of a single individual or organization. They can be made manifest only through the concerted effort of many individuals and organizations simultaneously.

We cannot emphasize enough the importance of this work. The research, development, and dissemination of the sacred alchemical technologies is of paramount importance to the entire human race. This activity should be supported by all those individuals who comprehend its importance and who have the ability to participate in, promote, or otherwise contribute to this essential endeavor.

We do not have a lot of time. The Cosmic Clock is ticking. The fiery Breath of God is on its way. Those of you who understand the message that we have tried to convey in this book should reflect and determine if there is any way you can assist in the global preparation. The Holy Spirit already is present among us. The Divine Messenger is coordinating our collective efforts. These efforts will not fail, but more workers of light are needed. More people are needed who are willing to stand up and be counted as instruments of the Light.

The time is rapidly approaching when the Light of God will set the Earth ablaze with celestial glory. The time is rapidly approaching when the darkness of the Night will totally disappear. Let us prepare ourselves for that amazing event. Let us join hands and walk into the Light together. Let us all go forth together to greet the Dawn of a new Day, full of joy and singing songs of thanksgiving and praise.

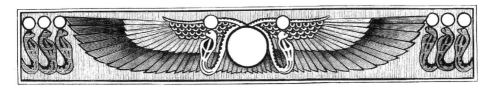

ABOUT THE AUTHOR

Robert Cox has spent many years living in Europe and India studying the ancient wisdom of the East and the West. In 1977, he obtained a Master's Degree in Vedic Studies from the MERU Institute, Switzerland. Between 1982 and 1991, he adopted a contemplative life and spent many hours every day immersed in silent meditation and contemplation. During that time he began to receive a series of intuitive insights and visions regarding the Sacred Science of the ancient Seers, and these cognitions have continued to unfold with increasing depth and clarity over the years.

In 1991, he left his contemplative life to pursue an active program of empirical research to explore his intuitive insights. For this purpose, he founded Agni Energy Research, L.P., a limited partnership established to perform research in the field of subtle matter-energy. This partnership is actively engaged in research to uncover the practical secrets of the Sacred Science and develop a whole spectrum of sacred technologies that utilize subtle matter-energy for the benefit of humanity. More recently, he founded The Celestial Science Foundation to promote the principles of the Sacred Science and coordinate and support research in the field of subtle matter-energy.

The author is available to give workshops, seminars, and conference presentations on the various subjects discussed in this book. Additional papers and audio tapes are available that go more deeply into these subjects. Anyone who would like to host a seminar or workshop, or receive a free catalogue of additional materials, is encouraged to contact the author through the addresses given below.

Robert Cox
PO Box 1322
Gulf Breeze, FL 32562
or
rob@celestialfire.com

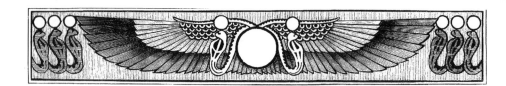

The Celestial Science Foundation is a spiritual and educational membership organization that has been founded to promote, coordinate, facilitate, and support the research and development of new sacred technologies that utilize subtle matter-energy for the benefit of humanity.

Because modern science has not achieved an understanding of the Universe that recognizes the existence of subtle matter-energy, many highly credentialed authorities may view research in this field as misguided and wasteful. Those pioneering researchers who are committed to exploring this field thus are open to various criticisms and are subject to substantial financial pressures. Because conventional funding sources rely heavily upon well-established opinion, funding for subtle matter-energy research is extremely difficult to obtain, if it can be obtained at all.

The Celestial Science Foundation has been formed to help meet the needs of researchers in this field, and give them the spiritual and financial support that they deserve. It is a spiritual organization that adheres to the following tenets:

1) A subtle life force or love essence pervades the entire Universe.

2) This subtle life force is the very stuff out of which everything in Creation ultimately is composed.

3) The life force may be understood as the subtle form of matter-energy that mediates the relationship between the gross physical body and the all-pervading field of pure consciousness.

4) As both a spiritual and physical substance, the life force can be generated or enhanced by both spiritual and physical means.

5) The life force can be increased through the spiritual practices that have been taught by various religious and spiritual traditions around the world.

6) In addition to these traditional spiritual practices, physical methods of generating the subtle life force must be researched, developed, and made available to everyone on our planet as soon as possible, so that the spiritual evolution of our planet may be accelerated dramatically.

Those who concur with these beliefs and would like to become a basic member of The Celestial Science Foundation may do so by sending their name, mailing address, phone number, and e-mail address (if applicable), along with an annual membership fee of $30 to:

The Celestial Science Foundation
PO Box 1286
Gulf Breeze, FL 32562

This will enroll one as a member in the Foundation and will entitle one to receive a bimonthly newsletter as well as two free audio tapes by the author over the course of the year.

Those who would like to make an additional contribution over and above the membership fee are welcome to do so. Because the Foundation has not yet received non-profit status, membership fees and any additional small contributions to the Foundation are not tax-deductible at the present time.

Those who wish to make larger contributions to the Foundation (amounts of over $1000) may receive a tax deduction by making their contribution payable to one of our sponsoring organizations. For more information please contact the Foundation at the address given above or by e-mail at csf@celestialfire.com.

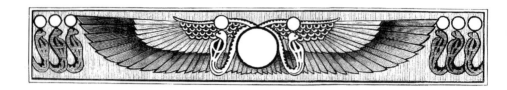

1. See *Rasanavam.*

2. Ibid.

3. *Srimad Bhagavata* 11.15.3–7.

4. See Levi, *Transcendental Magic,* 10–11.

5. See Hudson, "White Powder Gold."

6. See Nader, *Human Physiology.*

7. Revelation 4.1–8 New English Bible.

8. The field of pure consciousness is not composed of ordinary matter. It is composed of *exotic matter,* which displays the properties of a nonlocal, globally correlated superfluid, and carries a negative (minus) energy density. In an unpublished paper entitled "A Vedic Model of Vacuum Dynamics" (1995), the author argues that the superfluid of consciousness corresponds to the negative (minus) energy continuum of modern physics. In this paper, the vacuum of modern physics is analyzed using a two-fluid model. All the positive energy states are assumed to represent the normal objective phase of the vacuum, which carries all of the vacuum's thermal energy, entropy, and inertia. The negative energy states are assumed to form a subjective superfluid, which supports global correlations, has zero entropy, and is capable of inertia-free superflow, which can take place at superluminal speeds. According to this model, the vacuum superfluid not only is devoid of all positive thermal energy, but it actually possesses minus energy. This means that its internal energy is less than zero. As such, it can be said to be colder than absolute zero. Nevertheless, the vacuum superfluid is not frozen because it is composed of subjective consciousness and not ordinary objective matter. It represents the subjective organizing power of Nature, rather than the objective matter that gets organized. Thus, it ultimately transcends all considerations of hot and cold. We have described it as colder than absolute zero merely to indicate its ability to instill crystalline order in all things.

9. Ezekiel 1.4–13 New English Bible.

10. Scorpio is the eighth astrological sign counted from Aries. Among other things

it symbolizes physical death. It also symbolizes the spiritual transformation that occurs at the time of death. The most common symbol of Scorpio is the scorpion, which signifies the painful aspects of death from a physical viewpoint. The scorpion thus represents the lower physical nature of the sign. The higher spiritual nature of the sign is represented by an eagle, signifying the phoenix, which rises out of the ashes of death to attain immortality. This higher spiritual symbol was the one used by the Biblical prophets.

11. See Jochmans, "Top Ten Prophecies."

12. The best types of meditation allow the practitioner to transcend the ordinary thinking level of the mind and experience finer or subtler levels of thinking, eventually transcending even the subtlest level of thinking to experience unbounded pure consciousness. The experience of unbounded pure consciousness represents the simplest, least excited state of human awareness, where the mind is completely silent and still, yet fully awake within itself. Today there are many different types of meditation techniques on the market, taught by teachers from different traditions and backgrounds. I do not claim to be an expert regarding all of these different techniques. For over twenty-five years now I have faithfully practiced the technique of Transcendental Meditation as taught by His Holiness Maharishi Mahesh Yogi, and I can personally attest to the power and effectiveness of this technique in delivering the experience of pure consciousness. While other meditation techniques may also be effective in this regard, I cannot attest to them on the basis of my own experience.

13. Svetashvatara Upanishad 3.19. See *Brahmopanisat-Sara Sangraha*.

14. See Yogi, *Maharishi Vedic University*, 53.

15. When they are seen with the subtle senses, the currents of subtle matter-energy resemble luminous filaments of fire. This is because the filaments are composed of tiny charged particles, which radiate photons of light as they traverse their helical paths. The currents of subtle matter may be understood as plasma vortex filaments. A plasma is a gas composed of a nearly equal number of oppositely charged particles. Ordinary plasmas, such as those present in a neon tube, an electric discharge, or a lightning bolt, generally consist of ionized atoms and free electrons. Subtle plasmas consist of subtle charged particles, which are trillions of times smaller than electrons. These subtle plasmas pervade the so-called empty space that lies between stars and galaxies, and form vast cosmic filaments and vortices. When these filaments and vortices are apprehended through the faculty of nonlocal intuition, the celestial regions appear to be blazing with luminous flames of fire. For this reason, the subtle matter-energy may be called celestial fire.

16. The word chitta is synonymous with *mahat*. In the ancient Vedic system of Samkhya, which enumerates the most basic elements of Creation, chitta or mahat is considered the first and most subtle material substance created from the unmanifest field of primordial Nature. Although chitta is a material substance, it

nevertheless because of its subtlety is capable of reflecting pure consciousness. The predominating quality in chitta is *sattva* (physical lightness and spiritual purity). Chitta is the precursor and material basis *(upadana karana)* of all other material elements, which are nothing other than vortical modifications *(vrittis)* of chitta.

These other material elements, including elementary particles and atoms, are generated from the all-pervading subtle field of chitta through a cosmic churning process. This is compared to the process of churning milk to generate coagulated lumps of curd. The coagulated lumps of curd correspond to the galaxies and stars scattered throughout the Universe. See chapter 30 for a more elaborate description of the cosmic churning process.

17. Chi has two aspects: (i) *Tai Chi* or unpolarized subtle matter, and (ii) the *yin* and *yang* energies, which constitute the polarized condition of subtle matter. In its unpolarized neutral condition, the field of subtle matter-energy is capable of reflecting pure consciousness, which is experienced as unbounded transparent wholeness. In its polarized condition, the field of subtle matter energy manifests itself as the dance of feminine (yin) and masculine (yang) energies, from which the entire Creation emerges.

18. *Hermetica*, Libellus 12.1.

19. Subtle matter may be understood as a physical substance composed of tiny charged particles. Unlike photons, which move in straight lines, possess zero charge, and are massless, subtle particles move in helical paths, and possess both charge and mass. However, the mass possessed by subtle particles is extremely small. Generally speaking, subtle particles are trillions of times smaller than an electron (the smallest known elementary particle), and have trillions of times less mass and electric charge.

20. Prometheus was the Greek Titan who stole the sacred fire from the gods and gave it to human beings on Earth. For this act, he was severely punished, and the entire Earth was destroyed in a great flood.

21. *Visnu Purana* 2.5.2.

22. *Hermetica*, Libellus 3.147.

23. Although subtle particles are distinct from all known elementary particles, they are analogous to *virtual particles* within the physical vacuum. They interact with subquantum modes of the electromagnetic field.

24. Adapted from Wilson's translation of the *Rig-Veda Sanhita* 10.5.3.4.

25. The following three quotations are from *Hermetica*, Libellus 10.22–25.

26. In the Vedic tradition, the transcendental wholeness, which contains an infinite number of finite Universes or Cosmic Eggs within itself, is called the *Akshara Brahman*—the Imperishable Wholeness. The Cosmic Eggs within this transcendental wholeness are arranged in a perfectly symmetrical manner resembling atoms in a crystalline lattice. This transcendental lattice of Universes is infinite, eternal, and

indestructible, and is the true abode of the immortal gods and seers. Because each crystallographic cell in this infinite lattice of Universes displays a cubic structure, it may be understood as the true Philosopher's Stone or Salt, which is indistinguishable from the Absolute.

27. *Hermetica,* Asclepius 3.16.

28. See Genesis 2.10–14.

29. Adapted from Sargeant's translation of the *Bhagavad Gita* 15.1.

30. Ibid. 15.3.

31. According to the Vedic Seers, the Cosmic Egg endures for approximately 311.04 trillion years before it is dissolved into the field of primordial matter-energy *(pradhana)* from which it arose. This period of time is called Supreme *(para),* because nothing within the field of Creation can last longer than the Creation itself. It thus serves as the fundamental unit of time by which Eternity is measured. See *Visnu Purana* 1.3.

32. See Crosswell, *Alchemy of the Heavens,* 191–192.

33. See Becklin, Gatley, and Werner, "Far-infrared Observations of Sagittarius A."

34. Laviolette, *Beyond the Big Bang,* 239.

35. Although we may use male and female terms to refer to the Universal and Galactic Beings, these divine beings intrinsically are devoid of sexual attributes. The gender terms "Father" (for the Universal Being) and "Mother" (for the Galactic Being) are used only for the sake of consistency within a metaphoric model of Reality, in accordance with ancient tradition. The Universal and Galactic Beings should be viewed as fully enlightened asexual cosmic beings, who can manifest either male or female attributes at will.

36. See Crosswell, *Alchemy of the Heavens,* 194.

37. Adapted from Sargeant's translation of the *Bhagavad Gita* 11.12–13.

38. In the Vedic tradition the glorious human beings that dwell on the Worlds of Light at the center of the galaxy are called the *pitris* (spiritual ancestors). The Vedic Seers located Pitri Loka in that portion of the sky corresponding to the signs of Scorpio and Sagittarius. On the basis of modern astronomical observations we now know that the center of the Milky Way galaxy lies in this same direction.

39. Adapted from Wilson's translation of the *Rig-Veda Sanhita* 10.10.9 verses 1, 2, 4, 6, and 7.

40. As one's awareness expands to encompass larger and larger scales of time and space, the music of the spheres unfolds from higher to lower frequencies of primordial sound. Eventually, the song of divine Love begins to sound like rolling thunder in one's awareness, and all individual harmonies become merged into the universal

sound of the Cosmic Hum.

41. Bunson, *Dictionary of Ancient Egypt,* 130.

42. Katha Upanishad 1.6.17, *Brahmopanisat-Sara Sangraha* [alternatively numbered 2.3.17 in *Eight Upanisads*].

43. Mundaka Upanishad 3.1.7. See *Brahmopanisat-Sara Sangraha* and *Eight Upanisads.*

44. Ibid., 2.2.7.

45. In the Vedic tradition, the lower self is called the *jiva* (breathing self) or *kshara purusha* (perishable soul). See *Bhagavad Gita,* trans. Sastry, chapters 13 and 15.16–17.

46. The spiritual eye is the subtle counterpart of the gross eye. It resides in the subtle body, and enables us to see spiritual forms and phenomena.

47. Sheldrake, *Presence of the Past,* xviii.

48. Ibid., xvii.

49. Ibid., 108.

50. "Morphic resonance involves a kind of action at a distance in both space and time. The hypothesis assumes that this influence does not decline with distance or time." Ibid., 109.

51. The various species of mineral, plant, and animal life that exist on our own planet are not the only types that exist in the Universe. Many other species exist on other planets. In addition, other types of nonhuman intelligent life forms exist on planets different from the Earth. Because of the dissimilarity between these beings and Earth-based life forms, the morphic fields associated with such beings do not resonate strongly with those on our planet. We have not introduced discussion of alien life forms into our narrative because we feel this would unnecessarily complicate our essential message.

52. "It is shown how, within the framework of general relativity and without the introduction of wormholes, it is possible to modify space-time in a way that allows a spaceship to travel with an arbitrarily large speed. By a purely local expansion of space-time behind the spaceship and an opposite contraction in front of it, motion faster than the speed of light as seen by observers outside the disturbed region is possible. The resulting distortion is reminiscent of the 'warp drive' of science fiction. However, just as happens with wormholes, exotic matter will be needed in order to generate a distortion of space-time like the one discussed here." Alcubierre, "The Warp Drive."

53. The term "negative" as used here does not mean "bad" or "evil." It means "minus." Exotic matter is a type of matter that has a minus mass-energy density.

54. This is the first principle presented in the Emerald Tablet, considered to be the most authoritative of all alchemical texts. See chapter 29 for a complete translation of this text.

55. The Central Galaxy is a spiral galaxy with four spiral arms. The sacred Vedic symbol known as the *swastika* is the esoteric sign of this Galaxy.

56. Such descriptive practices were common with the ancient Seers. For example, the Upanishads, the portion of the Vedic literature that deals with the nature of the higher Self, often use the term *atmani* "higher Selves" to refer to the Eternal Self (atman being equivalent to Brahman). Nevertheless, the higher Self also is described as "non-dual" *(advaita)*.

57. Adapted from *Eight Upanisads,* Gauda Pada's Mandukya Karika, 4.91–93, 98.

58. The term kurukshetra is used in the Bhagavad Gita to denote the battleground between the forces of light and darkness. This battleground corresponds to the luminous disk of the galaxy. The worlds that lie within the luminous disk of the galaxy are neither Worlds of Light nor worlds of darkness. They lie between the two extremes. This is where evolving souls incarnate to perform action, so that they eventually may evolve towards the Light.

59. In the Vedic tradition, the higher self (atman) also is called the *Sakshin* (Witness). The Egyptian word for the gods is *Neters,* which literally means the "Watchers."

60. Adapted from *Eight Upanisads,* Mundaka Upanisad, 3.1.1–4.

61. *Hermetica,* Libellus 1.13b–15, 121–123.

62. The chitta vrittis are polarized modifications of chitta, which manifest a predominance of either masculine (yang) or feminine (yin) energy. These modified subtle particles display helical or spiral motions. Hence they are described as *vrittis* (derived from the root *vrit,* "to turn, revolve, rotate"). The vrittis are vortical in their nature, resembling quantized whirlpools or tiny tornadoes within the field of chitta. Such phenomena in nature are described scientifically as vortex filaments. The vrittis display a stringy appearance, and correspond to the rays, streams, or nadis of subtle matter-energy that pervade the subtle body.

63. The celestial body formed of pure chitta also is called the causal body *(karana sharira).* It alone is capable of reflecting pure consciousness. In the Yoga Sutras of Patanjali, the celestial body of the higher self, formed of pure chitta alone without modifications, is called the self-referral form of the seer *(drashta svarupa).* When the seer is established in this self-referral form, he or she is said to be in the state of Yoga (union). The seer then becomes a knower of his or her own birthless and immortal Self (atman).

64. *Hermetica,* Libellus 16.9.

65. The celestial body of the higher Self can travel nonlocally (faster than light) because the celestial body is not upheld on the basis of physical forces. It is upheld on the basis of nonlocal pure consciousness alone. Because pure consciousness is nonlocal, it can project itself and its manifestations (on the level of chitta) anywhere in the Universe without being limited by the speed of light.

66. Maitri Upanishad 6.13. See *Brahmopanisat-Sara Sangraha.*

67. The celestial rays that consist of unpolarized subtle matter resemble hollow tubes filled with pure consciousness. Upon entering into such a ray, an individual soul (whether mortal or immortal) may travel at nonlocal speeds to its designated destination. When an ordinary human being dies, his or her mortal soul enters into the ray of celestial fire that connects our planet with the center of the galaxy, and is then conveyed to the throne of God that resides at the center of the galaxy. This corresponds to the central star, which appears to the deceased soul as a blazing light filled with divine love. There the soul is presented with a review of its life on Earth, and then dispatched to a new world or returned to Earth depending upon the nature of its karma. Enlightened souls do not go to the center of the galaxy—they proceed directly to the center of the Universe. This nonlocal transportation is not instantaneous, although practically speaking it is close to that. The journey to the center of the galaxy covers 27,000 light years, but is traversed by the mortal soul in a matter of seconds. This illustrates the nature of the celestial highways.

68. The entire ninth mandala of the Rig Veda is devoted to the praise of the Soma, the Nectar of Immorality, which is said to be purified by flowing through a woolen filter, called the avi.

69. In the Vedic texts, there is an ancient myth that Agni, the messenger of the gods, once disappeared from the Earth and could not be found. All of the gods hunted for him everywhere throughout Creation, but he could not be found anywhere. Eventually they located him. He was hiding inside a hollow reed submerged beneath the waters.

70. A few thousand years ago the arrow of Sagittarius was aimed almost directly at the center of the galaxy.

71. We plan to expand upon this highly condensed description of this great journey in a subsequent book.

72. *Dionysiaca* 38.35.

73. See *Plato's Cosmology.*

74. *Dionysiaca* 38.424–31.

75. See Santillana and von Dechend, *Hamlet's Mill,* 256. See also Laviolette, *Beyond the Big Bang,* 209–210.

76. See Santillana and von Dechend, *Hamlet's Mill,* 257–258.

77. The subtle fusion processes described here are the exact opposite of the subtle fission processes that occur in the regions of dark matter. Subtle fusion processes manifest the quality of sattva (physical lightness and spiritual light) while subtle fission processes manifest the quality of *tamas* (physical inertia and spiritual darkness). Also see note 123.

78. This principle was used by the ancient Egyptian and Vedic Seers to develop simple levitation technologies that still remain beyond the grasp of modern scientists.

79. The awakening and refreshing influence that propagates around the Earth just before dawn is caused by the luminous life force of the Sun that precedes its actual rising.

80. Certain ancient Seers and prophets were so intensely filled with the Holy Spirit that they were considered to be embodiments of the Divine Messenger. The list of such prophets includes the ancient Seer Hermes Trismegistus, the Biblical patriarch Enoch, the Middle Eastern prophet Idris, as well as the Central and South American visionaries Viracocha, Zamna, Queztacoatl, and Kukulcan.

81. *World Book Encyclopedia,* vol. 15, 358.

82. Rundle-Clark, *Myth and Symbol,* cited in Bauval and Gilbert, *Orion Mystery,* 188.

83. Although this myth is alluded to in the Rig Veda, it is most fully developed in the Brahmanas and Puranas.

84. See Gilbert and Cotterell, *Mayan Prophecies,* 3–5.

85. Cited in Santillana and von Dechend, *Hamlet's Mill,* 163–164.

86. Ibid., 213.

87. See Gilbert and Cotterell, *Mayan Prophecies,* chapter 6. See also Aveni, *Empires of Time,* 254–255.

88. Sahagun, *History of New Spain,* cited in Aveni, *Empires of Time,* 254.

89. Aveni, *Empires of Time,* 255.

90. See Gilbert and Cotterell, *Mayan Prophecies,* 131.

91. See "Parallel between Indian and Babylonian Ritual."

92. See Santillana and von Dechend, *Hamlet's Mill,* 125.

93. The powerful nourishing and evolutionary influence of such groups has been carefully studied by numerous scientists and published in reputable journals. For a review of some of this research see Yogi, *Maharishi Vedic University,* 277–288.

94. "As the numbers 1,296 and 864 were the key to unraveling the astronomical and geodetic secrets of the Great Pyramid, they may in due course resolve the mysteries of the Mesoamerican pyramids. Is it a coincidence that a circle of 1,296,000 units has a radius of 206.265 units and that 20.6264 is the length of both an English and an Egyptian cubit, that the Hebrew shekel weighs 129.6 grams, and the English guinea 129.6 grains, and the measure of the Most Holy in Solomon's Temple is 1,296 inches? Not only was the number 1,296,000 the numerical basis for astronomical measurements as far back as the records are traceable, it was also the favorite number in Plato's mystic symbolism." Tompkins, *Mysteries of the Mexican Pyramids,* 256.

95. See Genesis 6. This is also true in Vedic astrology or Jyotish, where the full cycle of nine planetary periods *(dashas)* is equal to 120 years.

96. For a review of this data see:
http://www.leland.stanford.edu/~meehan/donnelly/paleo2.html.

97. *Hermetica,* Asclepius 3.25.

98. Ibid., 3.25–6.

99. Ibid., 3.26.

100. Coe, *Breaking the Maya Code,* 275–6.

101. Rig Veda 10.191.2–4, translation by Maharishi Mahesh Yogi.

102. The worlds of darkness lie in the regions that extend beyond the rim of the luminous disk of the galaxy.

103. *Hermetica,* Libellus 16.13–16. The translation has been adapted to translate the Greek word *daemon* as "nature spirit."

104. Ibid.

105. The cycles of time are designed to allow the structure of the Earth and all beings that dwell upon it to evolve and change. To use a crude analogy, it is as if the bones of the Earth receive a chiropractic adjustment every 13,000 years. At the end of each Dark Age, the hard surface crust and tectonic plates shift and adjust into new positions that more efficiently can accommodate the new levels of subtle energy infused into the planet at the beginning of each new Golden Age. When the level of subtle energy in the Earth is very low compared to the level of subtle energy in the illuminating wave, sudden violent Earth changes can occur. This is analogous to making a chiropractic adjustment when the patient is tense and the muscles are stiff. A forceful adjustment made under such conditions can be painful and cause serious damage. On the other hand, when the level of subtle energy in the Earth approaches the level of subtle energy in the illuminating wave, the contrast is reduced, the Earth changes are more gentle, and minimal damage is incurred. This

corresponds to a chiropractic adjustment when the patient is relaxed and the muscles are loose. Under such conditions, the adjustment can be painless and improve the general well-being of the patient, rather than cause damage.

106. Genesis 6.4 New English Bible.

107. Ibid., 6.5–8.

108. Ibid., 6.17.

109. According to the ancient legend, Prometheus carried the sacred fire to the Earth from the celestial regions in a "hollow reed." This hollow reed represents the pillar of celestial fire that descended onto the Earth at the onset of the Age of Aquarius, some 26,000 years ago.

110. For a summary description of the Asuras, see Fausboill, *Indian Mythology*, 40ff.

111. Mason, *Ancient Civilizations of Peru*, 163.

112. See *Nature*, and *New Scientist*.

113. Rand Flem-Ath, outline of *When the Sky Fell*, cited in Hancock, *Fingerprints of the Gods*, 468.

114. Cited in Santillana and von Dechend, *Hamlet's Mill*, 325.

115. See references cited in Hancock, *Fingerprints of the Gods*, chapter 51.

116. Ibid., 472.

117. Schneider and Londer, *Coevolution of Climate*, 88.

118. Hibben, Frank C., *The Lost Americans*, cited in Hapgood, *Path of the Pole*, 275ff.

119. For a more complete review of the evidence pertaining to this destruction, see Hancock, *Fingerprints of the Gods*, chapters 27 and 51.

120. See Ginzberg, *Legends of the Jews*, vol. 3, 22.

121. Cambrey, *Lapland Legends*, cited in Allan and Delair, *When the Earth Nearly Died*, 301.

122. Allan and Delair, *When the Earth Nearly Died*, 304.

123. Dark subtle matter represents a form of subtle matter in which *subtle fission* processes predominate. Fission processes tend to break down complex aggregates of subtle particles into more elementary systems. When this occurs, the system tends to absorb light rather than radiate light. The apparent weight or mass of the system also appears to increase, because it possesses more inertia. In the Vedic tradition, this type of subtle matter was said to possess the quality of tamas—inertia or darkness. Luminous subtle matter, on the other hand, represents that type of subtle matter in which *subtle fusion* processes dominate. Fusion processes represent processes of self-organization, whereby more elementary units of subtle matter become fused together to form higher order systems. When this occurs, the system

tends to radiate light rather than absorb light, becoming luminous. The apparent weight or mass of the system also tends to decrease, because of a reduction in the inertia of the system. In the Vedic tradition, this type of subtle matter was said to display the quality of sattva—spiritual purity, physical lightness, and luminosity. Because these two qualities are directly opposed, they tend to destroy or neutralize one another. However, a dynamic balance of these two qualities is necessary for the sustained existence of all forms of matter and life. In the Vedic tradition, the dynamic balance between the forces of darkness and light was denoted by the term *rajas*—passionate dynamism. Through the power of rajas, light is transformed into darkness and darkness into light in a way that sustains the status quo of the system. Under the influence of rajas, the system neither evolves nor devolves—it merely sustains its current level of existence. In order to evolve very quickly, one must take recourse to the quality of sattva; it is the means to achieve true spiritual victory.

124. It has been scientifically shown that a large group of individuals practicing transcendental meditation (TM) together in one location can have a dramatic positive influence on the trends of society in the surrounding area, even though there is very little direct contact between the meditation group and the surrounding society. This effect, which was discovered in 1974, has been termed the Maharishi Effect after its discoverer, Maharishi Mahesh Yogi. See Yogi, *Maharishi Vedic University*, 277–283.

125. See Filby, *The Flood Reconsidered.*

126. *The Epic of Gilgamesh,* 61.

127. Cited in Hancock, *Fingerprints of the Gods,* 188–9.

128. Ibid., 192.

129. Ibid., 193.

130. Ibid.

131. Ibid., 193–4.

132. Ibid., chapter 51.

133. See Fausboill, *Indian Mythology,* 40ff.

134. This does not refer to initiation into some spiritual technique that the aspirant must practice. It refers to initiation into the state of enlightenment. This initiation always is an act of pure grace. No technique or practice is competent to deliver one to the other shore. The state of enlightenment cannot be obtained through karma or action. Karma or action may prepare one to receive the Light, but the Light of enlightenment always is given as a gift through an act of pure grace. Those who are qualified to give this ultimate gift are the enlightened masters and seers, as well as the Divine Messenger. To give the gift of enlightenment, the enlightened masters do not have to physically travel to the individual. The masters are endowed with subtle

rays of consciousness that can extend anywhere on the planet and bestow the gift of enlightenment. The enlightened masters thus can remain hidden away in seclusion, while at the same time tending the flock of souls under their care.

135. See Wood, *Legacy,* 51.

136. Ibid., 52.

137. See Yogi, *Maharishi Vedic University.*

138. See *Manetho,* 231. See also Murray, *Splendour That Was Egypt,* 12.

139. See Gilbert and Cotterell, *Mayan Prophecies,* 200.

140. Prior to the flood, the northern Mediterranean regions were sparsely populated because of the cold climate of the Ice Age. Therefore the majority of the enlightened Seers came from the regions on the southern and eastern shores of the Mediterranean.

141. Photographs of these engravings may be seen in the recent book by Daniken, *Eyes of the Sphinx.*

142. See West, *Serpent in the Sky,* 100.

143. See Daniken, *Eyes of the Sphinx,* 172.

144. See Jochmans, "Top Ten Out-of-Place Artifacts."

145. See Bunson, *Dictionary of Ancient Egypt,* 107.

146. For example, in the ninth Mandala of the Rig Veda, Soma is described as the milk of heaven (RV 9.51.2), which flows in streams to the dear places of heaven (RV 9.12.8).

147. See Jochmans, "Top Ten Out-of-Place Artifacts."

148. See Leviticus 10.

149. See Bunson, *Dictionary of Ancient Egypt,* 65.

150. Ibid.

151. Ibid., 172.

152. See *Egyptian Book of the Dead,* 150.

153. The connection between the ankh symbol and the Divine Messenger (Thoth) is revealed by the fact that the hieroglyphic sign used to write the term "ankh" is a "created ibis," a bird sacred to and symbolic of the Divine Messenger. However, in Egyptian art the representation of the ankh as an ibis is rare. Most of the papyrus drawings and wall engravings represent the ankh as above, using the sign of the Egyptian cross.

154. Hancock, *Fingerprints of the Gods,* 255.

155. In the dramatic reenactments of the Osirian myth that became popular

towards the end of the Egyptian civilization, the resurrection of Osiris sometimes was symbolized by the physical erection of a Djed pillar. This was meant to serve as the mooring post of the soul during its celestial sojourn among the gods.

156. This is taken from *The Alchemical Catechism* of Baron Tschoudy, ed. E. A. Waite, available online in the Alchemical Virtual Library at http://www.levity.com/alchemy/tschoudy.html.

157. West, *Serpent in the Sky,* 125.

158. Ibid., 136.

159. It is well known that the Egyptians received a large portion of their precious metals from ore deposits in the Sinai peninsula, where they operated mines from the earliest antiquity. The communities of metallurgists in this region must have had access to many ancient secrets of the Old Kingdom. More than likely, these secrets were passed down from generation to generation over the centuries. Did the Egyptian ambassador to the Sinai become privy to certain ancient secrets that later were depicted on his tomb? See Sitchin, *Stairway to Heaven,* 70.

160. This comparison was first made by Sitchin in his book *Stairway to Heaven,* 71.

161. The quotations in the following discussion of this illustration are drawn from *The Egyptian Book of the Dead.* See plate 2.

162. This finds corroboration in Exodus 35.30–34. There Bezalel is described as an expert metallurgist, skilled in preparing copper, silver, and gold. This is significant because Bezalel was the divinely inspired craftsman who Moses appointed to prepare the Bread of the Presence.

163. See Hudson, *Superconductivity and Modern Alchemy.*

164. See West, *Serpent in the Sky,* 131.

165. See Lubicz, *Sacred Science,* 182–183.

166. Ibid., 130–131.

167. There are a number of excellent books on this subject that recently have been published. These include Bauval and Gilbert, *Orion Mystery,* and Hancock and Bauval, *Message of the Sphinx.*

168. See Hancock, *Fingerprints of the Gods,* 201.

169. Ibid., 200.

170. Although it is likely that most of the sacred sites originally were marked by nothing more than a sacred pillar atop of which was perched a fiery benben, at certain sites more ambitious projects may have been undertaken. There is growing evidence that the Sphinx, the Valley Temple, the Osireion, and even the great stone bases of the Pyramids at Giza may have been constructed during this very early epoch, when the previous Golden Age was at its peak.

171. See Wallis Budge, *Fetish to God,* 147. See also *Ancient Egyptian Book of the Dead,* 11.

172. See *World Book Encyclopedia,* vol. 1, 328.

173. This translation was adapted by the author. See *Emerald Tablet.*

174. *Rasataramgiri* 5.2.

175. See *Rasanavam,* chapters 11 and 12.

176. See Ray, *History of Chemistry,* 115.

177. See White, "Why Gurus are Heavy."

178. *Jerusalem Bible,* chronological table, 343.

179. Cited in Hancock, *Sign and the Seal,* 295.

180. Acts 7.22 New English Bible.

181. Exodus 16.13–15 New English Bible.

182. Exodus 16.31 New English Bible.

183. Exodus 16.32–35 New English Bible.

184. Exodus 35.30–33 New English Bible.

185. Exodus 35.11–14 New English Bible.

186. Adapted from Sargeant's translation of the *Bhagavad Gita* 3.10–11.

187. Mahanarayana Upanishad 79.11. See *Brahmopanisat-Sara Sangraha.*

188. In Vedic Science, the field of primordial matter energy is called Prakriti, and is considered completely unmanifest. The first created product or manifestation of this field is chitta or mahat—corresponding to subtle matter-energy. The Vedic myth illustrates the mechanics by which subtle matter-energy is generated from the field of primordial matter-energy. According to our interpretation of this myth, these mechanics involve rotating mass.

189. See Hudson, "White Powder Gold, Part 1," 28.

190. Ibid., 31.

191. See Hudson, *Superconductivity and Modern Alchemy.*

192. See "Inertias of Superdeformed Bands."

193. See Hudson, *Non-Metallic Forms.*

194. Revelation 2.17 New English Bible.

195. See the story of the revival of Innana in Wolkstein and Kramer, *Innana: Queen of Heaven and Earth,* 60–89.

196. Genesis 5.

197. Genesis 5.23–24 New English Bible.

198. See *The Apocryphal Old Testament,* 170.

199. See Mackenzie, *The Royal Masonic Cyclopedia,* 200–202.

200. Maronite Patriarch of Lebanon, cited in Sitchin, *Stairway to Heaven,* 181. According to this particular legend, the mountain fastness of Baalbek was built by Cain, the son of Adam, in the year 133 of Creation. Cain also had a son named Enoch. Apparently the site at Baalbek originally was named after this Enoch, the son of Cain.

201. 2 Kings 2.11 New English Bible.

202. John 20.26.

203. Luke 24.39–41 New English Bible.

204. Mark 16.19 New English Bible.

205. A physical form is visible to our ordinary eyes, while a celestial form is visible only to the eyes of the enlightened Seers.

206. Adapted from Wilson's translation of the *Rig-Veda Sanhita* 10.10.7.

207. See Rig Veda 10.2.9.

208. See Gardner, *Bloodline of the Holy Grail,* 347.

209. Exodus 25.10–22 New English Bible.

210. For example, see Leviticus 10.

211. Numbers 4.5–6 New English Bible.

212. Exodus 26.31 New English Bible.

213. For a review of the documented reports of fiery emanations coming from the Ark, see Hancock, *Sign and the Seal,* 274–276, 285–287, 354.

214. See Leviticus 16.2.

215. See Hancock, *Sign and the Seal,* 275.

216. Tyson, "God-Making," 107.

217. Exodus 19.18 New English Bible.

218. Exodus 34.29–35.

219. *Hermetica,* Libellus 4.3–5.

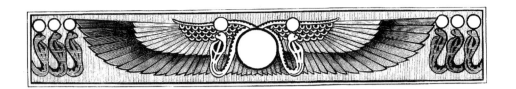

Ancient Texts

The Apocryphal Old Testament. Ed. H. F. D. Sparks. Oxford: Clarendon Paperbacks, 1989.
The Jerusalem Bible. London: Eyre & Spottiswoode, 1968.
The New English Bible, with the Apocrypha. Oxford University Press and Cambridge University Press, 1970.

The Ancient Egyptian Book of the Dead. Trans. Raymond Faulkner. London: British Museum Publications, 1989.
The Egyptian Book of the Dead. Trans. Raymond Faulkner. San Francisco: Chronicle Books, 1994. [this edition includes illustrations]
Manetho. Trans. W. G. Waddell. London: William Heinnemann, 1940.

Dionysiaca. Trans. W. H. D. Rouse. 1940.
Plato's Cosmology: The Timaeus of Plato. Trans. Francis Macdonald Cornford. New York: The Library of Liberal Arts, 1957.
Plato. *Timaeus and Critias.* London: Penguin Classics, 1977.

Hermetica: The Ancient Greek and Latin Writings Which Contain Religious or Philosophical Teaching Ascribed to Hermes Trismegistus. Ed. and trans. Walter Scott. Boston: Shambala, 1993.
"The Emerald Tablet." Richard Smoley. *Gnosis* 40 (Summer 1996), 17–19.

The Bhagavad Gita. Trans. Winthrop Sargeant. Albany: State University of New York Press, 1984.
The Bhagavad Gita: With the Commentary of Sri Sankaracharya. Trans. Alladi Mahadeva Sastry. 1897. Reprinted, Madras: Samata Books, 1977.
Brahmopanisat-Sara Sangraha. Trans. Vidyatilaka. Sacred Books of the Hindus, vol. 18, part 1. Ed. Major B. D. Basu. Allahabad: The Panini Office, 1916. Contains translations of excerpts from numerous Upanishads.
Eight Upanisads: With the Commentary of Sankaracarya. 2 vols. Trans. Swami

Gambhirananda. Calcutta: Advaita Ashrama, 1957–8. Vol. 1 contains Isa, Kena, Katha, and Taittiriya Upanisads. Vol. 2 contains Aitareya, Mundaka, Prasna, and Mandukya (with Gaudapada's *Karika*) Upanisads.

Mahanarayanopanisad. Trans. Swami Vimalananda. Mylapore, Madras: Sri Ramakrishna Math, 1957.

Rasanavam. Ed. Praphulla Chandra Ray, and Harischandra Kaviratna. Bibliotheca Indica, Nos. 1193, 1220, and 1238. Calcutta: Asiatic Society of Bengal, 1901–1910. Sanskrit text.

Rasataramgiri. Ed. Haridatta Shastri, et. al. Delhi: Motilal Banarsidass, 1965. Sanskrit text.

Rig-Veda Sanhita. Trans. H. H. Wilson, et al. 1850–88. Reprinted, Delhi: NAG Publishers, 1977–8.

Srimad Bhagavata. 4 vols. Trans. Swami Tapasyananda. Madras: Sri Ramakrishna Math, 1980–82.

The Visnu Purana. 2 vols. Trans. H. H. Wilson. Reprinted, Delhi: NAG Publishers, 1980.

The Epic of Gilgamesh. London: Penguin Classics, 1988.

Modern Works

Alcubierre, M. "The Warp Drive: Hyper-fast Travel within General Relativity." *Classical and Quantum Gravity* 11 (1994): L73–L77.

Allan, D. S., and J. B. Delair. *When the Earth Nearly Died.* Bath, U. K.: Gateway Books, 1995.

Aveni, Anthony F. *Empires of Time, Calendars, Clocks, and Cultures.* New York: Kodansha America, 1995.

Bauval, Robert, and Adrian Gilbert. *The Orion Mystery.* London: William Heinemann Ltd., 1994.

Becklin, E. E., I. Gatley, and M. W. Werner. "Far-infrared Observations of Sagittarius A: The Luminosity and Dust Density in the Central Parsec of the Galaxy." *Astrophysical Journal* 258 (1982): 135–142.

Bunson, Margaret. *A Dictionary of Ancient Egypt.* New York: Oxford University Press, 1991.

Cambrey, L. de . *Lapland Legends.* New Haven and Oxford: 1926.

Coe, Michael D. *Breaking the Maya Code.* London: Thames & Hudson, 1992.

Crosswell, Ken. *The Alchemy of the Heavens.* New York: Anchor Books, 1995.

Daniken, Erich von. *The Eyes of the Sphinx.* Berkley Books, 1996.

Fausboill, V. *Indian Mythology According to the Mahabharata.* London: 1902.

Filby, Frederick A. *The Flood Reconsidered: A Review of the Evidences of Geology, Archeology, Ancient Literature, and the Bible.* London: Pickering and Inglis, Ltd., 1970.

Flem-Ath, Rand and Rose. *When the Sky Fell.* Canada: Stoddart, 1995.

Gardner, Laurence. *Bloodline of the Holy Grail.* Shaftesbury, Dorset: Element Books, 1996.

Gilbert, Adrian G., and Maurice M. Cotterell. *The Mayan Prophecies.* Rockport, Massachusetts: Element, 1995

Ginzberg, Louis. *The Legends of the Jews.* Philadelphia: The Jewish Publication Society of America, 1911.

Hancock, Graham. *Fingerprints of the Gods.* New York: Crown Publishers, 1995.

Hancock, Graham. *The Sign and the Seal: The Quest for the Lost Ark of the Covenant.* New York: Touchstone, 1992.

Hancock, Graham, and Robert Bauval. *The Message of the Sphinx: A Quest for the Hidden Legacy of Mankind.* New York: Crown Publishers, 1996.

Hapgood, Charles H. *The Path of the Pole.* New York: Chilton Books, 1970.

Hudson, David. *Non-Metallic, Monoatomic Forms of Transition Elements.* British patent.

Hudson, David. *Superconductivity and Modern Alchemy.* Workshop given in Dallas, Texas, February 10 and 11, 1995. A videotape recording is available through The Eclectic Viewpoint, PO Box 802735, Dallas, TX, 75380. A transcript is available online (as of March, 1996) at: http://www.monatomic.earth.com.

Hudson, David. "White Powder Gold, Part I." *Nexus* 3, no. 5 (August 1996); and "White Powder Gold, Part II." *Nexus* 3, no. 6 (October 1996).

"Inertias of Superdeformed Bands." *Physical Review C* 41, no. 4 (1990): 1861–1864.

Jochmans, Joseph Robert. "Top Ten Prophecies for the Year 2000." *Atlantis Rising* 2.

Jochmans, Joseph Robert. "Top Ten Out-of-Place Artifacts." *Atlantis Rising* 5.

Laviolette, Paul. *Beyond the Big Bang.* Rochester, Vermont: Park Street Press, 1995.

Levi, Eliphas. *Transcendental Magic.* York Beach, Maine: Samuel Weiser, Inc., 1995.

Lubicz, R. A. Schwaller de. *Sacred Science.* Rochester, Vermont: Inner Traditions International, 1982.

Mackenzie, Kenneth. *The Royal Masonic Cyclopedia.* Wellingborough: Aquarian Press, 1987.

Mason, J. Alden. *The Ancient Civilizations of Peru.* London: Penguin Classics, 1977.

Murray, Margaret A. *The Splendour That Was Egypt.* London: Sidgwick & Jackson, 1987.

Nader, Tony. *Human Physiology: Expression of Veda and the Vedic Literature.* 2d ed. Vlodrop, The Netherlands: Maharishi Vedic University, 1995.

Nature 234, (27 December 1971): 173–4.

New Scientist, (6 January 1972): 7.

"A Parallel between Indian and Babylonian Sacrificial Ritual." *Journal of the American Oriental Society* 54 (1934): 107–128.

Ray, Praphulla Chandra. *History of Chemistry in Ancient and Medieval India.* Ed. Priyanaranjan Ray. Calcutta: Indian Chemical Society, 1956.

Rundle-Clark, R. T. *Myth and Symbol in Ancient Egypt.* London: Thames and Hudson, 1991.

Sahagun, B. de. *General History of the Things of New Spain.* Trans. A. Anderson and C. Dibble. Santa Fe: School of American Research; Salt Lake City: University of Utah Press, 1953.

Santillana, Giorgio de, and Hertha von Dechend. *Hamlet's Mill.* Boston: David R. Gordine, Publisher, Inc., 1977.

Schneider, Stephen, and Ramli Londer. *The Coevolution of Climate and Life.* San Francisco: Sierra Club Books, 1984.

Sheldrake, Rupert. *The Presence of the Past.* Rochester, Vermont: Park Street Press, 1995.

Sitchin, Zechariah. *The Stairway to Heaven.* New York: Avon Books, 1980.

Tompkins, Peter. *Mysteries of the Mexican Pyramids.* Harper & Row, 1976.

Tyson, Donald. "God-Making." In *The Golden Dawn Journal, Book III: The Art of Hermes.* St. Paul, Minnesota: Lewellyn Publications, 1995.

Wallis Budge, E. A. *From Fetish to God in Ancient Egypt.* Oxford: Oxford University Press, 1934.

West, John Anthony. *The Serpent in the Sky.* Wheaton, Illinois: Quest Books, 1993.

White, David Gordon. "Why Gurus are Heavy." The Divinity School, University of Chicago. Publication facts unknown.

Wolkstein, Diane, and Samuel Noah Kramer. *Innana: Queen of Heaven and Earth.* New York: Harper & Row, 1983.

Wood, Michael. *Legacy, the Search For Ancient Cultures.* New York: Sterling Publishing Co., Inc., 1992.

The World Book Encyclopedia. Chicago: Field Enterprises Educational International, 1968.

Yogi, Maharishi Mahesh. *Maharishi Vedic University—Introduction.* Holland: Maharishi Vedic University Press, 1994.

World Wide Web Resources

Numerous sites provide information from a wide range of perspectives on the topics discussed in this book. Sites that may be interesting to explore (current as of April, 1997) include the following:

Egyptology Resources at http://www.newton.cam.ac.uk/egypt/index.html

Egyptian Book of the Dead, complete online translation by Sir E. A. Wallis Budge at http://www.lysator.liu.se/~drokk/BoD

The Book of Enoch, from the Apocrypha and Pseudographa of the Old Testament, online translation by R. H. Charles (Oxford: The Clarendon Press) at http://wesley.nnc.edu/noncanon/ot/pseudo/enoch.htm

Hermes Trismegistus, The Archaic Underground at http://marlowe.wimsey.com/~rshand/streams/scripts/hermes.html

The Alchemical Library at http://www.levity.com/alchemy/home.html

Sites related to alchemy available at http://www.levity.com/alchemy/related.html

An overview of Vedic literature and how to order it: The Age of Enlightenment Mall, New World Books at http://www.aoem.com/Bookstore/BookPages/BooksVedic.html

Sites devoted to various theories of catastrophic Earth changes available at http://www.access.digex.net/~medved/catlink.html

What on Earth Happened in 3200 B.C.? Paleoclimatic Evidence of Dramatic Events at that Time at http://www.leland.stanford.edu/~meehan/donnelly/paleo.html

Annotated bibliography of technical works on the possibility of faster than light phenomena, including interstellar travel, available at http://lerc.nasa.gov.80/other_groups/PAO/html/warp/bibliog.htm

Information on free energy, gravity control, various electronic devices, and health available at http://www.keelynet.com

Information on David Hudson's research of monoatomic high-spin elements, producing a white powder with extraordinary properties at http://www.monatomic.earth.com

Atlantis Rising Magazine on the Web, covering various ancient mysteries and esoteric issues at http://www.aa.net/~mwm/atlantis/atrise2.html

Esoteric Web Link Index, 479 places to go at http://www.AccessNewAge.com/links/index.html#index01

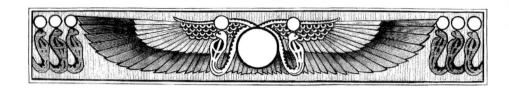

Aaron 303
Abydos 245
Adam and Eve
  fall of 138
  illustration 138
Adams, John 301
Agni. *See also* Divine Messenger
  and kundalini 141
  as divine hawk (shyena) 143-144
  identified with Pleiades 151
  illustration in form of divine hawk 143
Akkadian texts 152
Alaska, and evidence of pole shift 190-192
Alchemical Catechism 236-237
Alexander the Great 253-254
Alexandrian Library 254
American Philosophical Society 301
Amrit
  gift of Lord Dhanvantari 259-260
  identified with ambrosia from Aquarian
    urn 268, 276
  produced by churning Milky Ocean 275-
    276
Ani
  illustration 243
  Papyrus of 230-231, 242-244
Ankh 232-235
Antarctica
  evidence of pole shift 190-192
  ice sheets, illustration 191
Antiquities of the Jews 264
Anu (or An) 152
Anubis 244-247
  illustration 245
Ap-uat. *See* Anubis
Aquarius
  and the Eridanus 124-125
  beginning of Age 15-16
  compared with Lord Dhanvantari 260,
    268, 276

epochal transition at beginning of Age
    18-19
  identified with Ganymede 268
  illustration 269
  knowledge of celestial fire given at last
    Age 184
  now at junction between Pisces and 185
  resurgence of knowledge of alchemy in
    Age 267-269
  signs of the four living creatures 26-28
  urn of 125, 268-269, 276
Ark of the Covenant 302-307
  danger of 228, 303
  example of sacred technology 39
  illustration 302, 304
Ashva-Medha ritual, and Pleiades 151-152
Ashvattha Tree 56-58
Asuras 182, 184
  churning Milky Ocean 271-275
Atlantis 202-203
Atum-Re
  creation myth 75-76
  identified with benben stone 237-238
  in Hathor Temple engravings 225
  symbolized in illustration of Taurus 121
Ayurveda 259-261
Aztec
  eagle and serpent myth 144
  eagle and serpent, illustration 145
  New Fire Ceremony 149-150
  serpents (double-helix), illustration 137
Baalbek 288
Babylonian myth, and pole shift 190
Bauval. *See* Hancock
Bekaa. *See* Baalbek
Bennu bird
  ashes carried to Heliopolis 242
  described with illustration 142-143
  worshipped in form of benben stone
    237-238

Bezalel 266-267

Bhagavad Gita
celestial form of God 64
Tree of Life embodiment of the Veda 58
Tree of Life—Ashvattha Tree 56

Borneo celestial tree/Pleiades myth 149

Brahma, Universal Being 73

Bread of the Presence. See Manna

Buddhism, and rejection of ritual 213

Byblos 234

Caduceus
ankh related to 233-234
described with illustration 136
Krittika (Pleiades) related to 150-151
represented by alchemical furnace 258
represents divine bird 141
similarity to DNA double-helix 139
standard of Divine Messenger 136

Central Galaxy of the Universe
and divine correspondence 97-100
Central Sun as seat of Universal Being 55
described 50-51
Divine Messenger link between Earth and Creator abiding at 134-135
Eridanus (stream of celestial fire) descends from 123
in direction of Taurus 122
Mount Olympus and the Eridanus 124
roots of the Tree of Life 56

Central Sun of the Central Galaxy
central star of the galaxy corresponds to 62-63
dwelling of Atum-Re in Egyptian tradition 76, 225
emanation of celestial fire 55-56
Mouth of God 104
network of celestial rays streams from 113
seat of the Universal Being 55
symbolized by Ashva-Medha ritual 151-152
symbolized in illustration of spiritual ascension 232-233

Chambers of Light 313-315

Chinese legend of flood and pole shift 201

Christian tradition. See also Holy Spirit
blood and body of Christ 286
Jesus Christ, ascension of 289
rejection of ritual 213

Corpus Hermeticum 255-256, 313-314

Cosmic Egg
(s) infinite number of 55
and divine correspondence 97
cosmic body of the Creator 73
fourteen stages of evolution within symbolized by Ashva-Medha 151-152
fringes of, the branches of the Tree of Life 56
represented by Hermetic vessel 257
seven-layered structure of the Universe 47-49
structure of the Universe in the Revelation of John 24-25
transcending through path of knowledge 120

Cosmic Lotus, transcending through path of knowledge 120

Creator. See Universal Being

Critias, and Atlantis 202

Denderah
illustration of Temple at 224
Temple at 223-227

Devas
churning Milky Ocean 271-275
in Mahabharata 184

Dhanvantari 259-260
identified with Aquarius 268, 276
illustration 260

Dictionary of Ancient Egypt 229

Divine Ka
and enlightenment 100-101
and the immortal soul 102
at the heart of celestial beings 71-72
awakening of 82-83
awakening of galaxies and stars 275
body of the higher Self 104-106, 111-112
centaur represents evolution of elemental souls into 118
Egyptian tradition 75-76
in the human heart 71-72, 76-77
non-local travel 297
nourished with Bread of Life 244, 247
nourishment of 78
rays of celestial fire emanate from 111
Vedic tradition 73-75

Divine Messenger. See also Agni; Hermes; Holy Spirit; Mercury; Thoth
agent of Universal Being 119

and kundalini 139-141
and the flood 185
body emanates from Central Sun 56
Caduceus standard of 136
coordinates higher Self and lower self
    106-107
delivers cosmic life-breath of God 120-
    121
Divine Presence of God 48
founder of Hermetic tradition 255
in the Revelation of John 21-24
myths of the Pleiades 146-153
nature and function 133-136
periodic descent 24
restoration of Golden Age after cata-
    clysm 195
return of 308
Tree of Life body of 56, 58
widely represented as divine bird 141-
    145
Divine Presence
    carried by Divine Messenger/Tree of Life
      56
    Central Sun seat of in Universe 233
    extended throughout Creation by Divine
      Messenger 134
    filling cloud surrounding Ark of the
      Covenant 228
    fills the pillar of celestial fire 4-5
    in one's own heart 77
    in subtle matter technologies 39
    seven aspects constitute Divine
      Messenger 48
Djed pillar
    described 228-229
    illustration of spiritual ascension 232-234
    illustration, with high-voltage insulator
      229
    symbol of Osiris 234-236
Earth World
    described 66
    described in Vedic literature 289
Edfu Temple texts 248-250
Egyptian Book of the Dead. See Ani,
    Papyrus of
Egyptian Cross. *See* Ankh
Egyptian tradition 219-254. *See also*
    Atum-Re; Djed Pillar; Hathor;
    Heliopolis; Osiris; Pyramids; Thoth
Alexandrian Library 254

ancient source of sacred technologies
    221-222
Ani, illustration 243
animal skins used in chambers of light
    241
Ankh 232-235
Anubis 244-247
Anubis, illustration 245
ark used for storage of temple gods 305
benben stone 237-239
bennu bird ashes carried to Heliopolis
    242
bennu bird described with illustration
    142-143
bennu bird worshipped in form of ben-
    ben stone 238
Bread of Life 242-247
Builder Gods 248-251
chamber of light 239-242
chamber of light, illustration 240, 242
churning process of galactic creation
    273-274
Denderah 223-227
Divine Ka described 75-76
Divine Ka nourished with Bread of Life
    244, 247
divine knowledge of the stars 69-70
Edfu Temple texts 248-250
emergence from prehistory 220
Field of Reeds 114
gold as basis of spiritual resurrection
    236-238
hidden legacy 251-253
Horus and churning process of galactic
    creation 273-274
Horus, followers of 224
Horus, son of Osiris 235
Isis 234-236
levitation technology 247-248
Manetho 219, 224
Menes first mortal king 220
mines in Sinai 244
Nephthys 235-236
Nile valley sacred sites 248, 295
path of action 205-206
pillar of light 239
prehistory 219-221
Ptolemies collect ancient knowledge 254
Pyramid texts 253
remnants of the lost tradition 253-254

rites of immortality 229-231, 285-286
Set and churning process of galactic creation 273-274
Set, brother of Osiris 234
Sphinx 27-28
Sphinx, hidden chambers 251-252
Sphinx, illustration 252
spiritual ascension 231-234
subtle matter radiation device, illustration 223
subtle matter radiation technology 222-229
symbolic nature of language 237-238
Taurus 121
unification of Upper and Lower Egypt, illustration 274
Uraeus, description and illustration 139
Einstein, Albert
Earth-crust displacement theory 189-190
Theory of General Relativity 90-91
Elijah, ascension of 287-289
Elisha 288-289
Emerald Tablet 22
text 256
Enclosing Serpent, transcending through path of knowledge 120
Enoch
identified with Thoth and Hermes Trismegistus 287
identified with Thoth-Hermes 255
knowledge preserved underground 288
Enoch, ascension of 287
Eridanus 123-125
Exodus 264-267
Exodus, Book of, and Ark of the Covenant 303
Ezekiel and signs of the four living creatures 26
Field of Reeds
network of celestial rays 114
Thoth 199
Utnapishtim 199
Franklin, Benjamin 301
Freemasons, and Great Seal of the United States 301
Galactic Being. See also Milky Way Galaxy
and central star of the galaxy 63-64
body of 61-62
churning of the Milky Ocean 274

connected to Earth by galactic ray 116-118
Divine Ka at the heart of 77
life span 60-61
oversees evolution of planetary environment 119
stars offspring of 68
Galactic civilization 66-67
and celestial Yugas 160-161
Worlds of Light compose 299
Ganymede
compared with Lord Dhanvantari 260
identified with Aquarius 268
Garuda 144
Genesis, Book of
Enoch, ascension of 287
longevity of Biblical patriarchs 287
Nephilim 182-183
Tree of Life 56
Giza. See Pyramids
Great Seal of the United States 300-301
Greek tradition. See also Hermes
Aquarius compared with Lord Dhanvantari 260
Eridanus—river of celestial fire 123-125
Ganymede compared with Lord Dhanvantari 260
golden fleece 113
myth of Phaethon 123-124
Nonnos and Phaethon myth 123
Phoenix described 142
Phoenix, illustration 141
Plato and Phaethon myth 124
Pleiades 146-148
Prometheus 183-184
Titans 182-184
Hancock, Graham and Robert Bauval 27-28, 297
Hathor 225-227
Djed pillar depicted in Temple engravings 228
identified with Isis 235
illustration 226
Temple at Denderah 223-227
Hawaiian myth of Makalii, or Pleiades 148
Hebrew tradition. See also Ark of the Covenant; Moses
Aaron 303
Adam and Eve and the Tree of Knowledge 138

alchemy 264-267
Bezalel 266-267
Elijah, ascension of 287-289
Elisha 288-289
Exodus 264-267
Manna 265-267, 282, 286
Nephilim 182-183
siddhis 8
Sinai 303, 306
Heliopolis
ancient seat of Egyptian wisdom 219
bennu bird ashes carried to 242
original benben stone worshipped at 76
original pillar of light located at 239, 242
periodic world renewal with return of
bennu bird 142-143
Heliopolitan tradition. See Egyptian tradi-
tion
Helios Sun God (Phaethon myth) 123
Hermes. See also Divine Messenger
illustration 134
presides over healing arts 136
son of Zeus and Maya 146
Hermes Trismegistus 255-256
Chamber of Light 313-314
Emerald Tablet ascribed to 22
Enlightened Seers described 53
identified with Thoth, Enoch and Idris
255, 313
Hermetic tradition 255-259. See also
Hermes Trismegistus
Emerald Tablet, text 256
Kali Yuga 164-165
Mind, the substance of God 37
mortal and immortal bodies 111
nature spirits 179
Ouroboros 259
roots in Egypt 254
seven-layered structure of the Universe
47
Supreme and Universal Beings described
55
Thoth-Hermes, father of alchemy 255
Herodotus 242
Highest Heaven. See Central Galaxy of the
Universe
History of Egypt (Manetho) 219
Holy Bread. See Manna
Holy Grail 293
Holy Spirit. See also Divine Messenger

Divine Presence of God 48
inspires new thinking in sandhi periods
166-167
represented as white dove 141
represented in the Caduceus 141
Horus
churning process of galactic creation
273-274
followers of 224
son of Osiris 235
Huy, tomb of 239-242
Idris 255
Inuit flood legend 200-201
Iraq, clay tablets. See Utnapishtim
Isis 234-236
Islam, and rejection of ritual 213
Island of Jewels. See Central Galaxy of the
Universe
Isle of Flame. See also Central Galaxy of
the Universe
in Egyptian creation myth 76
Isle of Paradise. See Central Galaxy of the
Universe
Jefferson, Thomas 301
Jesus Christ, ascension of 289
John, Revelation of. See Revelation of
John
Jones, Sir William 217
Josephus
Enoch 288
Exodus 264-265
Jubmel, and flood legend 194
Julius Caesar 254
Jyotish (astrology) 115-116
Ka. See Divine Ka
Kenan 287
Krittika (Pleiades)
in Ashva-Medha ritual 152
related to Caduceus and May Pole cele-
bration 150-151
Kundalini, illustration 140
Lappish flood legend 194
Leo
and Egyptian prehistory 219
and the Eridanus 124
epochal transition at beginning of Age
18-19
signs of the four living creatures 26-28
Mahabharata 184
Mahalalel 287

Manetho 219, 224

Manna 265-267, 282, 286

Manu and the deluge 201-202

Marduk, and pole shift 190

Maya (one of the Pleiades)
  Divine Messenger from specific direction 146
  May Pole celebration 146-148
  Sun aligned with in month of May 146

Mayan
  beginning of Long Count 220
  calendar predicts day of Illumination 168
  New Fire Ceremony 149-150
  temples aligned with celestial events 13

Menes 220

Mercury. *See also* Divine Messenger
  illustration 134
  presides over healing arts 136

Mesoamerican tradition. *See* Aztec; Mayan;
  Peruvian; Navaho; Inuit

Mesopotamian tradition. *See also*
  Sumerian
  drum ritual and the Pleiades 152
  flood legend 198-200

Message of the Sphinx, The 27-28, 297

Methuselah 287

Midrashic flood legend 193-194

Milky Way Galaxy 59-67
  center connected to Earth by galactic ray 116-118
  center in direction of Sagittarius 117
  correspondence to Central Galaxy of the
    Universe 66-67
  current age 61
  Orion in direction of outer arm 298
  our solar system in, illustration 65
  stars offspring of the Galactic Being 68

Moses
  Ark of the Covenant 302-307
  birth and Exodus 264-267
  on Mount Sinai 303, 306
  Stone Tablets 305-306
  trained in Egyptian wisdom 265, 302

Mount Meru, and deluge 202

Mount Olympus as Central Galaxy 124

Mouth of God 104

Nagas, representing polarized subtle energy 144

Navaho flood legend 194

Nebuchadnezzar 267

Nephilim 182-183

Nephthys 235-236

Nile valley sacred sites 248, 295

Noah, role played by Utnapishtim 198-200

Nonnos and Phaethon myth 123

North American flood legends. *See*
  Navaho; Inuit

Nu or Nun 76

Old Kingdom. *See* Egyptian tradition

Orion constellation 297-299, 300

Osiris
  Field of Reeds 114
  in Papyrus of Ani 243-244
  myth of 234-236
  symbolized by Djed pillar 228

Ouroboros 259

Peruvian
  flood legend 200
  myth of terrestrial gods 184-185

Phaethon 123-124

Pharaoh 264-265

Phoenix
  as immortal Divine Ka 111
  described 142
  illustration 141
  relationship to bennu bird 237, 242
  symbolized by eagle in Great Seal of the
    United States 300

Pisces
  end of Age 15-16
  now at junction between Aquarius and 185

Planetary Being
  and solar ray 116
  cosmic life-breath awakens every 13,000
    years 126
  enlightenment of 298
  Mother Earth 2-3
  sacred mounds 250

Plato
  Atlantis 202
  Phaethon myth 124

Pleiades 146-153
  Agni identified with 151
  Ashva-Medha ritual 151-152
  Borneo celestial tree myth 149
  center of the Universe in direction of 4
  Divine Messenger from direction of 133
  Hawaiian myth of Makalii 148
  illustration 147

in Greek tradition 146-148
in sign of Taurus 122
May Pole Celebration 146-148
Mayan/Aztec New Fire Ceremony 149-150
Mesopotamian drum ritual 152
Vedic tradition 150-152
Prometheus 183-184
Ptolemies
builders of Temple of Hathor 223
collection of ancient knowledge 254
Pyramid texts 253
Pyramid Texts of Unas 230
Pyramids
aligned with celestial events 13
and Orion constellation, illustration 297
capped with benben stone 295
gateways to the cosmos 296-300
Great Seal of the United States 300-301
levitation technology 247
Orion constellation 297-300
research of Hancock and Bauval 27
rites of immortality 230
secret purpose of 295-300
Rasayana 260-261
Revelation of John 20-28
and Central Sun of the Central Galaxy 55
and the seven-layered structure of the Universe 47-48
Manna or white Stone 283
Rig Veda
collective enlightenment—samitti samani 172
Divine Ka 74
Soma verses 292-293
Roman tradition
Mercury presides over healing arts 136
Mercury, illustration 134
temple at Baalbek 288
Rosicrucians 301
Sagittarius
and the Eridanus 125
centaur, illustration 118
direction of central star of the galaxy 62
galactic ray from direction of 117-118
Sagittarius A*—central star of the galaxy 62-64
Sanskrit, compared to Greek and Latin 216-217

Sapta Lokas or seven heavenly worlds 47
Scorpio
and the Eridanus 124
signs of the four living creatures 26-28
Set
brother of Osiris 234
churning process of galactic creation 273-274
Seth 287
Seventh Heaven. See Central Galaxy of the Universe
Sheldrake, Rupert, and theory of morphic fields 84-85
Shiva
animal skins 241
mercury (Hg) identified with 261-262
Shukadeva 289
Siddhas 285, 291
gateways to the cosmos 296-299
Sinai
Hebrews in 303, 306
mines in 244
Solon, Phaethon myth 124
Soma
acquired by Agni in form of divine hawk 143
captured by Garuda 144
Milk of Heaven, compared with milk of Hathor 226
preparation of 291-294
spiritualized substance 286
verses from Rig Veda 292-293
woolen filter 114
Specifications of the Mounds of the Early Primeval Age 250
Sphinx 27-28
Builder Gods 248
hidden chambers 251-252
illustration 252
Stonehenge
aligned with celestial events 13
weight of stones 288
Sumerian
flood legend and Utnapishtim 198-200
sculpture (double-helix), illustration 137
tablets describe Bread of Life and Water of Life 286
Sun
as celestial being 68-71
Divine Ka at heart of 71-72, 77

relationship to Phoenix, bennu bird, and gold 237
residence of higher Selves 106
solar ray 116
Supreme Being 45
  and celestial luminaries 68-69
  and pure consciousness 30-31
  and the Universal Being 54-55
  described 52
  divine Love 68-69
  Garuda celestial vehicle of 144
  higher Self emanation of 102-104
  merging with through path of action 120
  merging with through path of knowledge 120
  Mouth of God portalway to and from 104
  symbolized by Ashva-Medha ritual 151-152
  Vedic creation myth 73-75
Taoist tradition
  alchemy 263-264
  chi 37, 263
  currents of subtle matter 82
  Golden Elixir 286
Tat 314
Taurus
  and the Eridanus 124-125
  direction of Central Galaxy 122
  illustration 121
  signs of the four living creatures 26-28
  symbolizes creative power of Central Galaxy 121-122
Thompson, Charles 301
Thoth. See also Divine Messenger
  attributes 255
  father of alchemy 255
  Field of Reeds 199
  illustration 135
  location of sacred mounds 249-250, 295
  physical description 134
  presides over healing arts 136
  symbolized by baboon 227, 233
Thoth-Hermes 255
Timaeus
  Atlantis 202
  Phaethon myth 124
Titans 182-184
Tree of Knowledge, illustration 138
Tree of Life 56-58

branches as vortex filaments 23
connects mortal and immortal soul 107-108
Tutankhamen, King 239
  tomb of 70
Tutu 243
United States, Great Seal of 300-301
Universal Being
  Creator in the Revelation of John 21
  described 54-55
  Divine Ka at the heart of 72, 77
  galaxies cells in the body of 70
  life span 60
  presides over evolution of human civilization 118-119
  Vedic creation myth 73-75
Uraeus, description and illustration 139
Utnapishtim, and flood legend 198-200
Vasuki 273
Vedic tradition 207-218. See also Agni; Soma
  alchemy 259-263
  Amrit produced by churning Milky Ocean 275-276
  Amrit, gift of Lord Dhanvantari 259-260
  Ashva-Medha ritual 151-152
  Ashvattha Tree 56-58
  Asuras 182, 184
  Asuras churning Milky Ocean 271-275
  Ayurveda 259-261
  beginning of celestial Kali Yuga 220
  bhasma (ash) 282, 292
  celestial Yugas or Ages 160-161
  chitta 36
  chitta and chitta-vritti 109-110
  collective enlightenment—samitti samani 172
  currents of subtle matter (nadis) 82
  describes Earth World 289
  Devas churning Milky Ocean 271-275
  Dhanvantari 259, 260
  Dhanvantari, illustration 260
  Divine Ka 73-75
  Dwapara Yuga described 163-164
  four levels of existence 30-31
  fourteen stages of evolution 151-152
  Garuda 144
  individuals attaining Worlds of Light described 289
  Jyotish (astrology) 115-116

Kali Yuga described 164-166
Krita or Sat Yuga described 161-162
kundalini 139-141
kundalini, illustration 140
language of Nature 210-211
life spans of the Universal and Galactic
    Beings 60-61
Maharishi Mahesh Yogi 217-218
Manu and the deluge 201-202
mercury (Hg) identified with Shiva 261-
    262
Milky Ocean and galactic creation 60-61,
    271-275
Milky Ocean, churning of, illustration
    272
modern understanding of Vedic texts
    216-218
path of knowledge 205-206
Pleiades 150-152
preparation and consumption of the
    Soma 291-294
Rasayana 260-261
recent transition in celestial Yugas 161
Sanskrit compared to Greek and Latin
    216-217
sapta lokas or seven heavenly worlds 47
Shiva and animal skins 241
Shukadeva 289

Siddhas 285, 291
siddhis 7-8
spectrum of Creation 45
tapas 128-129
Treta Yuga described 162-163
universal gods described 51
Vasuki 273
Veda and the sacred mantras 208-210
Vedic education 214-216
Vedic Rishis 207-208
Vedic yagyas 211-213
yagya 270-273
Yugas or Ages on Earth 158-160
Washington, George 301
Worlds of Light
    and knowledge of sacred technologies
        221
    described 66-67
    Earth soon transformed to 131-132
    outposts of Galactic civilization 298-300
    permanent status as 171-172
    residence of higher Selves 105-106
    spiritualized matter in 283
    technology available upon transformation
        to 156
    Vedic tradition describes individuals
        attaining 289
Yogi, Maharishi Mahesh 217-218